MW00386577

You
&
God

An Invitation to Radical Living

You
&
God

An Invitation to Radical Living

Fred Miller

 Evangel Publishing House

Nappanee, Indiana 46550

You and God: An Invitation to Radical Living
Copyright © 2006 by Fred Miller

Requests for information should be addressed to:
Evangel Publishing House
2000 Evangel Way
P.O. Box 189
Nappanee, Indiana 46550
Phone: (800) 253-9315
Internet: www.evangelpublishing.com

A free Small Group Study Guide is available for each chapter at
www.fredmillerglorifygod.com

Unless otherwise noted, all Scripture quotations are from the New
International Version (North American Edition). Copyright © 1973, 1978,
1984 by International Bible Society. Used by permission of Zondervan
Publishing House.

All rights reserved. No part of this publication may be reproduced, stored in a
retrieval system, or transmitted in any form or by any means—electronic,
mechanical, photocopy, recording, or any other—except for brief quotations
in printed reviews, without the prior permission of Evangel Publishing House,
P.O. Box 189, Nappanee, Indiana 46550.

Edited by Kathy Borsa
Cover Design by Matthew Gable

ISBN 10: 1-928915-89-2
ISBN-13: 978-1-928915-89-8
Library of Congress Catalog Card Number: 2006929947

Printed in the United States of America

10 11 12 13 EP 8 7 6 5 4 3

TABLE OF CONTENTS

Foreword

This book has been growing in me for over 30 years—though I never actually thought it would come to this. That changed when publisher, Roger Williams, sent me an E-mail asking if I had ever thought of writing a book. I thank God for people like Roger who help unlock dreams in other people. Others have done this for me throughout my life—igniting sparks.

In similar ways, it's my prayer that this book will ignite something special in you, something that draws you irresistibly and joyfully to the heart of God. I believe it's what you and I have been made for and what our hearts truly long for.

The pages that follow are an attempt to talk about God's intentions for the Christian life, and to do it in ways that are both systematic and memorable. I do this partly for myself because my mind needs handles to grab onto when life becomes a bit hard or fuzzy. But I also do it for those I love and teach. Of course, if your mind doesn't work sequentially like mine, just jump around in the book all you like. It builds throughout the three parts, but I think you can benefit anywhere you roam!

It's my goal to speak about the Christian life in ways that touch the heart— not just the mind. I want to help your spirit connect with God's Spirit at the place of desire, so that you *want* to follow Jesus—not just feel that you *should*. God's ways are good—and they should *feel* good.

So this is a very spiritually-focused book. Something is always happening between you and a loving God—at least He *wants* something to be happening. So if I could offer a word of advice to you as you read this book it would be this: *Take your time, and listen for God.* Too often people feel they need to get through a book in a certain period of time. They see it as a task to accomplish rather than an encounter to have. If this book takes you several months to read—or even a year or two—and it's shaping a love-relationship between you and God that will last beyond the reading, that's worth far more than another completed book on the shelf.

At the beginning of each chapter you'll be encountering a parable. It's the unfolding story of a man who meets God. This story parallels the teaching content in the chapter that follows. I hope you can find yourself somewhere in it—or that it will awaken something you long to see in yourself. That's why Jesus told parables, and it's why I've written this quite-extended one.

You'll also notice that I've chosen to highlight key Scripture texts throughout, as well as referencing many others. It's my hope that you will be more captivated by God's words than mine and that, by seeing them stand out in the text, you will grow in your love for the One who inspired them. The references are there to aid you in any further study you may want to do on these themes.

The questions at the back of each chapter are for self-reflection (something we don't tend to do enough of when we read) and for helping you apply the material in your life. They help you *listen,* and not just learn. These questions can be used privately, but I would encourage you to study this book with some friends if at all possible—perhaps a Sunday school class or a home group. The questions will bear the most fruit if they are shared and discussed with other spiritual friends.

I want to thank Evangel Press for allowing this book to take on the size of a handbook and allowing me the freedom to speak to what I consider to be the major discipleship issues facing Christians today.

This book has so many people's marks upon it. Foremost is my wife Cathy who has been a wonderful encourager to me throughout my life and has lovingly believed in this project from the start. (Her frank and loving critique of one of my first drafts of Chapter 1 was humbling but invaluable!) I'm also deeply grateful to my son, Jeff Miller, my brother, Doug Miller, and church elder, Jeff Reed, for reading the entire manuscript and providing thoughtful suggestions throughout—most of which I heeded. Special thanks, also, to Paul Pat, Mark Alexander, son, Brian Miller, and son-in-law, Eric Hansen, for their insightful contributions. Also I must thank my parents, Dick and Esther Miller, for the Christ-centered home environment they gave me and for supporting me in my varied vocational paths which helped shape God's work in me. Finally, I'm grateful to Evangel Publishing editor, Kathy Borsa, for her probing questions and fine-tuning of the manuscript, all done in a professional but gracious manner.

Two primary churches have formed the context in which the contents of this book have been formulated, taught, and lived out—New Covenant Church and Cumberland Valley Brethren in Christ Church. They have loved me, challenged me, and given me the wonderful opportunity to be a pastor to them, working these principles out with real people in real life. I feel privileged to have walked with Jesus beside them.

Then there are those men and women who submitted their thoughts to the discipline of writing so that people like me can be challenged to think with the mind of Christ without the time and expense of formal theological education. Their writings fill my bookshelves and I am deeply in their debt.

But greatest thanks goes, of course, to the One who has drawn me to His glory and love in a way that is altogether satisfying. I can't imagine life without Him.

If you would like to share your thoughts, questions, or personal journey as you read this book, I'd love to hear them. My contact information is at www.fredmillerglorifygod.com.

PART ONE

Spiritual Foundations for Daily Living

Life comes at us hard every day. There are hundreds of decisions to make, multiple tasks to accomplish, and people to relate to. Work, family, church—they all want a piece of us. It can feel overwhelming at times—or just numbing.

Maine is known for its lighthouses. Perched high above the rocky coastline of the Atlantic Ocean, strategically positioned lenses of varying thicknesses allow a simple light source to be concentrated in a rotating beam that can be seen for miles away. By these lighthouses, ships are guided at night or in stormy, foggy weather to the safety of the harbor. To a tourist, they appear quaint and picturesque. To the traveler at sea, they are life-giving.

The first three chapters of this book lay out the biblical foundations for living the Christian life. They serve as a spiritual lighthouse for people who need to see more clearly in the midst of life's demands and pain. To the casual bystander who is uninterested in spiritual matters, they will seem quaint. To the traveler who seeks God—they, too, are life-giving.

In these pages I invite you to a love-encounter with Jesus as He truly is, to a passionate pursuit of the glory of God in your everyday life, and to the delight of joy. These are foundations for life. Your life and mine.

The image of the beacon is an important one. Something has to penetrate the busyness of our lives and information overload we experience every day. Something has to shout truth and hope into our minds and souls when our emotions begin to take over. These first three chapters are that beacon for me.

You should know that the chapters that follow these three become increasingly practical. But true foundations for life must always start in the heart and the mind, not in behavior. If we build the foundation well, the house we build on it will handle anything the world (or our crooked inner world) can throw at us.

I've chosen to begin with Jesus, the center of it all. Then we'll take a few steps back to behold the greatness of our God. Then, in the third chapter, we will end in joy. Life can't get any better than these.

Chapter 1

A Very Important Question: What Does God Require?

A Parable

There once was a man who lived in a land of great pain. For generations the people endured a disease that showed itself by boils on the skin. Some cases were mild and others were quite serious. Various cures were invented by the people to minimize the pain, but no one could actually get rid of them. Most people just learned to accept life with boils, including the suffering that went along with them.

One day while walking about the town, the man sat down on a nearby bench. Beside him was a leaflet. Out of curiosity he picked the leaflet up and began reading it. He was shocked to hear the author say that the disease would eventually kill them! Apparently, this was the reason many had been dying at earlier ages than normal. To avoid this early death, the pamphlet said he had to drink from a special spring in a nearby land. The King of that land had blessed these waters so that those who drank them would not die from the boils.

The pamphlet had quoted an ancient spiritual book called The Breath, *which the man had read on a few occasions.* The Breath *was a collection of the King's sayings, stories, and history with his people. The man had some degree of respect for the book, but also something about the pamphlet resonated as true to him as well. (And he figured, "Better safe than sorry!")*

So he gathered all his possessions, along with his wife and his children, and set out from the land of his birth to go to this new land. After several days on the road, he finally came upon a group of small villages. To his delight, these people, too, had come searching for this water. They said it was a spring about a mile away.

The man and his family went there immediately and drank from the spring. The experience filled them with joy, for they knew they were now safe from the disease's death. They returned to the village to settle with their new boil-covered friends.

A village leader told them, "All you need is one drink," but some people returned to the spring multiple times just to make sure the powers "took." They didn't want to take any chances.

Unfortunately, their spring experience didn't do much to ease the suffering caused by the boils. And the pain continued to feed a spirit of discontentment among the people as it always had.

Occasionally people would decide to leave the village and return to the old country, searching for something better than the life they knew. A few would actually get an adventurous desire to go see this King who made the spring. But that was a rare occurrence.

Since no one had died in several years, the villagers were mostly content. The man and his family saw it as an improvement from their previous life. They were safe from the disease's death—and as far as they were concerned, that's what it was all about.

What is Jesus Up To?

My comfortable, Christian world was shaken one night as I attended an InterVarsity Christian Fellowship meeting at Drexel University. I was a freshman and I had come to the big city of Philadelphia with a solid Christian upbringing. But I wasn't prepared for what I heard that night. They were studying a small blue-covered book (which title escapes me). It was essentially a verse-by-verse study of Mark 10, where Jesus answers a question posed by a rich young man about what he must do to inherit eternal life.

Jesus first told him to obey God's commandments. When the man said he did, Jesus then told him to sell all he had, give the money to the poor, and then come follow Him. The man's response was to walk away in dejection. The amazing thing was that *Jesus didn't call him back to talk further! He let him go!*

I remember the author suggesting with a tinge of sarcasm that perhaps Jesus would benefit from taking a few popular, personal-evangelism courses. That way he could become more "effective" to help this man see his sins, confess them, and then lead him through a "sinner's prayer" so he could be forgiven and go to heaven when he dies. Then perhaps Jesus would have realized that bringing up that stuff about the man selling his possessions and giving money to the poor was teaching a salvation based on works, not faith. It was obvious that Jesus had a lot to learn!

Of course, this is absurd but it did raise some interesting questions. Why did Jesus make it so hard for this man? Was this encounter an isolated instance—or did Jesus relate to others this way? Was Jesus' teaching on salvation different than the apostle Paul's? Furthermore, why have our modern-evangelism message and methods strayed so far from the Master's!

Growing up in independent and Baptist churches, I had heard all my life that salvation was obtained by "accepting Jesus as my personal Savior." So if I believed I had sinned (which I did), and if I believed Jesus died to take the penalty for my sin (sounded good to me!), then all I had to do was tell Jesus that's what I believed, and I could be forgiven and avoid hell (and that sounded *really* good to me!).

All the preachers, evangelists, Good News Clubs, and tracts I had ever encountered gave that simple message—and there seemed to be many Bible verses to support it. From my personal experience, the only downside to this was that since salvation was tied to my faith at a particular moment in time, I often doubted whether my faith was strong enough the last time I had "prayed the prayer"—so I regularly repeated it just to be sure. Which meant I got "saved" a couple of dozen times in my youth. One's eternal destiny was not something you fooled around with!

But now I was faced with something different. I was studying passages in the Bible I had never seriously looked at before. In particular, I was listening to Jesus Himself, as presented by Matthew, Mark, Luke and John. And what I was seeing was making a whole lot of sense.

A Disturbing First-Century Encounter With Jesus

In the years that followed, I studied the Scriptures, I read about the beliefs of the early church, and I broadened my Christian reading. I came to be amazed at how anyone could read the Bible and still reduce the Gospel to avoidance of hell. There was so much more and it shouted from almost every page of Scripture!

Perhaps an encounter with Jesus, as it happened 2000 years ago, will make this more clear. Imagine yourself sitting in a grassy field near Capernaum, just off the northern shore of the Sea of Galilee, surrounded by a few hundred other curious people. Jesus is speaking, and He's quite interesting—actually, impressive for an uneducated builder from Nazareth.

You're trying to figure Him out. You've been hearing numerous stories about people being healed by Him. And the other day, when you were in town a sandal maker told you about his cousin seeing Jesus multiply a few fish and some bread to feed several thousand people! Something inside you stirs at the thought that this could actually be for real!

So here you are, listening to him for the first time. And you realize it's not just His teaching that has you hanging on every word—it's Jesus Himself. There's something about the way He talks—and looks at people—that draws you. It's sort of like seeing a sparkling waterfall after a four-hour hike on a hot, hazy, humid day. Or like waking up after being asleep for several years.

Much of what He says really resonates with you. But some things are, well, quite confusing—like when He starts talking about Himself. Phrases like "Son of Man," "Son of God," and "the Way, the Truth, and the Life" leave you wondering, "Who is this guy, anyway?" And His stories often just add to the confusion. You wish sometimes He would just say it straight. Why does He have to make it so hard to understand?

His voice suddenly rises in pitch, and the passion in His heart grabs your attention: "I am the bread of life. Whoever comes to me will never be hungry, and whoever believes in me will never be thirsty" (John 6:35 NRSV). A number of people begin arguing about what He means. Frankly, you, too, are a little perplexed. He doesn't seem like a crazy man from the desert. (You've seen some of them!) But this talk of never being hungry and thirsty again is pretty strange. And Jesus' explanation only makes it worse:

> *"Very truly, I tell you, unless you eat the flesh of the Son of Man and drink his blood, you have no life in you. Those who eat my flesh and drink my blood have eternal life, and I will raise them up on the last day" (John 6:53-54 NRSV).*

What in the world is He talking about? It sounds like some kind of cannibalism, where people who "eat" and "drink" Him get to have "life!" But you recall that He just talked about "coming to me" and "believing in me." They're *relational* descriptions. Jesus keeps putting Himself at the center of this life. Which begs the question, what does He mean by "life?" He seems to speak not just of unending existence but of a *present quality* of life—a kind of life that belongs to God.[1]

Jesus' words are having a disturbing effect on some who are listening to Him. They're turning away and leaving. Jesus is just too confusing. Others detect He's looking for more commitment than they want to give. Listening to Him is one thing; committing to Him is another.

Then Jesus looks at His twelve disciples and says words that will ring in your ears for years: "Do you also wish to go away?" [The man named Peter answered,] "Lord, to whom can we go? You have the words of eternal life" (John 6:67-68 NRSV).

You're now alone in your thoughts. The choice He was presenting has become clear to you. Either you have this ongoing "eating/drinking" relationship with the person of Jesus, or you can say good-bye to eternal life—which includes real life on earth as well. The choice is before you. Whom will you join, the crowd or the Twelve?

The Narrow Gate and Narrow Path

This scene from John 6 further illustrates the collision course I was on during that freshman year in college. Jesus had come to bring something deeper and wider and more wonderful than I had previously known. And, His expectations were more demanding than I had previously known.

If this modern-day belief that salvation comes from merely believing with our minds that Jesus died to take away the guilt of our sins was only an isolated teaching in the Christian world, this chapter would not be very relevant to many readers. But this isn't the case. It has permeated the church at large—especially with children's evangelistic ministries, tract societies, evangelists, and television personalities.

Consider the following texts that concur with the John 6 passage above. Whatever view we develop of the path to salvation must, in the end, include these. We can't just ignore them or somehow place them *after* salvation is received. These describe the *entrance* to life, not just the path.

> • "But small is the gate and narrow the road that leads to life, and only a few find it" (Matthew 7:14). Jesus says that it's not easy to get His life. The entrance and road are small. Few find it. And many people, like that rich, young man in Mark 10, don't want to go in. It's too restrictive; it's too hard; it's too costly—as Jesus warns in Luke 9:57-62 and 14:28-33. Both the gate *to* salvation and the path *after* salvation are narrow.

> • "Not everyone who says to me, 'Lord, Lord,' will enter the kingdom of heaven, but only he who does the will of my Father who is in heaven. Many will say to me on that day, 'Lord, Lord, did we not prophesy in your name, and in your name drive out demons and perform many miracles?' Then I will tell them plainly, 'I never knew you. Away from me, you evildoers!'" (Matthew 7:21-23). Jesus says that mere religious words and mere religious deeds don't get us into heaven. Something else is needed. We might expect Him to say that the problem for these people is a lack of true faith—and that would likely be true. But that's not what He says. He says what's lacking is doing the will of the Father. Clearly, obedience is not optional. (See also Acts 5:32 where God gives the Holy Spirit "to those who obey him.") This is *not* salvation by works. It is salvation by a faith that naturally wants to please the Father—both in Jesus' day and ours.

Some will be shocked that their very public "faith" was insufficient. God requires something more.

• "Then he said to them all, 'If anyone would come after me, he must deny himself and take up his cross daily and follow me. For whoever wants to save his life will lose it, but whoever loses his life for me will save it. What good is it for a man to gain the whole world, and yet lose or forfeit his very self?'" (Luke 9:23-25). How does one receive the Gospel and save his life? Jesus says he must die to the self-life to receive the God-life. He must "lose his life." Salvation according to Jesus isn't mere freedom from judgment, it's freedom from self-rule. Dallas Willard says that this means being "apprenticed" to rabbi Jesus, learning to think, desire, and act like Him. A disciple is "someone who has decided to be with another person, under appropriate conditions, in order to become capable of doing what that person does or to become what that person is."[2] You *must* be a disciple.

• "Repent and be baptized, every one of you, in the name of Jesus Christ for the forgiveness of your sins. And you will receive the gift of the Holy Spirit" (Acts 2:38). "I have declared to both Jews and Greeks that they must turn to God in repentance and have faith in our Lord Jesus" (Acts 20:21). Repentance (Greek *metanoia*) means literally "to change one's mind." It is a decision to turn *from* sin and a decision to turn *to* God in the way we live. Thus, *it's not enough to admit sin—we must desire to turn from it!* This is the way salvation has always been presented to people throughout the Scriptures. God hasn't changed the rules. Yes, specific life changes resulting from repentance may take some time. But, with repentance, there can be no doubt that the heart is now inclined to obey God, and with that inclination significant change *will* come.

• "That if you confess with your mouth, 'Jesus is Lord,' and believe in your heart that God raised him from the dead, you will be saved" (Romans 10:9). Jesus is Lord. Following Him in obedience is required for salvation—not in perfection, but in the decision of the mind and heart to make *Him* our new

Master and no longer ourselves. This is the same thing as "repentance." And the common reference to Jesus as "Lord and Savior" in the New Testament further demonstrates that these are united, not separated.

Please understand this: I am not speaking of salvation by works. God's grace and our faith are the foundation of any rescue from our sin. But repentance is part of trusting in Jesus—and it's right there at the gate (Mark 1:15). Whether we come to Jesus at a moment's "decision" or over a gradual process, we all, at some point, "cross over from death to life" (John 5:24). That crossover point must include a repentant and trusting heart. From Adam to Job to Noah to Abraham to Moses to David and to Jesus, it's always been about both relationship and righteousness. And this all means that the gate to eternal life is not as wide as many think.

What is the "Gospel" Anyway?

So the entrance to salvation involves relationship, repentance and life-change. But we might wonder, "What, actually, is the good news Jesus came to bring? And what did the early church preach?"

Consider these statements:

> • Mark 1:14-15 "Jesus went into Galilee, proclaiming the good news of God. 'The time has come,' he said. 'The kingdom of God is near. Repent and believe the good news!'" Here Jesus equates the "kingdom of God" to the Gospel— which is the "rule of God" on earth through Jesus. God was setting up a new order of life *here* (not just in heaven), and *that* was the "good news!"

> • Acts 5:42 "Day after day, in the temple courts and from house to house, they never stopped teaching and proclaiming the good news that Jesus is the Christ." The Gospel (literally "Good News") is that Jesus is the "Christ," which is the Greek word for the Hebrew word Messiah, the Anointed One. Jesus is the One chosen by God for a work of salvation. 1 Corinthians 15:1-4 affirms this as well, saying "Christ died for our sins." The question, of course, is what about our sins did He save us from? We must first of all affirm the truth that God, through Jesus, saved us from the *penalty* of our sins.

This is affirmed explicitly in Mark 16:16, Acts 2:38, Romans 5:9 and 2 Timothy 1:10. For that we rejoice! But there is more:

• "...our great God and Savior, Jesus Christ, who gave himself for us to redeem us from all wickedness and to purify for himself a people that are his very own, eager to do what is good" (Titus 2:13-14). Here we see another equally-important saving work—saving us from the *power* of our sins. Thus we are delivered from our "wickedness" so we can become good, delivered from our impurity so we can become "pure," and delivered from our alienation so we can become "his very own." Jesus affirms this as well when He says He's come to "seek and to save the lost" (Luke 19:10). Lost people are not so much fleeing judgment as they are wandering from God and His goodness.

• Ephesians 3:7-8 "I became a servant of this gospel by the gift of God's grace given me through the working of his power. Although I am less than the least of all God's people, this grace was given me: to preach to the Gentiles the unsearchable riches of Christ." The "Gospel" is clearly all "the unsearchable riches of Christ." *All* of them. Is He our Savior? Absolutely! But He has come to save us from *everything* that alienates us from God, ourselves, and others. The "unsearchable riches of Christ" include more than forgiveness!

Recently I wanted a literature tract to use for a summer carnival outreach our church does every year. I browsed online through scores of tracts to find one that carried this kind of message. It was very slim picking. The vast majority spoke only about Jesus being Savior in terms of forgiveness. No unsearchable riches. No Lord. No Conqueror. No Bread of Life or Living Waters. Not only was their "gospel" too easy to obtain—it was way too small.

Getting it Right From the Start

A neighbor invited Cliff to his church when Cliff was twelve years old. Soon a Sunday School teacher asked him if he wanted to go to hell. Cliff said "no." So the teacher asked him to kneel down on the floor. Then she and the class prayed over him. He later wrote, "When they finished they got up and said I was saved (whatever that was)."

Four years later his dad kicked him out of the house and so he "decided to pursue religion" again. Shortly thereafter, at a revival meeting, a leader asked him if he was saved. Cliff said he was, but when the man discovered he was not baptized, that was taken care of that night ("for what reasons I don't know"). Over the next years he would often encounter people "getting saved again" because they felt they weren't really saved the first time. Even his associate pastor "got saved again." At age eighteen a church leader invited Cliff into his office, and, after some questions, determined that he was going to hell—so Cliff repeated the salvation prayer and was re-baptized later that day.

Cliff ended up going to a Bible college, memorizing over 500 verses, and converting 5-10 soldiers a week at a nearby military base, leading them "down the Romans Road"—a series of verses on salvation from the book of Romans. As he began his fourth year in Bible college, he met some Mormon missionaries. After extensive dialog with them and his professors, he decided to convert, leaving the college, a promised pastoral call, and a fiancé.

When I met Cliff, he had just returned from a successful mission in South Africa—and he was beginning to doubt the Mormon religion. After much love shown to him by my wife Cathy and me, and dialog about truth and experiencing our church, Cliff finally made the decision to leave the Mormon church, with all the intrigue and danger of a prison escape.

Cliff's story may be unique, but his experience is not. When salvation is equated with believing Jesus died for our sins, two dangers often follow. First, there is often an insecurity in the conversion because the primary evidence of the conversion is the words/prayer spoken, not the life lived. Months or years later doubts come as to whether it was sincere enough, so "the prayer" is said again (and again) just to be sure. (This was also my experience throughout my childhood.)

Second, it leads to a professing church and not a possessing church—a church that talks its faith but doesn't live it from its heart. I remember asking one young man what was holding him back from surrendering his life to Jesus. He pointed to a co-worker whose "walk" had little to do with his "talk." I've heard this story many times in different forms.

Not only has this easy-salvation doctrine harmed the name of Jesus and undermined the proclamation of His Good News to the world, it has taught tens of thousands of people that they're eternally safe because of a prayer they said years ago about accepting Jesus as their personal Savior. According to Jesus, these people have been deceived, and many of them are *not* safe. Out of love, these people must be re-evangelized with the full Gospel of Jesus.

When people realize repentance and obedience is a necessary part of the gospel, they will live lives in the fear of God as well as the love of God, and there will be spiritual power and God's presence among them. They will know that fruit is proof of faith.

I heard a speaker tell the story of an elderly Mennonite man being asked by a very zealous Christian if he was a Christian. The man thought for a moment, then answered, "Ask my neighbor." The point isn't that we obtain salvation by works, the point is that the proof of our faith is *in* our works. By them we make our "calling and election sure" (2 Peter 1:10).

So if churches are to return to the Gospel as taught by Jesus and the early church, what will it take? What will it take to make this truth clear again—that *we must actually love and follow Jesus from the start*—and not just believe in His atoning death on the cross for our forgiveness? I believe it will require the following:

Believe All of Jesus. The church must recognize that to "believe" in Jesus Christ is to "trust, rely upon" (Greek *pisteuo*) Him for all that He is for us. We can't subdivide Him. Yes, He is our Savior from the penalty of sin, but He's also our Savior from the *power* of sin. And He is the Teacher of what is true and right and Lord and Master over everything our lives touch. To believe is to trust in Him *completely.* So when we lead people to salvation through Jesus, we should make it clear that to have faith in Him is to trust Him, at minimum, to be their Teacher, Forgiver, and Leader. He doesn't give us the option of picking and choosing which parts of Jesus we trust in and which we don't— He just says *believe in Him*! (Note John 3:16, Acts 16:31, Romans 10:9.) As Donald Guthrie notes in his *New Testament Theology*, "the hearers were expected to commit themselves to all that Jesus Himself stood for—i.e. His whole mission."[3]

Unite the Gospels and Letters. We must unify the Gospels of Matthew, Mark, Luke, and John with the letters of Paul, James, Peter, and John. They speak of one consistent salvation and one consistent response to Jesus. Think about this: When Jesus was on earth, He offered forgiveness of sins and fullness of life through a faith relationship with Him—and He hadn't even died for those sins or risen from the dead yet! When people believed in Jesus for eternal life, the cross and empty tomb were not on their minds—following Him was. Did God then make it easier to be saved *after* the Cross and Resurrection than when Jesus Himself was on earth telling people to believe in Him? No! There is one Gospel in the New Testament, and it's rooted in repentance and loving faith in Jesus.

Embrace All Salvation Metaphors. To be "justified" (Romans 3:24) is to be "made right with a person." It refers to the legal world, where someone is declared free of guilt in a courtroom. In the Scriptures, though, we are pardoned *and declared righteous* by the Judge. As wonderful as this is (and it really is wonderful!), there's more to salvation than justification. Scripture also uses images of "redemption" (Galatians 4:5), "reconciliation" (2 Corinthians 5:18) and "adoption" (Ephesians 1:5), each of which portray God as a Father who wants to restore us to a loving *relationship* with Him. Thus we are saved not only from judgment but *from alienation and from sin's controlling power.*

Brian McLaren, in his book *A Generous Orthodoxy*, addresses this limited understanding of Savior: "Even as Savior, though, we limited Jesus to saving us from hell, which explains why we have had comparatively little interest in his saving us from greed, gossip, prejudice, violence, isolation, carelessness about the poor or the planet, hurry, hatred, envy, anger, or pride."

Rejoice in Grace—and Affirm its Conditions. The grace of God is the ultimate foundation for our salvation. By definition it is "his love to us that we don't earn." God didn't choose Israel because they were righteous. They weren't. And neither does He choose us because of our righteousness. (We aren't.) The unrelenting, indestructible love of God to us in our sinfulness is perhaps the hallmark of the Christian faith. So we can say, appropriately, that His grace is *unconditional* because we don't have to "earn" God's love by certain behaviors.

Nothing I say in this book will take away an ounce of glory from the God of this grace. But we must not push a glorious attribute of God to places God Himself has not taken it. It does not magnify God more by insisting that grace is *only* unconditional if the Bible itself teaches that it is also *conditional.*

God's grace is conditional in the sense that we must repent and believe in order to receive it. Repentance and faith aren't "works," as Ephesians 2:8-9 makes clear. But they are conditions. And grace is *also* conditional in the sense that much of God's empowering and nurturing grace throughout the Christian life comes only when our hearts are humble (James 4:6), holy (Hebrews 12:14), and trusting (Psalm 32:10).

Some people emphasize that grace is "free." (This word is sometimes added to our English translations to amplify the Greek word for "gift," but "free" is not actually a separate word in the Greek New Testament.) To contemporary ears, this added word "free" often obscures the conditional aspect of grace that requires a proper heart response on our part to receive God's gift of salvation.

For example, I may give you a car as a gift without requiring that you earn it, but it's still a gift even if I ask you to promise to take care of it as a condition to your receiving it. You didn't earn the car. It's still grace. But you did satisfy a condition upon receiving it.

We must be careful that the wonderful grace of Jesus doesn't become "cheap" grace—as German pastor, Dietrich Bonhoeffer, described the kind of grace that costs us nothing. This grace is contrary to Jesus' statements that show that we must "lose" our life if we are to save it. Grace is not cheap. It has its conditions and cost.

Discipleship is Basic Christianity.   In the Bible, disciples are Christians and Christians are disciples (see Acts 11:26). There's no such thing as a Christian who isn't a disciple in the Bible. As Glenn Kaiser, lead singer of Rez Band and elder in the Jesus People U.S.A. said many years ago, "If Jesus isn't your Lord, he isn't your Savior, either." We must squarely face all Jesus' statements that make entry into the kingdom costly and hard (Matthew 6:15; 6:24; Mark 10:23; Luke 9:23).

Ron Sider, author of *The Scandal of the Evangelical Conscience* says, "I would think that evangelicals would want to get biblical and define the Gospel the way Jesus did—which is that it's the Good News of the *kingdom*. . . . embracing Jesus means not just getting fire insurance so that one doesn't go to hell, but it means embracing Jesus as Lord as well as Savior."[5] The "scandal" is that too many Christians live untransformed lives that look more like the world than like Jesus.

Works Must Accompany Faith—and Sustain Faith.   The conditions for *entering* the gate, *walking* the path, and *staying on* the path are all the same. It's about a *living* faith in Jesus, and works and obedience *must* follow (James 2:17). In fact, Paul tells us that we will be judged by our good deeds as well as our faith (Romans 2:7-8, 13).

The letter of 1 John is written specifically "to you who believe in the name of the Son of God so that you may know that you have eternal life" (1 John 5:13). Our assurance of salvation isn't based on a one-time profession of Jesus as savior from sin's penalty. Assurance is based on our: obeying God (1 John 2:4), walking as Jesus walked (1 John 2:6), discontinuing sin (1 John 3:6, 9), heeding the apostles' teaching (1 John 4:6), loving others (1 John 4:8, 20), receiving of the Spirit (1 John 4:13), *present* acknowledgment that Jesus is God's Son (1 John 4:15), and overcoming the world (1 John 5:4). John is clear—without these, we do not know God.

Further, we must acknowledge that, in Jesus' words, "he who stands firm to the end will be saved" (Matthew 10:22; 24:13). This is affirmed by Paul when he gives the conditions that believers are reconciled to God "if you continue in your faith" (Colossians 1:22-23) and "hold firmly to the word" (1 Corinthians 15:2). So a healthy "fear of the Lord" must be within us that always drives us back to the heart of God and an obedient, loving faith in Jesus. We can't believe once and then walk away from it. We must hold on—all the while knowing that He is also holding on to us because of our faith (1 Peter 1:4-5).

We MUST Enter the Rule of God!

Jesus' mission was to proclaim "the good news of the kingdom of God" (Luke 8:1) and His disciples did likewise (Acts 8:12). The "kingdom" of God is the "reign" or "rule" of God. In other words, the kingdom isn't a locality but a spiritual reality. It's what happens when God's will in heaven happens on earth, as Jesus taught His disciples to pray in Matthew 6:10.

Imagine, for a minute, an invisible reality that is intertwined with what we see with our eyes, hear with our ears, and touch with our hands. It's sort of like radio waves that are constantly moving through the air all around us, carrying TV shows, cell phone conversations, music and talk shows, and police signals—invisible to the eye, but present and detectable with the right electronic instrument. Jesus is saying there IS another reality around us (not just out in space somewhere)! It's the reality that we enter when we begin to love and follow Jesus.

Jesus' Sermon on the Mount is a clear articulation of life in this spiritual reality. This is how people live who lovingly follow Him. These aren't rules; they are values. They're what His disciples see as important because *He* sees them as important. The first ten verses particularly capture these values in what are commonly called the "beatitudes." Listen to these (including my interpretative paraphrases) and see if these describe the kind of life *you* want to live:

> *"Blessed are the poor in spirit* (those who know they need God), *for theirs is the kingdom of heaven.*
>
> *Blessed are those who mourn* (whose losses make them hungry for God), *for they will be comforted.*
>
> *Blessed are the meek* (those who gladly and humbly surrender to the rule of God), *for they will inherit the earth.*
>
> *Blessed are those who hunger and thirst for righteousness* (who treasure God's ways), *for they will be filled.*
>
> *Blessed are the merciful* (those who reach out to the hurting), *for they will be shown mercy.*
>
> *Blessed are the pure in heart* (those whose desires are God's desires), *for they will see God.*
>
> *Blessed are the peacemakers* (those who bring understanding and resolution to conflicts), *for they will be called sons of God.*
>
> *Blessed are those who are persecuted because of righteousness* (who suffer for doing what's right), *for theirs is the kingdom of heaven"* (Matthew 5:3-10).

This is His agenda, and He invites us to join Him. The choice is ours. Either we live under the rule of God or the rule of the evil one (1 John 5:19). "No one can serve two masters," says Jesus (Matthew 6:24). We must choose one ruler only. One kingdom only.

This concept of the kingdom is critical for us to grasp because it clarifies what following Jesus is all about, and it counteracts some common errors within contemporary Christianity.

We are not free in God's kingdom to do what we want to do. We are always submitted to the authority of the King. We're not our own—we are His. Whether we're a parent or a child, a church leader or member, a government official or a citizen, a boss or an employee, we all live under His authority as His disciples. This is often especially difficult for Americans who pride themselves in their independence, their state's rights, and their ability to make new laws, if they can convince their legislators to do so. In the kingdom of God, the executive branch (President), legislative branch (Congress), and judicial branch (Supreme Court) are all found in one Person. We have "pledged allegiance" to the King—from the start.

His rule starts with our hearts and leads to transformation. As King, Jesus rules our life purpose. He shapes our values and priorities, and He gives us new desires and longings that are spiritually oriented—not merely earthbound. When He has our heart, He has our life. Everything we do will have His fingerprint on it, from family relationships to entertainment pursuits, from how we spend our money to how we work at our jobs. Nothing is left untouched. There are no separate secular and sacred categories in the kingdom life. All is sacred and holy because all is ruled by Him—because He rules our hearts. Kingdom people are a changed people from the inside out, and this book will flesh that out in later chapters.

We are abundantly cared for by the King, and we need not fear or worry. As Jesus says, "But seek first his kingdom and his righteousness, and all these things will be given to you as well" (Matthew 6:33). Life under the rule of God is safe—not in the sense that we won't experience hardship and death (in fact He says they *will* come), but in the sense that He cares for us. Basic food and clothing is one expression of His care for us, but it's wider and deeper than that. So He tells us "do not worry about your life," because He is with us and He is good.

His kingdom involves a people, not just "me." We are not free to be isolated followers of Jesus. We are a holy, set-apart people that He wants to reign in and through, starting here on earth and into eternity. Thus the church is central to His rule (more will be said about this in Chapter 13). It isn't just an add-on to the King's agenda—it's fundamental to it. In fact, together, the church is at the heart of His glory on earth (Ephesians 3:21).

His rule is for the good of the whole world. God's rule is established to be a blessing to the whole world, just as Israel was to be (Genesis 12:3). (See Chapter 9.) As a city on a hill, we are a light to the world. We aren't to be insulated or isolated from our neighbors. God's purpose is to reveal the goodness and good news of Himself to them. The kingdom is an ever-growing and expanding kingdom.

You've already read the first installment of a parable that will be woven throughout this book. In it people meet a King. And He changes their everyday lives. Yes, in this parable many see Him with their physical eyes, but for the most part, He's not there physically. He lives in their hearts.

Years ago the King really did come to earth for a time. Then he left and sent his Spirit to live in us. So the kingdom goes on—invisible but visible. As Paul says,

> *"Since, then,* you have been raised with Christ, *set your hearts on things above, where Christ is seated at the right hand of God. Set your minds on things above, not on earthly things. For you died, and* your life is now hidden with Christ *in God. When* Christ, who is your life, *appears, then you also will appear with him in glory* [emphasis mine]" *(Colossians 3:1-4).*

Jesus invites you to His kingdom, where your true identity is "hidden," invisible to the normal eye. People can't immediately know you're His follower just by watching you walk down the street or work at your desk. But in reality, He is "your life"—a life that inhabits your being at your own request, and then invades your visible world with the markings of God Himself. And, if people hang around you long enough, what was "hidden" will certainly become visible.

As you can see, the presence of His kingdom in you is a whole lot more wonderful than just escaping judgment!

Are You Willing to Give a Costly Love?

So how are we to summarize this? What words can we use to answer the question posed in this chapter title: "What does God require of us?" When asked what the greatest commandment is, Jesus gave the following answer:

> *"'Love the Lord your God with all your heart and with all your soul and with all your mind.' This is the first and greatest commandment"* (Matthew 22:37-38).

At the heart of God is His desire for our love. The prophet Micah reminds us about the worshipful and obedient nature of that love when he answers this question:

> *"He has showed you, O man, what is good. And what does the LORD require of you? To act justly and to love mercy and to walk humbly with your God." (Micah 6:8).*

The people in the parable at the beginning of this chapter weren't interested in love. Gratitude, perhaps—but not love. They were content with safety without relationship, and it cost them nothing.

That isn't the picture Jesus paints. From the beginning of the Christian life to our last days on earth, His purposes are brimming with love. It starts with God's love for us, and culminates in our love for Him. Affectionate love. Self-giving love. Obedient love. There can be no salvation apart from love.

Yes, it grows and deepens over time, but to imagine a Gospel or a salvation that is separated from the *desire* to love God with all our heart, soul, and mind is unknown in Scripture. And it is foreign to the heart of God.

To all, young and old, regardless of what they have said to Jesus in the past, regardless of what kind of conversion experience they have, Jesus simply asks, "Do you love me?" As He tells His disciples,

> *". . . the Father himself loves you* because you have loved me [emphasis mine] *and have believed that I came from God"* *(John 16:27).*

Loving Jesus and believing Him are part of the same equation. There *is* no relationship apart from love.

And love, by necessity, is costly, just as God's love for us cost Jesus His life (1 John 4:10). To make God and His Son first in our hearts has radical implications. It means placing family love—including marital love—second to God (Luke 14:26). It means giving all material belongings to Him to use as He chooses (Luke 14:33). It means being willing to suffer for proclaiming His name and doing what is good (Matthew 5:10-12). It means obeying His teachings (John 14:23).

This kind of love can't begin or be sustained apart from God's work in our hearts and minds. The world is against us. Our old sinful nature is against us.

Satan is against us. We need the grace of God to start the journey, walk the path, and finish the course.

And know this: God's grace isn't forced on us. It must be appropriated by us through faith—not just because we desire to avoid eternal judgment, but because we are captivated by the purposes and love of God and because these purposes touch our souls with *life*. These things are truly "good news!" And that is the subject of the next two chapters—in fact, the rest of this book.

For Self-Reflection and Life Application

1. What might have been your reaction to Jesus if you were a first-century Jew listening to one of His teachings?

2. What attracted you initially to trust in Jesus? What attracts you *now* to continue to follow Him?

3. Is there anything in the way you personally speak about the Good News (Gospel) to others, or how your church invites adults, teens, and children to salvation and eternal life, that might need to be changed to reflect biblical teaching? If so, how might you sensitively go about addressing this?

4. In what ways might referring to Jesus primarily as "Savior" be biblically true; and in what ways could it mislead someone?

5. In what ways might the word "free" be helpful to describe the salvation God gives us through our faith in Jesus; in what ways might it not be helpful?

6. If you were talking to someone who had no previous exposure to Christianity and she asked you—"So what's the minimum requirement for me to become a Christian?"—what would you say?

7. How do you balance in your own mind the biblical necessity for good works with the concept of salvation by grace through faith?

8. How does the concept of being a participant in the "kingdom of God" affect the way you view your relationship to God?

9. Which values of the kingdom, as presented in the beatitudes, do you value but want to see more alive in your heart?

10. In what ways do you see yourself, or other people you know, in the opening parable?

Note: If this book is being used in a Sunday School class or a home study group, the author has written a "You & God" Small Group Study Guide. It is available free of charge at www.fredmillergloritygod.com. The guide provides reproducible participant sheets that summarize the teaching of each chapter and it provides discussion questions for a leader to use. Questions are designed to help a group discuss and understand the material, as well as apply the material with their hearts and lives. One or two "homework" assignments are suggested for each lesson. Little leader preparation is required.

---

[1] Colin Brown, ed., *The New International Dictionary of New Testament Theology,* Volume 3, Zondervan Corporation, Grand Rapids, 1978 p. 832.
[2] Dallas Willard, *The Divine Conspiracy,* Harper Collins Publishers, New York, 1998, p. 283.
[3] Donald Guthrie, *New Testament Theology,* Inter-Varsity Press, Downers Grove, 1981, p. 576.
[4] Brian McLaren, *Generous Orthodoxy,* Zondervan Publishing, Grand Rapids, 2004, p. 86.
[5] *Christianity Today,* April 2005, "The Evangelical Scandal," p. 72.

Chapter 2

Going for the Glory of God!

The man was working along the road, weeding one of his gardens, when an older woman traveling by called out to him. "Good morning," she said with a friendly air. The man returned the greeting with some reservation. He wasn't the outgoing sort, but the woman seemed nice enough.

"Is this the way to Lovelost?" she asked. He said it was—just down the road about 10 miles. She thanked him and explained that she was on her way to visit her son and her new granddaughter.

"Where are you from?" he heard himself ask, not really caring to know but feeling obliged to be cordial. It would turn out to be a very significant question.

"Oh, I'm from Kingcity, just over that mountain range," she said, pointing to a ridge in the distance. The man had seen the range many times, but he never wondered what was on the other side. He was quite content where he was. And safe. Far-off countries had no interest to him.

"Have you ever been there?" the woman asked with a tinge of excitement rising in her voice. The man confessed he had not. At this the woman brightened. Soon she was telling him all about it. It was where the King lived—along with thousands and thousands of citizens who loved Him. She said it was the most wonderful place.

The woman went into great detail and it was obvious Kingcity was a very special place to her. But one thing in her description stood out to the man— the King. His love for the people and his great wisdom were remarkable. When he met with the people, they would hang on every word, sometimes responding with song and shouts of joy and, at other times, with tears and on bended knee. This King was obviously pretty great, and the people confirmed it in their daily experiences with Him.

But the man was skeptical. "How much freedom does the King give people to do what they want to do in Kingcity?" he asked. He was thinking about his woodcarving business and his love for fishing—and his wife and children. He didn't want to go visit some place where someone—even a good king—ruled his every action. To him, the King had always been more of a helper than a ruler. He liked it that way.

The woman smiled, looked down at the ground to collect her thoughts, then moved her gaze to the man. "We have all the freedom we want," she said, with what seemed like a twinkle in her eyes, which made the man wonder if he knew what she was saying.

"I should get going," the woman said, "but sir, you really need to know something." The tone of her voice and the look of her face took on such deep love for him that it took him off guard for a moment. "The farther a spring is from the King, the less likely it has any protective powers from the disease. I urge you, please come to Kingcity." And with that she walked away.

Not safe? Was that possible? Might his village be "too far?" The thought of going to Kingcity filled him with both excitement and caution. Was there really more than just safety from the boils? His mind was racing . . . and dreams, long suppressed, began to rise deep within him.

God as the "One Thing"

I can't imagine a more important question to answer than "Why am I here?" It may not be the kind of question everyone thinks about while they're eating their morning cereal each day, but it would be wise if they did. And it would be even wiser to have an answer—in particular an answer that agrees with God's!

If we would ask people (including many Christians) their answer to this question, the answers would include, "to raise a family and love my kids," "to be successful in my job," "to be happy," or "to buy a certain kind of house in a certain kind of neighborhood in a certain kind of school district with a certain kind of car in the garage."

People are governed by many different life-purposes, though they aren't often consciously aware of them. At times, they will even compete for our allegiance. For example, the "relaxation and fun" goal can compete with the "spend time with the kids" goal. The "success at my job" goal can contend with the "have people like me" goal. This can contribute to a kind of life—purpose schizophrenia.

But what if there is one over-arching life-purpose that integrates all of life's decisions and goals; one life-purpose that measures, critiques, and rules all others?

The Bible tells us that this is, indeed, the case. David speaks about "one thing" he asks of God and seeks (Psalm 27:4), and Jesus tells Martha that her worry about food preparation missed the "one thing needed" (Luke 10:41-42). Apparently, there *is* something out there that brings focus to all other desires.

Christians have offered many answers to what this "one thing" is. For some, it's evangelizing the world. For others, it's serving God. But many years ago I encountered an answer that has been reaffirmed to me over and over again as I have studied the Bible and lived it out in my own life. That unifying life principle is this: *We have been created to glorify God!*

What Does it Mean to "Glorify God"?

I've sung about glory—and probably so have you. From classic hymns to Christmas carols to contemporary songs, the word "glory" and "glorify" are often on our lips. I think, to many people, the word "glory" is synonymous with "praise," but that doesn't do the word justice.

In Exodus 16 the people of Israel were in the desert for about a month and a half after God delivered them from slavery in Egypt. They were complaining—again. This desert living was even less comfortable than Egypt was. At least back there they had meat and all-you-can-eat meals!

Then, in Exodus 16:7, God tells Moses that He will show His "glory" to the people in the morning. What happened in the morning? A flaky kind of bread miraculously lay on the desert floor. Their first reaction was to ask, "Manna?" which is Hebrew for "What is it?" And, as you might know, that's what they ended up calling it: Manna ("What is it?")! So the miracle of daily Manna became a display of God's glory—God's ability to do great things for them.

Then, in Exodus 16:10, we read that the people "looked toward the desert, and there was the glory of the Lord appearing in the cloud." What was this glory? Exodus 24:17 tells us: "To the Israelites the glory of the LORD looked like a consuming fire on top of the mountain." Here, God's glory was the brilliant light of fire.

Shortly thereafter Moses made this request of God: "Now show me your glory" (Exodus 33:18). God responds, "I will cause all my goodness to pass in front of you, and I will proclaim my name, the LORD, in your presence. I will have mercy on whom I will have mercy, and I will have compassion on whom I will have compassion. But, you cannot see my face, for no one may see me and live." Here God's glory is described as His "goodness," but it, too, may have been manifested by light since Moses had to be placed in the crack of a nearby rock to avoid seeing the light and dying.

In the Old Testament the Hebrew word that is translated "glory" in our Bibles is the word "kabod," which means literally "heavy in weight." It implies something that is important—something very significant. So God receives kabod, or glory, by anything that shows He is important or great.

In the New Testament, the Greek word translated "glory" is the word "doxa," from which we get our word doxology. Doxa means "something that radiates from the one who has it, leaving an impression behind."[1] We might say that the sun has glory, since it gives out light and causes other objects around it to be lit up.

So we can summarize the biblical meaning of glory as "greatness," which sums up all God's worth, His love, His holiness, His transcendence, His power, His eternal nature—all the attributes that together make God so wonderful and so glorious.

I've spent time explaining this word because it's not a word that is often used in our normal everyday conversation. But think about it—*if we've been created for the purpose of glorifying God, then we better have a firm understanding about what that means!* How sad to think that we could get to the end of our lives and think that we did well, only to find that we were aiming at the wrong thing!

Consider these statements about our purpose for living:

> [God is describing His people:] "... whom I created for my glory, [emphasis mine] *whom I formed and made" (Isaiah 43:7).*

> "... *to him be glory in the church and in Christ Jesus throughout all generations, for ever and ever!" (Ephesians 3:21).*

> *"May the God of peace, who through the blood of the eternal covenant brought back from the dead our Lord Jesus, that great Shepherd of the sheep, equip you with everything good for doing his will, and may he work in us what is pleasing to him, through Jesus Christ, to whom be glory for ever and ever. Amen" (Hebrews 13:20-21).*

God's glory is to be the focal point of our lives. As I have considered the biblical descriptions and uses of glory, I've concluded that the goal of glorifying God has two components: knowing and showing.

Consider the moon. Any glory (greatness, brilliance) the moon has is due to the sun. The moon is just a rock in the sky. In fact, without the sun, most of us wouldn't even know the moon is there! But it *knows* the glory of the sun because the sun's rays shine on it. And then it *shows* that glory to us at night as it reflects the sun's rays down on us. In these ways, the moon *glorifies* the sun.

Or let's take this metaphor one more step. We *know* the glory of the sun when it hits our bodies and warms us. It's an experiential knowing. We feel it and think, This is good! (except, of course, if we're exposed too long to the sun's rays and get sunburn). Once we've known the goodness and glory of the sun, we can then *show* its glory when the sun's rays radiate off us, enabling people to see us. So we glorify the sun both by knowing and showing the sun's rays.

And so it is with us and God. We glorify God when we *know* His greatness experientially, and when we *show* His greatness visibly to others—in that order. We can't show what we first don't know. If we try to skip the knowing, our showing will be seen for the shallowness it really is. It's like a shiny red apple that's not yet ripe inside—one bite and we see it was all show. Our families, sports buddies, and office mates who see us in real-life situations will know whether our talk is just fluff or whether it's substance.

The church has had a pattern of trying to show God's greatness without knowing it. It's easier to look spiritual or talk about it than it is to actually *be* spiritual. It's easier to sing in a choir than to speak gently to our children, and it's easier to build big new church buildings than it is to treat all races as equal. But knowing God first changes all that. I love the phrase attributed to Saint Irenaeus, "The glory of God is man fully alive." Fully alive. Fully connected to God. Fully encountering daily life in the presence of the Glorious One.

I'm fully alive when I see the purpose of every created thing around me and worship God because of it. I'm fully alive when someone loves me in spite of my weaknesses—and when I love someone in spite of theirs—and both connect me to the God who is love. I'm fully alive when I offer my body's abilities back to God by serving others. I'm fully alive when God is actively shaping my attitudes to be more like Jesus. And when I'm fully alive, God is glorified—because a person whose being is alive with the purposes of God is a person who knows and shows that God is great!

Yes, we were made for this (Psalm 8:5)! As John Eldredge puts it in *Waking the Dead*, "I daresay we've heard a bit about original sin, but not nearly enough about original glory, which comes *before* sin and is deeper in our nature. We were crowned with glory and honor."[2] That vision is vital if we are to become who God intends for us to become. We have been given a created glory as a human creature, and a redeemed glory as His adopted child by faith. Together they offer us greatness—a greatness that flows from *His* greatness.

A Radical Shift

> *"Not to us, O Lord, not to us but to your name be the glory, because of your love and faithfulness" (Psalm 115:1).*

Have you met this fork in the road—the one that gives you the two choices of promoting yourself or promoting God? Robert Frost wrote: "Two roads diverged in a wood, and I—I took the one less traveled by, And that has made all the difference."[3]

Most have taken the road well traveled. And it's full of self-glorifiers, people who promote their own agendas and greatness. But the road less traveled is filled with the glory of God. It's chosen because of His great "love and faithfulness." Taking that fork "has made all the difference."

Now this requires no small shift in our hearts. We are "me monsters" who crave praise, success, comfort, pleasures, fairness, respect, and love. To give this all up in order to promote the greatness of God is a mortal blow to our ideas about life. Fear begins to creep in. We wonder, "If I promote God, what will happen to *me*?"

A number of years ago I knew a man who was deeply caught in a web of anger and criticism. I asked him, "Why don't you give it up? It's destroying your life. What's holding you back?" He thought a bit, then answered, "I don't know who I might become—and that scares me." Until we see God's glory as including His love, it can be an unnerving thing to let go of the pursuit of our own glory. Fear is a very powerful force.

I can think of nothing more life changing than to pursue glory in God rather than in ourselves or others. This is no small shift because, frankly, we're able to obtain just enough glory from our other pursuits that we can sometimes get by without feeling a deep need to do anything different. But eventually the day comes when that relationship goes sour and that success fades and your body fails and the glory fizzles. In fact, it never was all that you thought it was.

There's an interesting text in Isaiah 50 that challenges us about where we go for light in our lives:

> *"Let him who walks in the dark, who has no light, trust in the name of the LORD and rely on his God. But now, all you who light fires and provide yourselves with flaming torches, go, walk in the light of your fires and of the torches you have set ablaze. This is what you shall receive from my hand: You will lie down in torment" (Isaiah 50:10-11).*

It's tempting to light our own torches, especially when God's light seems too hard to find or when He delays its delivery. Trusting in God is not something we're very practiced at. But in the long run, relying on ourselves is disastrous. God says torment is what we'll get in the end.

One of my favorite experiences as a father was reading C. S. Lewis's *Chronicles of Narnia* to my children. (It was one of the few times I could hold my twin boys' attention for more than 10 minutes!) In the fourth book in the series, *The Silver Chair,* a young girl named Jill is very, very thirsty. To her delight she comes upon a stream. But she is immediately horrified by seeing a huge lion by the stream. She's perplexed. She's thirsty but she's also scared to go near the stream. When the lion speaks to her and invites her to drink, it only adds to her confusion.

"'Will you promise not to—do anything to me, if I do come?' said Jill.

'I make no promise,' said the Lion.

'Do you eat girls?' she said.

'I have swallowed up girls and boys, women and men, kings and emperors, cities and realms,' said the Lion. It didn't say this as if it were boasting, nor as if it were sorry, nor as if it were angry. It just said it.

'I daren't come and drink,' said Jill.

'Then you will die of thirst,' said the Lion.

'Oh dear!' said Jill, coming another step nearer. 'I suppose I must go and look for another stream then.'

'There is no other stream,' said the Lion."[4]

Like the person who fears flying and is thus hindered from seeing some amazing parts of the world, fear can keep us from seeing—and experiencing—some wonderful things about God. If we believe God caused our parent to die prematurely or if we believe He indifferently watched as we got laid off from work, or if we believe He will ruin our lives if we follow His sexual restrictions, then we will miss out on much love from Him. We will decide to explore alternative streams. Instead of running into the arms of the Lion (Christ), we often learn the hard way—that there are "no other streams."

Substitute Glories

Alternative streams are downright foolish. Tantalizing—but foolish.

> *"Has a nation ever changed its gods? (Yet they are not gods at all.) But my people have exchanged their Glory for worthless idols. Be appalled at this, O heavens, and shudder with great horror," declares the LORD. "My people have committed two sins:* They have forsaken me, the spring of living water, and have dug their own cisterns, broken cisterns that cannot hold water [emphasis mine]" *(Jeremiah 2:11-13).*

God told His people that He had given them glory. They had been given greatness because they had been given His love, His salvation, His law, His prophets, His mercy, and His presence. But let the heavens shudder with great horror at this thought: They had traded it in for the idols of the nations around them! What foolishness! What nonsense! How could they possibly have done such a thing?

I first encountered this passage with full force when reading Larry Crabb's book "Inside Out." It was one of those milestone books in my life. I realized that my heart was far worse off than I had imagined—and that God's love was far greater than I had dreamed.

It has been a sobering process, occupying many years of my life, to face the ways I have exchanged God's glory for my own. Few were obvious and intentional. Most people didn't even see them. But they were there. The pivotal question was, Where *did* I go to quench my soul's thirst? Was it to my quick mind and my sharp analysis (even if flawed)? Was it to my biblical knowledge and strong convictions? Or maybe it was to my loving and accepting family? Even in the "Lord's work" we can find substitute religious glories. They're often the hardest ones to detect.

Israel's foolishness—their sin—was thus twofold: They gave up what could have satisfied them, and they chose what didn't satisfy them (their cisterns were "broken"). We don't often use cisterns anymore, but, in the days before deep wells and city water, they were invaluable. Cisterns were usually constructed out of limestone and formed into a basin designed to collect rainwater for later use. When cisterns were broken, they offered no water. No satisfaction. So the people were doubly foolish—no God, and no satisfaction.

The sooner we recognize this, the better: God's ways are always better. They're not just right, they're *good*. They're satisfying. But unfortunately, this lesson doesn't come quickly to us. We've been taught from our childhood days to find glory in ourselves (and we, too, often pass on the same instruction to *our* children). As children we crave compliments about our cuteness, our intelligence, our athletic ability, and our work of art pinned on the refrigerator.

It's not that these are bad in themselves, but if they form the center of our worth, and if they cause self-glory without appropriate gratitude and humility before God, they can easily become substitutes for the glory found in Him.

God spoke some further relevant words through the prophet Jeremiah:

> *"Let not the wise man boast of his wisdom or the strong man boast of his strength or the rich man boast of his riches, but let him who boasts boast about this: that he understands and knows me, that I am the LORD, who exercises kindness, justice and righteousness on earth, for in these I delight"* (Jeremiah 9:23-24).

God isn't saying that we can't take joy in these human attributes. What He *is* saying is that they pale in comparison to knowing God. His kindness, justice, and righteousness are what we should take our greatest delight in. It's all about priorities. It's all about *one thing*. But it's usually not the way we have lived our lives up until now.

Indeed, this is a dramatic reorientation. To have lived years and years promoting our self-esteem through how we look, what (and how) we drive, how much we earn, how well we perform—and then to say that none of this really matters unless God is glorified in it—this is a shift of epic proportions!

Jesus once said,

> *"I am the vine; you are the branches. If a man remains in me and I in him, he will bear much fruit; apart from me you can do nothing" (John 15:5).*

Everything you and I run to for greatness, for glory, is of no ultimate value if our first nourishment does not come from the Vine.

I love my wife. And I love my three children, all of whom have now grown up. They all make me very proud to be related to them. But, if I ever seek to make them my primary glory, I will have robbed God. And I will be a fool. If I set them up as idols in my heart—looking to them for my "spring of living water"—I will have denied the glory I was made for and I will be ultimately disappointed along the way.

I met Lynn when his 32-year-old son (who was also his best friend) died unexpectedly. Through the grief and the funeral, Lynn came face-to-face with his own emptiness, which caused him to reconsider the God of his youth whom he had strayed so far from. He came to my office thirsty for purpose in his life, suspecting it had something to do with God. We chatted for some time and finally I asked him if he was a reader. He said he was, so I suggested that he read John Piper's *Desiring God.*

I saw him several months later and asked him how it was going. He said, "I wish someone had told me before that my purpose in life was to glorify God. It would have saved me a lot of heartache." Here are some words he wrote to a troubled friend a few years later:

> "Like many men I spent many years of my life chasing what I thought—or what I told myself—was expected of me. I had always been taught that I had to succeed. The only problem was, nobody ever told me what succeeding meant.
>
> When Chris died, I realized that everything I thought was important to me was really meaningless compared to what I then realized was really important. One day I woke up and realized that my family

wasn't counting on my being president of the company, or living in a big house, or having a net worth of a million dollars and retiring at age 40. It was me, myself, that thought all those things were necessary. It was MY ego that needed to be fulfilled.

I realized that the most important thing in the world is my relationship with God, then my family and my relationship with others. Sometimes we don't know what we have because we're looking in the wrong place. The happiness we really wanted is right there.

I tell you these things because I don't want you to fall into the same trap I did.

Your loving friend, Lynn."

Life is like an all-you-can-eat buffet, filled with all sorts of temptations for substitute glories. Every culture has them. And America offers them in supreme abundance! I can look to my athletic performance to define my worth. I can look to my political and national freedom as my greatest value. I can look to my clever wit to give me praise or my ability to avoid conflict to give me peace. I can even look to my church as a substitute glory (a common temptation for us pastors: "See how important I am—my church is growing and my people like me!")

But the foundational truth remains that we have been designed by our Maker to glorify *God*. It is His love for us and our love for Him that makes us truly great. Everything else is, at best, a glimmer of the real thing.

Do it All for Him

We have considered the depth of God's glory as it searches out our deepest desires and reorients them around His name. Now we consider the breadth of this glory.

> *"So whether you eat or drink or whatever you do, do it all for the glory of God" (1 Corinthians 10:31).*

It's really tempting for us to water this down a bit. Do I really have to eat to the glory of God? Or watch TV for the glory of God? What about how I style my hair? Or mow my lawn? Or prepare macaroni and cheese for the kids? Is there any area that can become absurd in pursuing God's glory?

Frankly, I don't think so. If there is any part of life that God *doesn't* want to be known in and shown as great in, then that part of life would cease to be ruled by Him. And it would be ruled by us. Or the Evil One. And that's not an option to the King of Glory. He pursues His own glory in *all* His works (which is very fitting for the One who has always existed and is the creator of all that is! The universe, by definition, is completely God-centered!).

But we must acknowledge the fact that certain activities don't seem to readily fit into this glorify-God category. How do I play *Uno* to the glory of God, shop for a shirt to magnify His greatness, or brush my teeth for His honor and fame? (Do I have to memorize Bible verses while I brush?) How do I perform routine and tedious tasks at my job and home so that God is glorified? What, exactly, does it mean to do *all* for the glory of God?

In future chapters we'll address this crucial question, but for now our focus will be on building our foundation securely. Part of that foundation is getting rid of any sacred/secular division in our thinking. The phrase "whatever you do" in the text above won't allow us to carve life up into these kinds of categories.

For example, we can't choose to glorify God at church and then *not* glorify Him in the car on the way home from church. We can't know the greatness of God while we're praying and then throw a "glorify God" switch off while we turn on a TV, or chat with a friend on the phone about what happened at our job that day. The switch is always *on*. It's all about Him being great in us and through us. Every heart's desire. Every thought. Every word spoken. Every action pursued.

Connie and her husband came to our church when their daughter began attending our church's youth group. Though Ashley had a lot of energy, she had never given her parents trouble as a child, so it wasn't easy for Connie to put up with children who misbehaved. She often found herself working with children, though, because she was skilled at administration, not because she truly loved them. Through listening to the preaching and the testimonies of others, she became convicted that God was more interested in the transformation of her heart to become like Jesus than He was about her wonderful deeds.

In her words, "This was a new concept to me, but as I continued to witness it week after week in both words and actions of many faithful church leaders and friends, and with the Holy Spirit's gentle nudging, I finally surrendered and allowed God to make the changes that he probably wanted to make in me for years. Much to my amazement, I started *liking* the kids! Then before I knew it, I started *loving* the kids—*especially* the ones who couldn't sit still, refused to listen and acted out! My entire attitude changed and my heart softened (actually, it all but melted!). No longer did I look down my nose at these "bad" children (or the parents who couldn't control them). Instead, I found a love in my heart that could only have been put there by Jesus himself—a compassionate, *real* love for the children who need it the most." Connie was meeting the glory of God and He was lovingly invading her whole life.

So God is the *one thing* that pulls all of life's purposes—and

problems—together. He's the Lover who sought us out, and gives us the privilege of loving Him in return. He's the Glorious One, the Bright One, the One
who all history points to and in whom all human values find their meaning. He
wants more than our gratitude—He wants our devotion and our love. He wants
our whole beings so that we can be fully alive in Him.

God's Glory in *Me*?

Now at this point you might wonder, How can I possibly live up to this?
When I turn to God he feels so distant—there's certainly no glorious pillar of
light in my bedroom. On my *best* day I feel about as bright as a flashlight. I
don't even want to think about my worst days. How can God glorify Himself
in *me*?" Listen:

> *"For God, who said, "Let light shine out of darkness," made*
> *his light shine in our hearts to give us* the light of the knowl-
> edge of the glory of God in the face of Christ. *But we have*
> *this treasure in jars of clay* to show that this all-surpassing
> power is from God *and not from us* [emphasis mine]"
> *(2 Corinthians 4:6-7).*

That image is so true, isn't it? "Jars of clay." Can't get more ordinary than
a clay jar. It's practically invisible on someone's shelf. And so fragile. No
glory there. And that's the point.

If there was glory in us, people would be attracted to *us*, not to God. Of
course, if you *do* have something great about you, like a great singing voice or
a great problem-solving mind or a great ability with children, that's okay. It
can still glorify God. But the reality is that people will mostly be inclined to
see *you* as great. So in your clay jar area—your fears, your insecurities, your
pride, your physical limitations—God has a chance to do something that will
make *Him* look great. Something that will "show that this all-surpassing
power is from God and not from us."

How does He do it? The text above says our experience of the "glory of
God" is "in the face of Christ." To see someone's face implies we must be
looking at Him. Intently. Consistently. Lovingly. Submissively. This isn't
some occasional thing we fit into our very important schedules and activities.
This is intentional, humble effort.

But it's not only us who look at Jesus. He is looking at us. Oswald
Chambers observes, "When the rich young man in Mark 10 failed to answer
Jesus' question correctly, the Scriptures say he looked at him and 'loved him.'"
This look of Jesus will require breaking your heart away forever from

allegiance to any other person or thing. Has Jesus ever looked in this way at you? This look of Jesus transforms, penetrates, and captivates. Where you are soft and pliable with God is where the Lord has looked at you. If you are hard and vindictive, insistent on having your own way, and always certain that the other person is more likely to be in the wrong than you are, then there are whole areas of your nature that have never been transformed by His gaze. 'One thing you lack...' From Jesus Christ's perspective, oneness with Him, with nothing between, is the only good thing."[5]

As we and Jesus gaze on one another, something happens—His light transforms these ordinary jars. So every time God does something in us, there is glory going on. Every time we cry out to Him in our anger and He calms our spirit, we see Him as great. Every time we love someone who didn't love us first, God is glorified. Every time we stop a critical comment from coming from our mouth, God is magnified. In you and me! It's our weakness—our clay jar reality—that causes His work in us to appear all the more glorious and bright!

To Glorify God is to Follow Jesus

You may be wondering how Chapter 1 on discipleship to Jesus relates to this chapter on the glory of God. The answer is that they are the same. To glorify God is the same as loving Jesus, and visa versa. In John 17 Jesus prayed for His disciples: "I have given them the glory that you gave me, that they may be one as we are one" (John 17:22). This kind of unity in which we are united as fellow disciples—just as Jesus and His Father are united—is an experience of the glory of God.

We know and show that God is great when, as followers of Jesus, we live with Jesus' heart and Jesus' love and Jesus' mind together. Those who follow Jesus glorify God because that's what Jesus, too, seeks to do (John 17:1). In the end, it's all about Him.

To glorify God is in the "DNA" of every living thing—even a rock and a mosquito (obviously some of His glory may take a bit of serious reflection to see!). In particular, it's what every *human being* is wired for, though we, of all creatures, can resist that glory.

So what will it be in your life? The microphone of heaven is held to your life. God is listening to what is picked up. And so are the people around you. Will they hear the sound that rumbles through the ages, *"God is great!"*?

For Self-Reflection and Life Application

1. In the opening parable, have you ever felt like the man at the end of the story? Or like the woman? If you answer yes to either one, in what ways?

2. Consider the advantages of having one life purpose (one thing) unite every desire, belief, action, and word in your life.

3. In what areas of your life would living for the glory of God create the most radical shift?

4. What might be some common hindrances (internal or external) to consciously living your life for the glory of God?

5. What substitute glories (broken cisterns) must you guard your heart against? Where do you tend to turn to quench your soul's thirst?

6. How do you personally react to Aslan's statement that "there is no other stream?"

7. In what areas of your life might living for the glory of God be a little puzzling as to how to actually live it out? (For example, how might you glorify God in choosing a hairstyle? Or watching the news?) Think about each example you come up with and reflect a little deeper about how you might know or show the greatness of God in this activity.

8. In light of our calling to "do it all for the glory of God," make a list of at least 20 things that you do in a typical week that know and show God's greatness (His love, power, holiness, wonder, grace, etc.), or that *could* be done to know and show His greatness.

9. Think about a time when your "clay jar" weakness was used by God to reveal His glory to you. What are some other areas of your life that could potentially be used by God to show that *He* is great and not you?

10. What motivates you most to want to live your life for the glory of God in all you do?

---

[1] Dictionary of New Testament Theology, Vol. 2, p. 44.

[2] John Eldredge, *Waking the Dead,* Thomas Nelson Publishers, Nashville, 2003, p. 14.

[3] Robert Frost, *The Road Not Taken*, 1920.

[4] C. S. Lewis, *The Silver Chair,* Collier Books, New York, 1970, p. 17.

[5] Oswald Chambers, *My Utmost for His Highest,* edited by James Reimann, Discovery House Publishers, Grand Rapids, 1992, September, 28.

Chapter 3

Pursuing Your Greatest Pleasure

The man looked down upon Kingcity with awe. There before him were miles and miles of neat apartment-like homes, clustered together in mini-communities surrounded by borders of gardens and parks. He could hear the faint sound of stringed instruments playing some joyful tune, and in the nearest park children were playing. He had never seen anything like it.

It was hard to imagine he was actually here. His conversation with the woman earlier had sent him into a week of inner unrest and intense self-reflection. His life in the village was, for the most part, quite comfortable, but he couldn't get the King out of his mind. Nor the woman's joy. Or her passionate warning.

What if he really wasn't safe after all? How could he truly know? What if taking that one drink from the spring near his village really didn't take away the disease's death grip? He found himself thinking back to the leaflet he'd read by that park bench years ago. Had the author ever visited Kingcity, or had he only lived in one of the outer villages?

"I'll only be gone about a week," he'd told his wife. She thought the whole thing was foolish, especially because he wouldn't be bringing home any income while he was gone. "I'm sorry," he said. "It's just something I need to do."

Walking the two day journey to Kingcity, he thought much about his life. His job had long ceased to give him joy. And his marriage wasn't much better. As far as he could tell, it was about like all the other marriages he knew. No fire. Just going through the motions of family life like others he knew did. But—at least there was fishing!

He was approaching the outer homes of the city by now and people were greeting him as if he was a longtime resident. "Certainly a friendly bunch," he thought. And then it hit him. Everywhere he looked he saw people whose faces and arms and hands were largely free from the ugly marks! A few had about as many as he presently had, but he recalled the woman's stories and realized that these individuals may have come to Kingcity with a worse condition of the disease than he had.

The man noticed something else—the King's presence didn't seem to take away all the people's hardships. Some appeared to be poor, and others clearly had physical disabilities. He saw some people doing rather hard jobs that he knew he certainly wouldn't want to do. Yet, there was something in their faces, something he was used to seeing in his village when rains fell after a drought, or when a baby was born, or when the town had its annual harvest picnic (though people had to be with the "right people" to have a good time). But this was different. And, from the woman's report, he guessed it had a lot to do with the King.

Suddenly he was aware of a commotion in a nearby playground. He walked towards the noise and noticed two teen boys exchanging heated words. A ball was lying on the ground, apparently from a game they had been playing. The man could feel anxiety growing in his spirit as he watched the boys trading verbal assaults. Then a fascinating thing happened.

A group of girls and boys slowly and gently walked between the two quarreling boys, forming a multi-layered wall. The man later described it as a "peace wall," not only because of what they did, but because of what he saw on their faces. Some had closed eyes (he assumed they were praying to the King) while others softly and lovingly spoke words of comfort to their feuding friends.

Within a few moments, the angry words had ceased. Adults had come by now (one looked like the father of one of the boys) and they, too, had the same spirit of contentment. No harsh words. No anxious frowns. Just small groups of love forming around each of the boys. Within minutes the two boys themselves were embracing.

The man watched in awe.

Getting Comfortable with Spiritual Joy

On a scale of natural emotion, where "0" equals the emotions of a door knob and "10" equals cheers, screams, and passion like Niagara Falls, I'm probably about a "5." A few things in life will propel me up to an "8"—like hitting a forehand smash in table tennis at game point or watching a tear-jerker movie—but, most of the time, I'm pretty moderate. Take gifts, for example. When my wife Cathy opens a present she likes, the *world* can hear her. (Okay, I exaggerate a bit.) When *I* open a present, she has to settle for a sincere "Thank you" and a smile.

When I was a teen there was one book of the Bible I had a hard time connecting with—the Psalms. They seemed way too emotional for me. I was more interested in what was *true*. Give me solid doctrine. Something to ponder and think about. Something to *believe* in.

But, of course, Christians are to "rejoice evermore!" So we would regularly hear a songleader exhort us, "Let's smile as we sing this next verse!" At the time this seemed like a reasonable thing to encourage, given the expression-less faces around me. But as I reflect upon this 40 years later, I can't help but believe that the reason so few were truly happy was because their primary joy as a Christian was limited to what they would get one day—heaven—and not what was happening in their lives day-to-day.

It wasn't until I went to college and encountered the spirited emotion of a charismatic house church, that God began to chip away at my cerebral reli-gion. It took many visits to that basement community to bring my walls down, but their sincerity and love finally got through to my heart. Reading Judson Cornwall's *Let us Praise* further weakened my "this is just the way I'm wired" argument as I saw numerous biblical references to spiritual emotion—often commanded by God. I began to see the truth that joy was God's intent for all. And even people with melancholy or phlegmatic personalities and people with left-brain oriented minds like mine could actually enjoy God!

I know many Christians who have little joy in God, but they have great joy in what this world offers. On the other hand, I know Christians who are quite happy in church worship gatherings (especially when the music touches their soul!) and thank God for every blessing they have, but whose joy falls apart in the normal pressures of their daily personal lives. I don't know if you identi-fy with any of these categories, but I invite you to join me in the pursuit of joy in God!

Created for Joy

When the writers of the *Westminster Shorter Catechism* wanted to sum up the purpose of human beings on earth, they condensed the teaching of Scripture with these words: "The chief end of man is to glorify God and enjoy Him forever." We have already affirmed the first phrase—we are here to know and show the greatness of God in our lives. Now we ask: What happens when we live this God-centered, God-glorifying life? What happens when we place God's agenda over ours and God's fame over ours? The answer is that we dis-cover that it's good! We actually enjoy it! Or, specifically, we enjoy *Him*!

When an angel appeared to some common shepherds on a Judean hillside 2,000 years ago announcing the coming of Jesus, it was to announce *joy*.

> *"I bring you good news of great joy that will be for all the people"* (Luke 2:10).

Note that's *great* joy—joy that lasts past the last worship song. And it will be for *all* the people—not just certain personality types.

So what is the source of this joy? "Today in the town of David a Savior has been born to you; he is Christ the Lord" (Luke 2:11). Matthew makes it more specific, ". . . he will save his people from their sins" (Matthew 1:21). This means we are delivered from *all* that sin enslaves us to, which means we're saved from sin's *power, presence,* and *penalty.* As we've seen in Chapter 1, it's a *full* salvation!

But it's not just what God saves us *from.* It's what God saves us *to!* Soon a throng of heralding angels joined that first angel and together they proclaimed to the shepherds, "Glory to God in the highest, and on earth peace to men on whom his favor rests" (Luke 2:14). So we are saved *to "peace."* This is really great news for all those who know the stresses of living day after day on this earth! We are also saved *to God's "favor"*—which is very good news for those who are quite aware that they fall short daily of God's holy standards.

These are only two examples taken from the Christmas narratives. The Scriptures are filled with these *from* and *to* couplets of salvation. Each time we see them, we have fresh reasons to have "great joy" and "enjoy Him forever."

So we should go through life *expecting* joy—not being surprised by it:

> • *Psalm 16:11 "You have made known to me the path of life; you will fill me with joy in your presence, with eternal pleasures at your right hand."*

> • *Psalm 19:8 "The precepts of the LORD are right, giving joy to the heart."*

> • *Psalm 43:4 "Then will I go to the altar of God, to God, my joy and my delight."*

> • *Nehemiah 8:10 "Do not grieve, for the joy of the LORD is your strength."*

Joy is to be ours both here in this life and in the one to come. It's as basic to our created identity as breathing. To not be joyful indicates that something is very wrong.

Joy and Happiness

Before we go any further, we need to address a common distinction made in Christian circles. That is between joy and happiness. It's common to hear

Christians refer to happiness as a response to circumstantial pleasure—like getting a pay raise or giving birth to a new baby—whereas joy is independent of circumstances. So, in this way of thinking, happiness is secular and joy is spiritual.

I began questioning this distinction a few years ago. In my investigation I discovered that the *Merriam-Webster Dictionary* defines *happiness* as "a state of well-being and contentment" and it defines *joy* as "a feeling of happiness that comes from success, good fortune or a sense of well-being." There seemed to be no clear distinction between these two words.

But did the *Bible* make a distinction between happiness and joy? There are three primary Greek words in the New Testament used to express joy or happiness. (1) *Chara* implies well-being and physical comfort. *Strongs Greek Dictionary* defines *chara* as "calm delight." This is the most common word in the NT for joy. (2) *Euphrosyne* implies a subjective feeling, especially in times of celebration. And (3) *agalliasis* refers to the outward expression of joy, especially in worship.

Each of these could be used to describe circumstantial joy and each could be used to describe spiritually-rooted joy. In fact, the New International Version of the Bible translates *chara* as "happiness" in Matthew 25:21 and 2 Corinthians 7:9. An example of how the Old Testament sees the two is in Psalm 68:3.

> *"But may the righteous be glad and rejoice before God; may they be happy and joyful."* (Or see also Ecclesiastes 3:12-13.)

Both happiness and joy can be the result of knowing God. So I am going to use these words interchangeably and not apologize for being happy in God! Both happiness and joy are expressions of being satisfied, delighted, and pleased in Him.

Joy: A Longing Fulfilled

The fact is, however, life is hard. And our emotions reflect that reality. A friend of mine called his two-year state of mind "spog," because it felt like a spiritual fog. Joy was hard to come by during this time. For some people this lack of joy can spiral down even further—all the way to depression.

I've pondered why this occurs. What's going on in my world that causes these mood changes—apart from any organic/chemical causes that some people may need to consider? This is important to know because, if I don't know what's causing it, I'll flounder about with no cure and often with little hope. But, if I've been created for joy, then I must not merely accept emotional dullness or constant discouragement as normal!

I have found two verses in Proverbs helpful in understanding the nature of joy:

> *"Hope deferred makes the heart sick, but a longing fulfilled is a tree of life" (Proverbs 13:12).*

> *"A longing fulfilled is sweet to the soul..." (Proverbs 13:19).*

Though these verses don't speak explicitly about joy, they elude to it. It's that "calm delight" that the Greek *chara* refers to. So I think it's reasonable to say that *joy is a longing fulfilled.*

Think about some time when you were happy or full of joy. Isn't it because some longing had just been satisfied? Someone complimented you—satisfying your longing for worth. The sun was shining—satisfying your longing for light and warmth after a string of cloudy days. A project at work turned out well—fulfilling your longing for accomplishment. Your child hugged you spontaneously—fulfilling your longing for love. The deeper the longing, the greater the joy is when it's satisfied.

The same thing applies to joy in God. If joy is the fulfillment of a longing, then it follows that for us to be joyful and happy in God, two things must happen: First, we must identify those longings that God has promised to satisfy. Second, we must pursue the fulfillment of those longings in God.

What are those longings that God wants to satisfy and therefore result in joy? Here are three major ones:

> • The longing for significance, worth, meaning, and purpose. We want our lives to count for something. At the end of the day—especially at the end of our lives—we want to look back and believe that we have made a difference; that it was good to be alive.

> • The longing to be loved, appreciated, accepted, cared for, and encouraged. We want someone out there to take interest in us and come alongside us in our times of need. We long to have someone pick us up when we fall, counsel us when we are confused, comfort us when we are hurting, befriend us when we are lonely, accept us when we fail, and find us enjoyable to spend time with.

• The longing for security, safety, and protection. The world is a risky world at times. We long to live life, knowing that our deepest fears will not come to pass—free from worry. We want to know that things will really be okay.

I'm indebted to the writings of pastor and theologian John Piper for his extensive treatments on this subject of joy. His little book, *The Dangerous Duty of Delight* is an accessible condensation of his larger work, *Desiring God*. In both he presents the biblical case that joy is not just the bi-product of the Christian life—it's our God-given goal.

He cites a number of reasons for this conviction, but his quotations of Blaise Pascal, the 17th-century, French, Christian philosopher and mathematician, are particularly enlightening. "All men seek happiness," Pascal writes. "This is without exception. Whatever different means they employ, they all tend to this end. The cause of some going to war and of others avoiding it, is the same desire in both, attended with different views. The [human] will never takes the least step but to this object (of happiness). This is the motive of every action of every man, even of those who hang themselves."[1]

Perhaps you'll need to think about this for a few minutes to confirm it in your own life, but I think you'll see it's true. The reason you're reading this book is to pursue happiness—whether you're reading it because you want to grow spiritually or because you want to please a friend who gave it to you or because you found it lying on a coffee table and you had nothing better to do. It's all motivated out of some pleasure for yourself.

Of course, this doesn't mean everyone finds the kind of happiness they are seeking. It merely means that the *pursuit* of happiness is inherent in every human being. It's part of the image we share with God, for God Himself pursues His own pleasure at all times. One example of this is Psalm 115:3, "Our God is in heaven; he does whatever pleases him."

Perhaps using the word *happiness* as a synonym for *joy* isn't comfortable to you and that's okay. I agree that it would seem somewhat strange to say you're pursuing happiness when you're yelling at your five year old for making your living room wall into impressionistic "art." But my primary goal here is to help us see that behind all our actions is the pursuit of pleasure at some level.

Our natural inclination is to pursue the satisfaction of particular longings: to feel good about ourselves, to be liked by others, to complete a task well (or quickly), to avoid conflict, to say what's on our mind, etc. The unfortunate thing, however, is that most people aren't even aware of the deepest longings that propel them toward happiness. They see only the surface, where longings for a steak dinner, a vacation at the beach, a pay raise, new clothes, or winning a championship are what drive them.

But you don't need God to pursue *these* longings. They're readily available without Him, which is why God seems so irrelevant to so many people. Who needs God when you can get happiness without Him?

I teach an online discipleship course, and one of my assignments to my students is to interview several non-Christians and ask a series of questions about why they have not been attracted to Jesus. A common response given is that they have no need for Him. Life is fine without God. Their longings are substantially met—which means either they haven't allowed themselves to face their deepest longings, or they *have* faced their deepest longings and have resigned themselves to the fact that nothing can or will ever fulfill them.

Until we recognize that our shallow longings for such things as money, power, and sexual excitement can never be sufficiently satisfied, and until we recognize that our deepest longings for significance, love, and security *can* be satisfied, we will keep eating at the wrong tables of delight. And it has the potential of killing us if we're not careful.

Delighted in God

So if we've been created for happiness, and if, in fact, we actually pursue it without even trying, then what's most important isn't that we must *pursue* happiness. It's that we must pursue the right *kind* of happiness—and for the right *reasons*. "I believe God wants me to be happy." I've heard those words many times in my ministry, often from women whose husbands no longer met their emotional needs. This time it was Laura (not her real name). Laura wasn't happy in her marriage and she believed happiness was her right—and now she had found someone who did make her happy. It wasn't that her husband had been unfaithful or abusive. He was just inattentive, insensitive, and preoccupied. If God loved her, Laura was convinced He would want her happily married. The obvious solution was a new man—and God had "answered" her prayer. Although her friends cheer her on, Laura has been deceived.

For Laura and each of us, we face a fork in the road. To pursue happiness/joy *in God*, or to pursue happiness/joy *apart from God*. It all comes down to this.

Let's say someone hurts you deeply. You have two very different choices. If you pursue your happiness *in God*, you will choose to find God's love sufficient for you and you will delight in offering forgiveness to this person. If, on the other hand, you choose to find your happiness *apart* from God, you will pursue the joy of bitterness and giving this person the cold shoulder (yes, there is a kind of joy in these things!).

We must also recognize something else here. Choosing between these two options—God and not God—can sometimes mean doing the *same* thing but with a different attitude. For example, you may put money in a church offering plate for two very different joy reasons. Your heart may be pursuing your happiness in God (and therefore you delight in the advancement of the kingdom of God that your money will bring), or your heart may be pursuing your happiness apart from God (and therefore you do it to please some inner sense of duty you have, or to keep your spouse happy, or to impress others). Same action, but different joy-pursuit reasons.

I love this text from Psalm 37:

> *"Delight yourself* in the Lord [emphasis mine] *and he will give you the desires of your heart"* *(Psalm 37:4).*

The order here is critical. God is first. Always. Our longings must find fulfillment in Him. There's nothing wrong with delighting in a new sofa, a song by a favorite artist, or a compliment. But if our fundamental delight isn't in the God who satisfies our deepest longings for significance, love, and security, then these earthly delights actually become idolatrous in our hearts. They act as substitutes for the primary satisfaction of our souls in God. "Delight yourself in the Lord. . ."

Proverbs 28:26 says, "He who trusts in himself is a fool, but he who walks in wisdom is kept safe." So if we look to a safe neighborhood, retirement accounts, therapy sessions, a strong military, and our own hands and mind to give us security rather than to the God who saves and keeps, then we have become fools. If we're looking for direction in life from government, bosses, spouses, favorite authors, our own passions, etc.—instead of seeing God as our Lord and leader—then we have again become fools.

Our basic longings are to be met by God. This means we are to pursue the things God gives, and we are to pursue them with a heart that honors Him. So enjoy that chocolate-mint ice-cream cone. Delight in that TV show that captures your imagination. Rejoice in your wife (or husband) as Proverbs 5:18 says we should! But delight in them as *gifts* from God and *submitted* to God. And, by all means, don't stop there.

Press on to know the fullness of life that Jesus brings: the fruit and gifts of the Spirit, the beauty of God's holiness, the sweetness of confessing sin to a God of grace, the power of His love to you—and through you to others. *This* is joy! Discover the longings of your soul that only are met by encountering *Him*.

> *"My soul finds rest in God alone; my salvation comes from him"* *(Psalm 62:1).*

"As the deer pants for streams of water, so my soul pants for you, O God. My soul thirsts for God, for the living God. When can I go and meet with God?" (Psalm 42:1-2).

One of my heroes from church history is George Mueller, the director of the orphanage in England that ministered to hundreds of children without asking any person for money. His first wife died after 40 years of marriage and then, after two years of marriage to Susannah, she developed typhoid fever. Her health plummeted and death was expected. He wrote these words in his journal: "I was enabled, through my knowledge of God, to take this cup out of the hands of my heavenly Father, as the best thing for me under the circumstances. I delighted myself in God. I was satisfied with his dealings with me, being assured that much good would come out of this to me."[2]

Mueller's delight was in the work of God in him, even in the face of possibly losing one of his earthly longings—a wonderful wife. George Mueller had it right.

In Jesus' closing words to His disciples a few days before His death, He spoke several times about joy:

"I have told you this so that my joy may be in you and that your joy may be complete [emphasis mine]" *(John 15:11).*

And to His Father He prayed, "'I am coming to you now, but I say these things while I am still in the world, so that they may have the full measure of my joy within them'" (John 17:13). "Complete" joy. "Full measure" of joy! This is no "come to church and sing a favorite upbeat song" joy. This joy isn't based on how well the pastor delivered the morning sermon and whether he was funny, personal, practical, or "meaty." This joy is based in spiritual realities, where God satisfies substantial longings.

So what are "these things" that Jesus says enable joy? Many statements in those chapters could be cited, but I think the following two capture the heart of what Jesus is referring to: "'Do not let your hearts be troubled. Trust in God; trust also in me'" (John 14:1). "'As the Father has loved me, so have I loved you. Now remain in my love. If you obey my commands, you will remain in my love, just as I have obeyed my Father's commands and remain in his love'" (John 15:9-10).

From the beginning of God's covenant to Israel, ("Listen, listen to me, and eat what is good, and your soul will delight in the richest of fare"—Isaiah 55:2), through the promises of Jesus, and right up until today, *joy is consistently found in a love relationship with God that shows itself by trust and obedience to what He has promised and commanded.* We will look at this further in future chapters, but for now, we must see that this orientation of all of life under the love and rule of God is the necessary beginning of joy.

Counterfeits and Barriers to Joy

Depending on Common Grace. One of the greatest hindrances to finding happiness in God is misinterpreting what His various blessings mean. Our addiction to earthly pleasures sets us up for the age-old problem of worshiping God's gifts rather than God Himself.

Thanksgiving holidays are a good example of this. The typical Christian family is thankful for "my family, our home, my health, and the freedom we have in America." But these are the same things most American Muslim or Buddhist families—even atheist families—are thankful for. One need not be a Christian to be a recipient of "common grace," which are general blessings God gives to most inhabitants of Planet Earth.

> *"He causes his sun to rise on the evil and the good, and sends*
> *rain on the righteous and the unrighteous" (Matthew 5:45).*

Larry Crabb points this out in many of his writings. In *The Pressure's Off*, Crabb says, "We're never more deceived than when we think we're living for God but in fact are living for His blessings."[3] The danger here is that when particular blessings are no longer present (either because they are removed or because we may go to live in a country where these particular blessings never existed), then we begin to doubt God's love—and we lose our joy. The ironic thing about this, of course, is that the very countries to which some Christians might move and *lose* their joy—because there is no TV, no electricity for hair blowers, no flush toilets, no supermarket choices, no microwaves, no social security, etc.—are the very same countries whose national Christians are *filled* with joy! Something is wrong with this picture.

The problem is that we have lost the simplicity of happiness in God and His promise to meet our basic needs, and we have substituted an individually-based, money-based, entertainment-based lifestyle that has *nothing to do* with the joy Jesus spoke about. In fact, many of our "blessings" are not given to us at all by God. They have been *grabbed* and *bought* by *us*!

The result is that spiritual joy has often been counterfeited by earthly joy. And the American church has, to a great extent, bought the deception. We have a hard time imagining joy apart from the "blessings" of a capitalistic, free enterprise economy, or apart from the "blessings" of democracy.

I put these words in quotes because though they include benefits to the follower of Jesus, they also hold great risks as well. The pursuit of happiness may be an inalienable right, and freedom may be a cherished value, but when people's minds and hearts are no longer tied to God, these pursuits will most certainly drift in the direction of whatever prevailing morality may be strongest at the time! And it is unlikely to glorify God.

Delayed Blessings. We must also acknowledge that some of God's blessings are painfully slow in coming—which causes us to look for happiness from sources that give us more immediate pleasure. One example of this delayed pleasure is in God's promise of tangible blessings.

For example, in Hebrews 11 Abraham is praised for obeying God in going to the Promised Land, even though Abraham never saw the promises of the Promised Land. What gave Abraham joy? He "was looking forward to the city with foundations, whose architect and builder is God" (Hebrews 11:10). In other words, by faith he was looking forward to heaven. That's quite a delayed blessing!

Some tangible blessings have to wait—even until heaven. In this "possibly delayed until heaven" category we would also put perfect physical health (2 Corinthians 5:1-2) and perfectly loving and united relationships (Mark 10:29-30). Life may not always be pretty here on earth, even for Jesus' disciples. (Or shall we say *especially* for Jesus' disciples, in light of such texts as Acts 14:22, "We must go through many hardships to enter the kingdom of God?")

Joy, then, must be found beyond such earthly blessings as the expertise of modern medicine and the hope of permanent marriage vows—as wonderful as these are. God isn't handcuffed and gagged when difficult things like terminal illnesses and shattered marriages occur. He's not fretting over how He will possibly make something good come out of these tragedies (Romans 8:28).

He's still there, eager to pour out Himself to any who seek Him with all their heart. It's just that the *expression* of joy we may be seeking will have to wait a few years or more, and we will likely need to realign our joy pursuit to deeper things—things God has *promised* to satisfy *now*.

Effort is Required. Let's be honest. Some of God's spiritual blessings that bring happiness aren't as easily accessible as an entertaining movie or a fun shopping spree. The happiness God promises can often require *work* (which often goes against the grain of our concept of the "good life"). Contentment in an unfulfilling marriage is work. Resisting self-condemnation requires effort.

What kind of work? The work of faith in the promises and character of God. The work of repentance, holiness, and love. Yes, they are enabled by the Spirit, but the surrender of mind and heart that releases them still requires spiritual effort. It doesn't surprise us, then, to find our hearts attracted to sources of joy that are sometimes more immediate, even if they don't last very long and even if they dishonor God. These temptations require effort to resist—effort of mind and heart and faith in a wonderful God.

Suffering. One further hindrance to happiness is the presence of suffering. How is it possible to be happy when we're also in pain? When a spouse stops communicating, when a child contracts a life-threatening disease, when a church goes through a crisis—these aren't joyful events. They rightfully result in sorrow, for they cause God sorrow, too (Genesis 6:5-6).

Life is filled with suffering and we must understand something very important here: suffering is not a hindrance to joy. In fact, according to the Bible, suffering can make us even more sensitive to deeper joy.

In the midst of the apostle Paul's persecution and terrible trials, he says he was

> ". . . sorrowful, yet always rejoicing . . . having nothing, and
> yet possessing everything" (2 Corinthians 6:10).

The pain is still painful. It doesn't disappear. But we can still be joyful! Why? *Because God is in us, with us, and for us!* Our love relationship with Him, His formation of godly character and faith in us, our expressions of love to others, and our hope of heaven all work together to give us joy even when painful things happen.

God's answer to delayed blessings and suffering is that He has given us His Spirit as a down payment. In the words of 2 Corinthians 5:5, "Now it is God who has made us for this very purpose and has given us the Spirit as a deposit, guaranteeing what is to come." Yes, the best is yet to come, but the taste we get now is very, very significant. It's so significant that when we taste it, we know the full banquet is a sure thing!

To summarize this section on counterfeit joys: we must be diligent about constantly submitting our longings to God. Why? Because our hearts are so easily inclined to be captured by self-serving pursuits rather than God-glorifying pursuits. Until God captures our hearts, the people and circumstances of this world will rob us of our joy every day.

So submit your longings to God and, when necessary, let Him change them, soften them, or readjust expectations about them. We will know when we have the real thing, and not a counterfeit, because joy that is found in God—and not just His gifts—can never be taken from us!

The Satisfaction of Being a Disciple of Jesus and Glorifying God

Now, let's pull these first three chapters together. We have seen that we have been created for joy, and that joy is found in a loving, trusting relationship with God Himself. All people pursue happiness. But it's the follower of Jesus who is best equipped to find it—and keep it!

Jesus has come "that they may have life, and have it to the full" (John 10:10). Full life is satisfying life. His kingdom is the pearl of great price that is worth selling all we own to get it (Matthew 13:45-46)! Those who live in the values of His kingdom (values like humility, pursuing righteousness, mercy, purity of heart, peacemaking, etc.) are called "blessed" or "happy" (Matthew 5:3-11). The point is this: *We follow Jesus not just because we should, but because it's good!*

Following God is good for us! And it *feels* good (not like some medicine that we're told "is good for you" but tastes like liquid cardboard!) We experience it as *chara*—"a calm delight." And it often even breaks through to *agalliasis*—"an exuberant joy!" These joy-expressions are connected, ultimately, to our experience of the greatness of God, as these passages show:

> • Psalm 34:8-10 "Taste and see that the LORD is good; blessed is the man who takes refuge in him. Fear the LORD, you his saints, for those who fear him lack nothing. The lions may grow weak and hungry, but those who seek the LORD lack no good thing."

> • Psalm 63:1-7 "O God, you are my God, earnestly I seek you; my soul thirsts for you, my body longs for you, in a dry and weary land where there is no water. I have seen you in the sanctuary and beheld your power and your glory. Because your love is better than life, my lips will glorify you. I will praise you as long as I live, and in your name I will lift up my hands. My soul will be satisfied as with the richest of foods; with singing lips my mouth will praise you. On my bed I remember you; I think of you through the watches of the night. Because you are my help, I sing in the shadow of your wings."

> • Philippians 4:4 "Rejoice in the Lord always. I will say it again: Rejoice!"

These passages speak about a joy, a satisfaction, a goodness that is attractive. It's compelling to the one who is seeking happiness—provided they are willing to give up their life to get it (Luke 9:24). That's always the catch with God! But the sooner we understand that, the sooner we can pursue the kind of happiness we have been created to know.

This is joy that doesn't go up and down according to events around us. It's joy that's present even when our job doesn't go well, even when our kids are moody, even when the bills are more than we have in the bank. *Because happiness is found in God and His life in us!*

Consider the tendency of many churches to emphasize obedience and rules. Godly behavior is prescribed in detail and deviation from the church's standards is met with judgment. Of course, obedience to God is a good thing. But it doesn't usually nurture joy—and love. Love cultivates obedience, but the reverse isn't necessarily true—obedience doesn't necessarily cultivate love. (Ask any child being raised by authoritarian parents.)

So what *does* bring about love for God? Longings fulfilled! And that's what I want. I want a relationship with God that is brimming with love with all my heart and with all my soul and with all my mind because God has satisfied my soul! That is the path to joy.

That visit to the house church during my college days began a shift in my heart from believing in God to loving God, from duty to happiness. Countless encounters with Him since then have moved me closer and closer to His heart, where increased longings of my soul have been fulfilled.

I heard these helpful words by John Piper some years ago, and they brought it all together for me: *"God is most glorified in us when we are most satisfied in him."* [4] Yes, that's it! He has made us for happiness, but it's a happiness that is rooted in *His* glory, not our own!

The more we pursue our greatest satisfaction in God, the more He will be known and shown as great—as glorious—in us. Our deepest longings will be satisfied and it won't be through a perfect marriage, a successful career, a certain body shape, or entertainment. Those often glorify ourselves—or something else or someone else. When we look to God and enjoy His presence, His power, and His purposes, we are deeply satisfied and God receives the glory for being the source of that satisfaction!

> *"He who did not spare us his own Son, but gave him up for us all—how will he not also, along with him, graciously give us all things? [emphasis mine]" (Romans 8:32).*

If we have been given "all things," and we "lack no good thing" in God, how can we possibly not be satisfied? Isn't that the real issue? Isn't it about whether we really believe that we have "all things" through our relationship with Jesus? And that the things *we* think we *need* to be happy really aren't necessary? Isn't our problem that we are in serious need of a taste-realignment? We must learn to savor the things of God so that we find them totally satisfying and joyful and good—far beyond what the world can offer.

One way I remind myself about where my greatest joy comes from is to periodically recall this list of seven spiritual blessings we have in Christ: Fellowship with God, Forgiveness of sins, Freedom from sin, Fullness of life, Family of God, Flow of Love to the World, and Forever life. Each of these highlight the fact that God is most glorified in us when we are most satisfied in Him. In other words, when I turn to God to obtain these seven realities, I experience the greatness of God (He is glorified) and my deepest longings are met (I am satisfied).

I've heard worship leaders say, "We haven't come this morning for ourselves, we've come for God. It's not about us, it's all about Him." Though these statements are well-intended, I don't believe they're biblical. Certainly it is true that the universe centers on God. And certainly it is true that the purpose of our lives is to glorify God—and that we often think too highly of ourselves. But it's also true that God wants to glorify Himself by saving us, filling us, changing us, sending us—and satisfying us! We must not feel guilty about benefiting from worship (or from any other spiritual activity) if it is God who is the center of that activity. God's glory and our joy are meant to be inseparable!

So come to church gatherings to be blessed and to be made happy—in God! And He will be glorified for being the one who made the difference in your life!

Freed from Unhappy Choices!

One of the most significant implications of this truth, that God is most glorified in us when we are most satisfied in Him, is that we are freed from having to decide between following Jesus and being happy. For example, the woman who feels trapped in a loveless marriage doesn't have to choose between the possible happiness of divorce and the possible unhappiness of staying in the marriage. God promises to satisfy her *in* the marriage, if she chooses to glorify God—and not herself—*in* the marriage. And the man who is tempted by sexual excitement doesn't need to choose between the sensual joy of sexual lust and the perceived unhappiness of sexual purity. God promises to satisfy him *in* his sexual purity if he chooses to glorify God—and not himself—*in* his sexuality.

I invite you to enter the world of joy. I invite you to enter the kingdom of God. It's a day-to-day reality that embraces God's life for you. Joy comes from joyfully surrendering to the rule of Jesus because you know that this will make God look great in you and that His greatness in you satisfies your deepest longings—which is for your greatest joy!

Because I believe these things, I commonly end my prayers with words like, "Lord, I ask these things for your glory, and our joy! Amen!" This is what God is up to in this world!

Are you willing to face the longings of your heart and begin to let God satisfy them? Perhaps you haven't wanted to let your heart dream like this for some time, but you're realizing that God is still in the bread of life and living water business. Yes, the full reality of satisfaction is yet to come when we enter the new heaven and new earth. But we should expect *substantial* joy now—here on this earth!

What longings of your soul has God promised to meet? Can you dare let them surface to the consciousness of your soul and feel their tug so God can begin to meet them? Can you let the Lord of the Universe invade your soul with His love so that He can glorify Himself in you and bring you joy?

> *"May the God of hope fill you with all joy and peace as you trust in him" (Romans 15:13).*

Joy is not automatic. It comes through trusting in God for all who He is for you in Christ.

So hunger for happiness. Thirst for joy. And pursue them as a devoted follower of Jesus for the glory of God! If this has stirred something inside you, but you still aren't sure exactly how to go about these things, I invite you to read on.

Be encouraged with this wonderful promise:

> *"Though you have not seen him, you love him; and even though you do not see him now, you believe in him and are filled with an inexpressible and glorious joy,* [emphasis mine] *for you are receiving* [present tense!] *the goal of your faith, the salvation of your souls" (1 Peter 1:8-9).*

God satisfies our longings—and inexpressible joy is our bonus.

For Self-Reflection and Life Application

1. What are some common sources/causes of your happiness in life? When you have identified them, what longing is each one satisfying?

2. How does the concept of being created to experience joy strike you? In what way has your background and past prepared you to embrace a joy-focused life? And in what ways hasn't it?

3. What do you think of Pascal's statement that "All men seek happiness?" Does it seem true in the hundreds of decisions you make each day? In what ways might this truth change the way you view life?

4. What does Psalm 37:4, "Delight yourself in the Lord and he will give you the desires of your heart" have to say to you about joy and how desires are influenced? How might you apply this in your own life in a practical way?

5. How might you tell the difference between being "happy in God" and in being "happy in God's gifts?" When might they be the same, and when might they be very different?

6. Which of the "counterfeits" or "barriers" to God's joy have you faced, and what might you do to address them?

7. If "God is most glorified in us when we are most satisfied in him," how might a person pursue his or her greatest joy when hurt or criticized by a friend?

---

[1] John Piper, *Desiring God,* Multnomah Publishers, Inc., Sisters, 1996, p. 16.

[2] Roger Steer, *George Mueller: Delighted in God,* Harold Shaw Publishers, Wheaton, 1979, p. 234.

[3] Larry Crabb, *The Pressure's Off,* WaterBrook Press, Colorado Springs, 2003, p. 82.

[4] Piper, *Desiring God,* p. 9.

PART TWO

Come, Become, and Love—a Framework to Live Our Lives for the Glory of God

You are being changed. To commit to living a Christ-centered, God-glorifying, happiness-pursuing life is radical in the eyes of the world—and maybe even in the eyes of some of the professing Christians you know. Something's stirring within you that you know is resonating with eternal things. This *is* the way life is supposed to be lived.

For some people, the truths in these first three chapters are enough to launch them into spiritual transformation. The dots are connecting in their minds and they're off and running! But for others (myself included), this will take me to the state park, but I still need a trail map to get around once I'm there.

These next six chapters are that map. They will give practical ways to know and show that God is truly great—right in the middle of your life. They summarize what it means in tangible terms to glorify God and to find your greatest joy in three heart-actions: *Come, Become,* and *Love.* This is what we have been made for.

Will it require work? Yes. Change? Absolutely. But even more so, these chapters are a further invitation to joy. I pray they will inspire you to live in the kingdom of His love, for this is the life the Spirit has come to give us—a life filled with the glory of God.

Chapter 4

Come—An Invitation to a Love Relationship With God

The man had scarcely been in Kingcity for more than a half hour when a stir moved through the streets. People began talking excitedly and started walking toward one of the larger parks nearby. The man mustered enough courage to approach a young couple walking by him. "What's going on?" he asked.

"You must be new here," the young man said. The traveler nodded. "Welcome to Kingcity," the young man said, smiling and embracing him— which took the man somewhat by surprise. The young man introduced himself and his female friend. He was a cook in a nearby restaurant and she was a manager at a local retail store.

"The King is making his visit to our neighborhood," the cook explained. The tone of his voice showed that this was something he looked forward to with great anticipation. "He travels throughout the city going to various neighborhoods each day. It's a highlight when he comes! Everyone stops what they're doing to go meet with him."

The man took a stab at the King's purpose. "Sort of like a town meeting where everyone gets to express their complaints to the King?"

The couple looked at each other and smiled, as if they, too, had once shared similar thoughts. "It doesn't work that way," the woman said. "His visits are times of special fellowship together—like when we spend time together," she said, looking at her friend. "They aren't times of just asking for what we want. They're times of talking together about all sorts of things. But mostly they're times of enjoying the King's love for us."

This seemed strange to the man because the King had always seemed distant to him. Real but distant. He knew about His love, but it was mostly related to the spring and his not having to die because of the boils. And occasionally he would want the King to bail him out of a particularly difficult situation (like the time his daughter fell from a tree and was unconscious for several hours). But to think of coming to the King for love—in any form the King should choose to give it—was a new concept.

"Of course," the young man spoke up, "these visits aren't the only times we come to Him. He's the King, you know. He's able to hear us and speak to us even when He's in other parts of the kingdom. When we first came to Kingcity we started to see how really needy we were—in our hearts and minds—and how He wanted to meet those needs. He's made a great difference in our lives." He smiled as he again exchanged smiles with the young woman by his side.

The man thanked the couple and began walking with the flow of the people towards the park. His mind drifted to his woodworking business and all the frustrations that came with it—deadlines, difficult customers, dry sales. Did the King want to be part of his life in these routine things? Then he thought of his marriage. Scenes flashed in front of him as he replayed their shared hurts over the last few years. Did the King want access there, too? This city and its people were taking him places his heart had never traveled.

An Oxymoron: Faith Without Relationship

Every now and then I'll meet people who will speak about their spiritual journey in terms similar to these: "I was raised in the church all my life, but it wasn't until *[fill in the blank]* that I realized God wanted to have a personal relationship with me." This is one of the startling realities in parts of the church today—that someone could actually be exposed to the teachings of Jesus and come away with a non-relationship style of faith! It's like a husband telling his wife one day, "I didn't realize that marriage was about relationship!"

Most of you reading this book will likely fall into the category of "evangel-ical." That is to say, you believe that the Bible is the Word of God, and you believe that a personal faith response to Christ is necessary for salvation. Therefore, it's unlikely that you heard a non-relationship type of faith preached from the pulpit. You've heard about God's love for you and God's desire for your love. However, that doesn't mean that you—or church people you know—haven't adopted a non-relational type of faith in practice.

If faith is seen as a mental assent to facts about God and Jesus—that is, Jesus died for my sins or Jesus is the Son of God—or if faith is mostly seen as living by certain religious behaviors, one doesn't need a relationship with God. Oh, He may come in handy when faced with an occasional crisis but, for the most part, He becomes irrelevant to daily life.

Contrast this to what we have seen about the life of the disciple of Jesus whose aim is to be *like* Jesus and have Jesus' life imparted to Him. Or contrast this to what we have seen about living for the glory of God in whatever you do. Relationship is at the very heart of our purpose in life. It is for relationship that we have been made "a little lower than the heavenly beings" and "crowned . . . with glory and honor!" (Psalm 8:5).

It is in God that we "live and move and have our being" (Acts 17:28). This is much more than getting saved. It is about love, worship, and longings fulfilled by the Giver of Life. It's about interacting—talking and listening to one another, feeling various emotions about one another, disappointing and giving joy to one another, and living out our distinct roles in that relationship. Does this describe how you relate to God in a typical day?

Come To God

There are times in my life that I lose focus. "Life" happens and I'm caught up in it. God's glory is the furthest thing from my mind, and I certainly don't see Jesus—because I'm not looking for Him.

It's times like this that I find it helpful to recall something simple— something that can begin to get my heart and my mind back on track. Throughout our home we have numerous digital clocks. When a power failure occurs in our area, these clocks either show a blank screen or they start over at 12:00. Either way, they're no longer calibrated to the correct time. If I were to order my schedule using these uncalibrated clocks, it would wreck havoc in my life. They need to be recalibrated to the correct time.

So it is with the state of our souls when life comes pressing in upon us, and we respond with thoughts, desires, words, and actions that don't correspond to the Truth. We need something to help us refocus. To recalibrate. We need some way to find "true North" again when our emotions are all over the place and old ungodly habits are kicking in.

I've found three simple words helpful to me in this pursuit. Each of these is a sign post that redirects me to how life is meant to be lived for the glory of God. They are *come, become,* and *love*. This chapter and the next will address the first of these—*come*.

In the beginning chapters of Genesis, God is described as walking in the garden where Adam and Eve were. But they're hiding among the trees from Him. They had just committed their first act of rebellion against Him. But instead of immediately punishing them for their act, He asks them a question: "Where are you?" (Genesis 3:9). Instead of the normal fellowship they had experienced up to this time, there was distance. Instead of *coming* to Him, they were now fleeing in shame. This theme of God calling out to His people to come to Him is seen throughout the Scriptures and culminates in the last paragraphs of Revelation,

> *"The Spirit and the bride say, "Come." And let everyone who hears say, "Come." And let everyone who is thirsty come. Let anyone who wishes take the water of life as a gift" (Revelation 22:17 NRSV).*

Stop for a moment and consider this. The Maker of the Universe, the Eternal Spirit, the Beginning and the End is inviting you to a relationship with Him! He desires to impart His life to you, a life that's marked by eternal realities. The fact is, it's not just longevity of life that we thirst for—it's *Him*! That's why Augustine said, "My soul is restless until it finds its rest in Thee." As a glove has been made for a hand, so we have been made for Him.

A woman came to me after her fiancé had suddenly left her. She was crushed. Her longings for relationship had been dashed. Though she had responded to Christ as a youth, she had turned her back on God when her father died in her teens. Now it was 26 years later. She was nursing many wounds and facing numerous challenges. She had been spending time at a local café owned by a couple in our church, Jim and Mary. Mary had offered her spiritual hope and eventually suggested she talk with me.

As I shared the good news of God's love for her—a God who wasn't the bad guy—her heart broke and, amidst tears of conviction and joy, she returned to the One who made her, died for her, sought her, and wanted to rescue her. She was ready to pass through the narrow gate of repentance and faith—a faith in all that Jesus was for her. She found peace for her restless soul. God freed her from being needy for a man in her life, though she certainly still desired one. She had come home to a relationship with the One who made her for Himself.

Perhaps one of the clearest expressions of this *come* invitation of God to us is found when the risen and ascended Jesus addresses the church in Laodicea that had grown cold, calloused, and self-satisfied:

> *"Here I am! I stand at the door and knock. If anyone hears my voice and opens the door, I will come in and eat with him, and he with me" (Revelation 3:20).*

Several things stand out in this text:

• ***Jesus is initiating the relationship.*** He is the one who is knocking at our door. The love invitation starts with Him. The Greek word translated "knock" here actually implies that His knocking is persistent. He is knocking—and He will *keep* knocking in order to issue His invitation to *come*.

• ***He's offering us something good—fellowship with Himself.*** In the culture of Jesus, eating was a time for conversation. People sat down and ate together (an unusual experience for many contemporary American families) and they talked.

They shared their lives, thoughts, and longings together. That's the kind of relationship God wants with us: fellowship, mutual dialog, and sharing our hearts together.

• ***We must respond to the invitation.*** He's not going to walk right in. The ball's in our court. It's our move. In the 19th century Holman Hunt painted a picture of Jesus, crowned with thorns and wearing a royal robe, holding a lantern and standing at a door overgrown with weeds—and no visible door latch. It was called *The Light of the World,* and Hunt said he became a Christian while he was working on it. This Jesus is not going to kick the door down and storm inside. He's done His part: He has come, taught, healed, died, risen, imparted forgiveness and new life—and now He knocks. For some people, it's the first time. For most of us, it's the millionth time. The Light of the World knocks and issues His invitation to us. It is simply, "Come." What will we do?

So Jesus wants to spend time with us. And maybe we *should* answer. After all, He's God! But could there possibly be any other reason to open that door? Could, perhaps, joy be behind it?

Something Bigger Than Prayer

At this point it's possible that you may be thinking something like, Yes, I know I need to have a better prayer life. My "quiet times" have been a little too quiet (or nonexistent) and my "devotions" have had little devotion about them. My mind wanders when I pray. I don't really feel like going to church prayer meetings. I often feel like I'm just talking to the ceiling.

If you've ever thought along these lines, take heart in the fact that you have a lot of company—including the writer of this book! Prayer isn't something that has come natural to me. I often would prefer to read, play, work, watch TV, pay bills, fix a squeaky door, or do a host of other things than pray. That's my natural tendency.

For example, my mind wanders like crazy when I try to spend long times in prayer. Add that to the fact that I'm a more task-oriented person than a people-oriented person, and that God Himself is invisible to the five senses (at least directly)—and prayer can become quite a chore.

This all changed significantly for me a number of years ago when I began to focus more on God's invitation to me to *come.* Instead of prayer being something I *should* do, I began to see it as a natural part of something bigger—to glorify God through a love-relationship with Him.

It had crushed my spirit to see prayer as a duty that had to be fulfilled at certain times of the day, for certain blocks of time, with certain prayer formulas and lists. I was bound by guilt, fueled by people telling me what my prayer life should look like, and I felt distant from the very God who I wanted to be close to.

So I decided to start over with a fresh slate. I decided to only be motivated by the loving call of a God whose invitation to *come* was a call to greatness. He was saying, Put your lists away. Put your schedules away. Stop letting other people define your relationship with me. Just *come*. Let's get to know each other.

I'm not against forms and structures of prayer. What I am cautioning against is a pattern of talking to God that is devoid of connecting to His heart and His goodness. I believe the word *come* captures that. It speaks of something bigger. It speaks of love—and relationship.

What Are We Coming To?

Now none of this will capture our interest if we're afraid of this beckoning God, if we feel unworthy to come to Him, or if we have all sorts of distorted ideas about who this God is.

For example, if you think He took your mother in death while you were still a child, you may have grown to resent Him for it and not be attracted to a love invitation from this kind of God. You may be hesitant to want to be loved by a God who you've been told controls and determines all the details of our lives, including every evil done to you and every disease and physical calamity that happens to you.

If you believe you can never be good enough to please this God because of your perfectionist tendencies or because you have certain sinful behaviors that have stubbornly plagued you for many years, you may not feel drawn by His invitation to *come*.

I'd like to share three fundamental beliefs that are critical for us to want to come to God. Let's face it: Why *should* we open the door and let Him in?

1. *God desires me.* Many of my days are quite ordinary. They aren't filled with deep spiritual experiences. In fact, I can go for hours without even being aware of any "knocking." But when I think about this truth—that God desires me—it becomes a powerful motivator to respond to His call to *come*.

Your response is not indifferent to God. He doesn't say, *come*, and then follow it with a "Whatever," as if your response doesn't really matter to Him. The truth is that He's longing for you to say "yes!" He is passionate about you.

Listen to how the apostle Paul puts it:

> *"And because you are children, God has sent the Spirit of his*
> *Son into our hearts, crying, 'Abba! Father!'" (Galatians 4:6*
> *NRSV).*

In other words, God wants your love so much that He gives you His Spirit who makes your heart *want* to relate to Him as an intimate Father. He has "lavished" His love on you (1 John 3:1) so that you could be His child. There's nothing about you that can stop His love from reaching out to you. If you have responded to Him in repentant faith, you are His child and He will continually knock until you answer. He wants your love—so He can fully pour out *His* love on you!

2. *God is good to me.* "Taste and see that the LORD is good; blessed is the man who takes refuge in him. Fear the LORD, you his saints, for those who fear him lack nothing" (Psalm 34:8-9). We have seen this already in Chapter 3, but this truth must be burned deeply into our minds. God wants to bless you with His goodness! When you relate to God by tasting Him, seeing Him, taking refuge in Him, and fearing Him, you "lack nothing" that you need. *Nothing.* His goodness actually *feels* good! You can taste it and see it!

If we truly believe this, why would we *not* want to come to Him? Why would we choose something else? He's knocking and He's bearing gifts with our name on them! Of course, this doesn't mean they're always the gifts we want—but they *are* the gifts we need the most! The ones that satisfy deep longings. The ones that bring us joy that no one can take away from us.

God is good—even when painful things happen. In fact, in pain we *especially* need His goodness.

> *"And we know that* in all things God works for the good
> [emphasis mine] *of those who love him, who have been called*
> *according to his purpose" (Romans 8:28).*

Can you imagine living by this verse? Really? Believing with all your heart that God is good—and He's good to you in the midst of *"all things?"* You would *run* to the door and fling it open, like a child hearing Grandpa and Grandma at the front door, knowing they came bearing Christmas gifts.

Opening the door to God in painful experiences is one of the most deeply spiritual experiences you can have in life. To see His goodness (and learn to recognize it) through eyes of love when hardships come your way is the ultimate expression of love to Him—and trust. It's a step into the heart of God.

3. *God is Full of Grace.* I can't imagine life without the reality of God's grace. My failures would condemn me. My easily-tempted heart would make me hide in the trees whenever I heard the Lord walking nearby. My recurring sins would enslave me. But praise God for His grace that rescues me from these prisons, despite my weaknesses.

Biblical grace is "any expression of the unmerited (unearned) love of God that comes in response to the needs of His people." It is both God's *accepting attitude* to us (Romans 3:24) and His *powerful action* to us (2 Corinthians 12:9; Romans 12:6) that come when we are undeserving of it. So our forgiveness is not earned, and our spiritual empowerment to live a holy life is not earned. They are gifts. We cannot boast of what *"I"* have accomplished.

As mentioned in the first chapter, this doesn't mean that God's grace is without conditions. The heart must be humble and repentant to receive the *fullness* of His grace. Nevertheless, Ephesians 2:8-9 tells us grace is a gift. It's one more reason why we should respond to God's invitation to *come*.

> *"And God is able to make* all grace *abound to you, so that in* all things *at* all times, *having* all that you need, *you will abound in* every good work [emphasis mine]" *(2 Corinthians 9:8).*

When this kind of God gives these kinds of promises, answering the door is not a hard thing to do! If we get these realities firmly imbedded in our minds—that God desires us, that God is good to us, and that His grace is *for us* in our inadequacies—then we will *sprint* into the arms of God frequently. We will "approach the throne of grace with confidence, so that we may receive mercy and find grace to help us in our time of need" (Hebrews 4:16).

So let me ask you: What picture comes to your mind when *your* God invites you (actually *urges* you) to *come* to Him? Is it the Good Shepherd of Psalm 23 in whose presence you "shall not be in want," and who leads you to waters and pastures that are exactly what you need to live well, and who protects and rescues you with His rod and staff? Is He someone you would want to spend a few minutes with or perhaps even a whole day with—or maybe eternity with?

Put simply, is your God the God of Scripture, the God who has revealed Himself in the relationship-seeking Jesus who is *Immanuel*, "God with us?" Or is He someone you have poorly pieced together from childhood, parents, experiences, books, and even past preachers, with the result that His invitation to *come* is not compelling to you at all?

What would it be like to see God as He truly is—and hear Him say to you in unmistakable personal terms, "_[insert your first name]_ , come"?

Driven to God by Your Needs

One of my favorite books on prayer is a classic written years ago by Norwegian pastor, Ole Hallesby, simply entitled *Prayer*. In the first chapter, Hallesby writes, "...helplessness is the very essence of prayer."[1] He goes on to say that many times we may feel frustrated in prayer because we don't receive what we ask for, but the reality is that the very cry for help touches the father-heart of God. "Your helplessness," he says, "is the very thing which opens wide the door to Him and gives Him access to all your needs."[2]

This principle is taught in John 15 where Jesus uses the branch and vine metaphor to illustrate this very point.

> *"I am the vine; you are the branches. . . .apart from me you can do nothing." (John 15:5).*

Of course we can do all sorts of things apart from Jesus, but we can't do anything of *ultimate value* apart from Him.

This text teaches us that we are needy. Branches need vines to grow. This text also teaches us that our neediness is met in the Vine—Jesus. It's through the cambium layer just under the bark of the vine that nutrients flow from root to vine to branch to fruit. So connectedness to Jesus is the means by which He meets our needs—not in our spouse, jobs, possessions, home, or abilities. It is in God, through Christ, that we find satisfaction, fulfillment, and fruit.

John Piper puts it this way: "The gospel commands us to give up and hang out a Help Wanted sign (this is the basic meaning of prayer)."[3] He also says, "Prayer is the turning away from ourselves to God in the confidence that He will provide the help we need. Prayer humbles us as needy, and exalts God as wealthy."[4] (See Appendix A for the prayers, "I Need You, I Praise You" that can stimulate a needy and praiseworthy heart.)

Do you see what is going on here? When we respond to God's love invitation, we are satisfied—and God is glorified! Our neediness exalts His provision. Our weaknesses give attention to His power. Our inadequacies highlight His sufficiency. When we are weak, then He shows Himself to be strong. We say along with King David,

> *"My soul finds rest in God alone; my salvation comes from him. He alone is my rock and my salvation; he is my fortress, I will never be shaken" (Psalm 62:1-2).*

This is a life-changing text. It orients our soul's confidence around God and "God alone." But these words stretch us because we look for rest and rock (security) and salvation (deliverance) from so many other things. We're well-practiced at seeking to have our needs met through relationships, our work, and all sorts of pleasures our culture offers.

But, we ask, aren't these things gifts from God as well? Can't God use them to soothe our souls? The answer is "yes," He can. But, before we go run to turn our TV on, check the Dow average, and expect our spouse to meet our every desire, we need to ask ourselves some hard questions—questions like: To whom (or what) do I turn for rest *first*? and To whom do I *ultimately* turn? Yes, God may use sunsets and music and a loving embrace to meet our needs, but these things can never be the ultimate source of our satisfaction.

These earthly blessings must be seen as gifts *from* Him, not substitutes *for* Him. One way we know if we are seeing them as gifts and not substitutes is to see what happens to our hearts if they're gone. Was it to God that we were *really* coming for help—or to the gifts?

This is often difficult for those who have trained their hearts to look to a spouse or a certain level of financial prosperity to meet their needs. If these earthly sources of joy should be lost to some degree, the disciple of Jesus is suddenly faced with the stark reality that these joys are neither guaranteed nor necessary parts of God's promised joy on earth. Their faith has become so attached to their culture that it is no longer to "God alone" they look but to His gifts.

When someone loses his job, he comes face-to-face with this question. Was God really his "fortress"such that he "would not be shaken?" What—or who—did he go to for rest? Where do *you* go to have your real needs met?

A Deeper Look at Our Needs

If God's call to *come* is essentially a cry of a needy heart to be satisfied in God, then we must first identify our needs and then learn how to get them.

The Challenge of Seeing Our Needs. We are not, for the most part, very reflective people. Our sight goes about skin deep. What I mean is that if people are asked what their needs are, they might list such things as more money, better health, better sex, happier marriages, a better job, etc. The question follows, however: Are these really needs? Think of it this way. Is it necessary for this desire to be met in order for me to know happiness in the kingdom of God?

Put this way, we realize that not all of our needs are really *needs*. I've found that one significant hindrance to our responding to God's love invitation to *come* is that we often ask God for what we consider to be a need and, when that isn't granted, we get disillusioned with God and pull back in our relationship with Him. So when cancer continues to eat away (or goes into remission and then returns) or our spouse is still as difficult to live with as before our request to God, we conclude, "Why bother with God? He really doesn't meet my needs."

But the reality is that our modern understanding of "needs" is more often defined by our feelings or by current pop psychology than by God. When the distraught wife comes to my office and expresses her pain about her husband with words like, "He's so caught up in his own world he has no time for my needs; I've been asking God to change him for years but he hasn't," what is really going on here from *God's* perspective? What does *He* see?

Yes, He sees a husband weak in love and in need of spiritual life. And yes, He sees a woman who is hurting and *coming* to Him. But there's something else. He also sees a woman who has perhaps become so fixed on her own goals of a happy marriage that she has lost sight of her spiritual identity and life purpose of glorifying *God* and finding her rest in Him alone. He sees a woman who has probably confused her needs and wants so that her *coming* to God has a more human agenda associated with it than a divine agenda.

God's understanding of needs is much more fundamental, more spiritual. When Jesus teaches His disciples how to pray using "The Lord's Prayer" in Matthew 6, He teaches them that their basic needs are essentially threefold:

- To glorify God (seeing Him as holy and honored; desiring His rule on earth).

- Physical essentials (daily bread).

- Spiritual life (to be forgiven and to forgive; freedom from temptation).

Ephesians 3:14-19 is another good list of our essential needs from God's perspective.

We must learn to see these as our *real* needs if we are going to find delight in coming to God to meet them. These are the things that are on God's heart. They are the things He longs to give us as expressions of His loving care for us. We mustn't confuse our desires (which we often call needs) and our true needs that God has promised to satisfy here on earth, lest we hang out in the playground of superficial longings and not press deeper into the living room where God awaits us with His real gifts.

The Challenge of Seeking Help for Our Needs. Proud people are not quick to seek help. They want to do it themselves and get all the credit for finding solutions to their problems in life. They don't want to be seen as weak by anyone—and that includes God. But Scripture says, "God opposes the proud but gives grace to the humble" (James 4:6). This means the proud are definitely off on the wrong foot when it comes to drawing close to God! We'll look more at pride in Chapter 7 but, for now, we see that it hinders *coming* to God. It blocks grace. It doesn't delight in God's glory because it's too preoccupied with self-glory.

So we must first see our needs as God sees them, and then we must seek God to satisfy those needs. This will take some time. It's a radical concept for many. Some will need to change the content of their prayers from self-centered motives to God-glorifying ones. (See more on this in the next chapter.) Others will need to begin redirecting their needs to God rather than to their best friends, TV, food, or their work. It's like teaching a child how to play a piano with all 10 fingers instead of using only two. Old habits can be hard to break, but the results of this change are wonderful. We have a love-invitation from God himself. He's inviting you and me to *come*.

When We Come and Feel Nothing

I recently played a game where all the participants wrote a pet peeve on a piece of paper and then another person would try to match our answers with their author. I wrote, "Lights left on for long periods of time when no one is in that room." Another pet peeve of mine is hearing preachers and authors make spiritual truth too simplistic. They make it sound really great until real people have to live it in the midst of their real lives! So I knew I must include a section in this book about times with God that feel like "no one's home up there." It's the proverbial "my prayers feel like they bounce off the ceiling" syndrome. This section has to be written not just because I know you've been there, but because *I've* been there—and honesty demands it.

I often wish that God would do the writing on the wall for me like He did in Belshazzar's Babylonian court in Daniel's day. (On second thought, that writing required a prophet to decipher and it was a word of judgment from God! Forget the writing on the wall.) Or how about talking to me through a burning bush, a dew-laden wool fleece, a talking donkey, or maybe a visible angel? (Have you ever noticed that God is really into variety?)

I can just imagine God shaking His head and lamenting, "My child, I chose to use some spectacular ways of communicating to a couple dozen specially-chosen people throughout all the centuries of humankind. Each of these people had great tasks to do for Me that cost them greatly. And you want Me to put you in the same category as Moses, Gideon, Balaam, and Mary? Do you want assignments like theirs, too?"

Well, if you put it that way . . . no. Actually, we make a mistake when we think that people like Abraham, Moses, Elijah, David, Isaiah, Mary, and the apostle Paul had normal encounters with God. They didn't. That doesn't mean we can't learn from them. It just means that we can't expect the same means of encountering God.

So far I have sought to make a case for the joyful (happy!) Christian life. But God is unlike any person we've ever had a relationship with. On the one hand, this is to be the most intimate of all relationships—particularly because the Holy Spirit indwells us. God isn't just "out there." On the other hand, it can feel a little bit like a guy trying to pursue a girl who's hard to get and who is more than a little disinterested. In C. S. Lewis' words, "God is not tame." He doesn't always act like we think He should.

Yet, Jesus is a friend—not just some unknown metaphysical entity. God is knocking to meet with us, not to play hide and seek with us. So we may be able to handle short periods of time where our *coming* seems mechanical, but if this goes on very long—or if we go through a difficult season in our personal lives without any experience of His presence—then our relationship is going to suffer.

I've heard the saying, "If you feel distant from God, guess who moved?" The implication is that I have. And who can deny this as a likely possibility? Isaiah 59:2 says, "But your iniquities have separated you from your God; your sins have hidden his face from you, so that he will not hear." Isaiah isn't talking about the need to be perfect but the need to confess our sins and turn to God to be changed. So a significant proportion of our emotional detachment from God is likely due to unconfessed and undealt-with sin in our lives.

Another emotion-killer is unreasonable expectations, which we will address in the next chapter. I personally believe this is one of the primary reasons so many Christians become disillusioned by prayer and pull back from a close love-relationship with God. Unreasonable expectations can kill any relationship, human or divine.

Furthermore, why must communication be emotional in the first place? Sure, we want to *pursue* joy and satisfaction in God, but this doesn't mean that every moment (or even every week) must include emotional elements. I have many good, loving conversations with my wife that aren't emotional at all, but they are very real and meaningful.

Perhaps the real problem is that we want to experience something from God. We want to see Him answer a specific prayer, bless us with a good doctor's report, have someone in the church praise us, or make us feel close to Him in *some* way. If these kinds of things don't happen, God seems strangely and uncomfortably quiet.

I knew a pastor who left the pastorate because of his wife's long and unsuccessful battle with cancer, which left him with three children. He went into a depression and felt abandoned by God. All he could hear was silence in response to his prayers. These "dark nights of the soul" can be painful if we have learned to trust in emotion and material blessings rather than God's sovereign—and often hidden—love. In times like this, we are called to persevere in faith, just as Abraham waited 40 years for God to answer His promise to Sarah to give them a child.

Now certainly part of this problem rests on us and how we listen for God. But there's another side to this question of emotionless communication. It's God Himself. As Philip Yancey points out in his book, *Searching for the Invisible God*, God reveals, but He also conceals. "We may not like to hear this, but it's true: God hides himself. Isaiah said it bluntly: 'Truly you are a God who hides himself'" (Isaiah 45:15).

God may be hiding just enough to require a sustained pursuit on our part. Which means that faith is a good thing on this earth. It's the way divine-human relationships work. It's part of a love-relationship with an Almighty God. So perhaps there's more to that hard-to-get girl than we first realized. Perhaps she *wants* to be found—by the right kind of person and the right kind of love.

My cousin, Bob, grew up in a solid, Christian family. When he was a teen, however, he rejected the biblical stories of God and became an agnostic. His mind saw no reason to believe in Jesus. College experimentations gave pleasure but no answers. Marriage and children came along, and he began going to church, primarily so his children would share his Judeo-Christian values. But all the while he hid his real unbelief. Years later he was visiting his parents' house and noticed a copy of Philip Yancey's *The Jesus I Never Knew*, laying on a table. The title intrigued him and he asked to borrow it.

For the first time, Bob encountered evidence for faith. "That book, and later others like *The Case for Christ*, convinced me that the resurrection of Jesus was an historical event. That single fact changes everything. God can be known, and in fact he wants us to know him, and proved himself to be God through mastery over death." His family rejoiced, but especially his Dad, who was ill with Parkinson's. A year later a four-day Emmaus retreat melted Bob's pride and brought him into a love-relationship with Jesus. In two weeks he would find himself in tears, proclaiming hope of eternal life at his Dad's funeral.

God wants to be known. And the resurrection of Jesus is one of His strongest calling cards.

Just Come

When it all comes down to it, our mere act of *coming* to God glorifies Him—because it reminds us of our dependence, our neediness, and our position before the One who is worthy of all greatness. It demonstrates that we are true disciples of Jesus because disciples *spend time* with their Rabbi in order to be like Him.

In the next chapter we will be looking more fully at what happens when we *come* to God but, it should be clear by now, that the mere turning of our hearts to God is an expression of knowing His greatness. Prayer formulas, self-centered prayers, and heartless prayer do not cultivate love. God desires prayer that cries out of need, that makes Him great in our hearts, and that is formed in the midst of intimacy with Him. It's not so much the words that are said, the length of time spent with Him, or the frequency of our meetings with Him. It's about the "godwardness" of our hearts.

David says it well:

> *"As the deer pants for streams of water, so my soul pants for you, O God. My soul thirsts for God, for the living God"* *(Psalm 42:1-2).*

So cultivate spiritual thirst. Identify your real needs. Even if all you can say is, "Oh God!" that is enough. God knows your heart. He can fill in the blanks. Your heart may be so thirsty, so desperate, so hurting, that no words seem adequate. But all He wants is you. That's all He's ever wanted from the first day you heard His knocking, and heard His voice call "Come," and opened the door. "Oh God!" It's the beginning of great things to come. It's why I wrote this prayer—to speak simply to God about what's most important to Him when my mind is weary from the battle:

> *"O God, glorify yourself in me, not for my will, but yours I plea.*
> *Give me your love and truth anew in all I want, think, say, and do."*

For Self-Reflection and Life Application

1. Describe what a relationship with God has meant to you at different times in your life.

2. Imagine God knocking at the door of your heart. What kinds of emotions rise within you at the thought of the Creator of the universe wanting to spend time with you? (Anxiety? Fear? Excitement? Calm?)

3. Read Psalm 103 and Ephesians 1 slowly and in the presence of God. Pause each time you read about some expression of God's love to you and then (1) meditate about that love-expression (mull over it for a bit in your mind and heart) and (2) thank God for it.

4. Have you experienced a dullness in prayer? If so, how have you typically dealt with it?

5. Which of the three truths mentioned about God do you most need to remember as you *come* to Him? Why? *(God desires me. God is good to me. God is full of grace.)*

6. What difference might it make in your *coming* to God to approach Him out of your *spiritual* neediness? What cautions must you take regarding your understanding of needs? Give some personal examples.

7. Think about a time when God seemed distant. What might you do next time this happens to keep your relationship with God honest and close?

8. Why is the mere act of *coming* to God such a delight to Him, even if you're weak, confused, struggling, hurting, or even upset with Him?

9. Spend some time with God right now by using the "O God" prayer at the end of this chapter to *come* to Him in your neediness. Pray it slowly and sincerely and from your heart's deepest longings for His glory and joy in you.

---

[1] Ole Hallesby, *Prayer,* Augsburg Publishing House, Minneapolis, 1959 copyright renewed, p. 20.

[2] Ibid., p. 21.

[3] John Piper, Desiring God , Multnomah Publishers, Inc., Sisters, 1996, second edition, p. 140.

[4] Ibid., p. 133.

Chapter 5

Come—How to Meet With a Great God

Soon the man found himself in an open area of Kingcity ringed with tall trees, flower beds, and benches. The open area was nearly filled with people of all ages, sitting on the grass and talking with one another. Then He came.

Somehow the man had expected something different. The person who ascended a small grassy knoll at one end of the park was not particularly handsome, and He certainly wasn't dressed in the royal garments of storybook kings. There was no crown. No glittering cape. In fact, there was nothing about Him that a visitor would think was kingly—except for one thing. His face. His eyes and smile had love written all over them.

As He looked out into the sea of faces that had become expectantly quiet, His words rang out with sincerity and authority. "Come. Let us celebrate our love!" And with that the people erupted into applause.

The man was not used to so much emotion, but he couldn't deny that love was in that park. It was also clear to him that the King had loved them first. These people had come to this city in the first place because this King had touched their souls deeply—so deeply that they had surrendered their very lives to Him.

For the next several minutes the King taught them about Himself, and how His laws were expressions of His love for them. He closed by reminding them that one of His greatest joys was having them come to Him throughout their day, in all circumstances and with all kinds of conversation. It was His desire that they would know the greatness of His love, and that this greatness would be shown to the world outside Kingcity as well. The people responded with spontaneous songs of praise to Him, and they continued for quite some time even after He had left them.

Soon people began to return to their jobs and homes and whatever they had been doing before the King had arrived. The man remained sitting on the grass, deep in thought. Something life-changing was taking place in him. He felt his heart being drawn to the King.

He didn't know how long he sat there, but in the end love won. There was more than safety from boils. There was the King! Tears flowed and deep soul-conversations took place between the King and the man, often requiring very few words. The man had never felt so transparent—and still so accepted—in all his life. If someone would have told him a week ago that he would be surrendering his life to someone without any fear attached, he would have laughed in their face. Now there was only relief and peace.

That moment was a turning point in the man's life. It was his entry into life as it was meant to be lived. Into joy that was independent of circumstances. Into a love-relationship with the King.

In the Presence of an Unseen Spirit-God

Let's review where we've come to so far. The purpose of our lives is to glorify God, and one of the primary ways we do this is through *coming* to God in response to His invitation—an invitation that is attractive and satisfying.

Now we are there. We've opened the door. We're face-to-face with God. Sort of. There's no face to see.

This God who beckons us in love is invisible to our eyes, except for a somewhat brief period of $3^1/_2$ years in which He went public in the person of His Son, Jesus. Apart from that incarnation, we're left with such contact points as His handiwork (creation), His image (human beings), His works (His dealings with human beings and His people, especially Israel and the church), His spokespeople (prophets and apostles), and His indwelling presence (the Holy Spirit).

We're certainly not lacking for any evidences of His entry into Earth, and we certainly aren't lacking for information about Him. But let's face it—it's still not the same as *really* being face-to-face.

Frankly, this complicates our relationship somewhat. We're in new waters here. Not only are we invited to a love-relationship with a *spirit-being*, but this spirit-being operates in ways and with thoughts quite different than ours. As the apostle Paul says,

> *"Oh, the depth of the riches of the wisdom and knowledge of God! How unsearchable his judgments, and his paths beyond tracing out! 'Who has known the mind of the Lord? Or who has been his counselor?'" (Romans 11:33-34).*

These barriers can seem almost overwhelming at times. Who *has* known the mind of the Lord? When He doesn't heal my crying young son's stomachache or bring unity in a church crisis, relating to this unseen God can be a lot of work! But Philip Yancey helpfully points out, *all* relationships are work! Why should we expect this one with a spirit-God to be any different?[1] The following are helps to me—and hopefully to you—when God's invisibility becomes a barrier to drawing near Him in love.

Expect a certain degree of mystery and incomprehension. Yes, God has revealed Himself, but we're still dealing with dimensions and realities far bigger than we know of here on earth. We still "know in part" (1 Corinthians 13:12) and we shouldn't expect to fully wrap our finite minds around God's infinite being and thoughts (Deuteronomy 29:29). We must accept mystery.

Expect some adjustments in understanding God's ways in a groaning world. Not all God's ways are mysterious. But even the things we *should* understand can be hard to understand if we only see things from the world's point of view. For example, "creation was subjected to frustration" by God (Romans 8:20). So this world isn't the way God designed it to be.

> *"We know that the whole creation has been groaning as in the pains of childbirth right up to the present time" (Romans 8:22).*

This means we should expect a significant amount of suffering and pain in this life until Jesus returns—even for His followers. (John the Baptist was beheaded and most of the apostles were martyred for their faith!) And though we can't expect to avoid hardship, we *can* expect His *spiritual* work in our lives to be the normal Christian life! (Romans 5:3-5).

Faith is required. Faith is at the heart of our relationship with God.

> *"And without faith it is impossible to please God, because anyone who comes to him must believe that he exists and that he rewards those who earnestly seek him" (Hebrews 11:6).*

Until that final day when faith and hope are no more and only love remains, faith must fill in the gaps of our limited understanding. In fact, God has purposely limited Himself in communicating with us so that faith *is* required.

When you lose spiritual focus, look at Jesus. "If we doubt God, or find him incomprehensible, unknowable, the very best cure is to gaze steadily at Jesus...."[2]

> *"No one has ever seen God. It is God the only Son, who is close to the Father's heart, who has made him known" (John 1:18, NRSV).*

He is "God with skin on," as Tom Skinner used to say. When the race is hard, it is He who we are to set our eyes upon (Hebrews 12:3). Gaze long and hard at Him, and let His love and truth draw you to Him and to His Father. All we really *need* to know about God is seen in Jesus.

Listen to His voice and respond to it. Open your heart to listen to Him as God speaks through His many channels of communication (Bible, sermons, Christian authors, mature Christian friends, etc.). Listen and then respond. Begin the dialog. It's the way all relationships begin.

The Russian Orthodox church leader and monk, Anthony Bloom, in his little book, *Beginning to Pray*, says, "We complain that He does not make himself present to us for the few minutes we reserve for Him, but what about the twenty-three and a half hours during which God may be knocking at our door and we answer, 'I am busy, I am sorry' or when we do not answer at all because we do not even hear the knock at the door of our heart, of our minds, of our conscience, of our life."[3] .

This relationship with an unseen God is, indeed, an adventure of love, truth, and wonder. And for all its mystery, we are also richly blessed with enough revelation to walk in a reasonable faith—and know the Lover of our souls.

Some Reflections about Frequency and Duration

As I mentioned in the previous chapter, one of the barriers to my affection for God was the rules people had developed about what prayer was to look like. One example of this was hearing inspiring stories about some great saint in the history of the church who would spend four hours in prayer every morning before starting his day. Any inspiration to me from these stories usually only lasted a few minutes.

I eventually concluded I was measuring my relationship with God on external things rather than internal. I was preoccupied with quantity more than quality. And I was being overly influenced by other people's spiritual experiences. (Gary Thomas's book, *Sacred Pathways,* confirmed what I had been sensing: we are wired to relate to God in different ways. He describes nine, affirming that my relational pattern with God doesn't have to look like someone else's.)[4]

When I looked at the Scriptures, I saw no formal meeting times prescribed by God. There's no three-times-a-day bowing in the direction of Jerusalem, no daily recitations of the Lord's Prayer—not even prescribed periods of fasting. There were descriptions, of course, of how David would meet with God morning and night and how Jesus sometimes withdrew early in the morning, but none of these are given as "go and do likewise."

What stood out to me, however, were the descriptions of a continual, throughout-the-day relationship with God:

• Psalm 16:8 "I have set the Lord always before me." This is a conscious decision to come into the presence of God throughout the day, setting His ways, purposes, truth, and life at the center of our hearts and minds.

• Ephesians 6:18 "And pray in the Spirit on all occasions with all kinds of prayers and requests." "All occasions" implies a responsiveness to life's events, coming to God in every human encounter, every emotional reaction to life, every situation. "Pray continually," in 1 Thessalonians 5:17, describes this same condition of constant fellowship with God.

Setting aside regular, planned times for this relationship can be helpful (just as they can be in a marriage relationship), and there are plenty of books available that describe how to make the most of these. But they aren't the core of the relationship. The core is moment-by-moment. A morning meeting with God was never meant to last for the whole day. Many can testify to the reality that this can quickly wear off.

I remember when my children were young I would sometimes seek some solitude in prayer in my den. One of my children came in once to complain about a sibling squabble, and my response was to feel somewhat irritated about being interrupted. Later I saw this as a sobering statement on the emptiness of my times with God. Yes, I may have been talking to Him. But certainly God's heart was not being infused into mine. My impatience exposed the self-centeredness of my meetings with Him.

God is much more interested in the quality of our meetings than the structure, frequency, or duration of them. He's more interested in the responsiveness of our hearts to His regular knocking than He is about our scheduled meetings with Him.

When I was in college, I did a number of things to help bring my mind into conscious fellowship with God. I wore a wooden cross around my neck for awhile, and I wrapped athletic tape around the end of my lacrosse stick to remind me to come to Him during practices and games. When I began working as an electrical engineer, I used water fountain trips as triggers to come to God, and in a later job, it was riding the elevator.

Frank Laubach, missionary and literacy champion, so desired this regular fellowship with God that he made it his aim to have conscious communion with God once every minute (and after much effort, practiced this successfully for many years). But most of us need to start at a slightly different place!

I would suggest establishing multiple "God connection" points throughout your day to train your heart to come into His presence. These may be meal-times, showers, work-breaks, car travel time, or waking up and bedtimes—any setting that occurs somewhat routinely that can begin training your mind and heart to come to God throughout your day.

These may only last 15 seconds, or a minute, or much longer. The goal is not quantity. It's glorifying God by coming to Him. It's reminding yourself that you're a disciple of Jesus and that you want His life to be imparted to you. It's about love and your joy in Him! It's a step into the fullness of the kingdom of God so that you, too, will be saying, "I will set the Lord always before me."

Three Settings to Hear God's Knocking

Planned God connections are helpful to begin the discipline of regularly coming to God throughout your day and reorienting your heart around God rather than your own self-focused desires. However, I would like to offer three *spontaneous* connection points that can also help move us to an "all occa-sions" love-relationship with God.

Emotional Connection Points. We see these throughout the Psalms. Emotions like depression (Psalms 42, 77), shame/guilt (Psalms 32, 51), fear (Psalms 27, 56), and spiritual darkness (Psalms 13, 22) were frequent entry points into God's presence. Jesus, too, went to His Father in Gethsemane amidst the emotions of His impending death for the sins of the world, and He often withdrew in prayer when He felt exhausted from ministry.

Besides His example, Jesus teaches us to *come* in the midst of our emotional needs:

> *"Come to me, all you who are weary and burdened, and I will*
> *give you rest" (Matthew 11:28).*

Psychology is right—we need to get in touch with our feelings. If we aren't aware of the emotions we're feeling, how can we come to God and allow Him to glorify Himself in the longings behind these emotions? How can He be great in us if we hide behind our personalities and self-justified feelings?

Let's face it, we might as well come out in the open with Him, because He already knows us inside and out. And if our goal is to glorify God and be sat-isfied in Him, there's no better place to start than at those many moments throughout our day when our emotions signal our need to *come*.

Relational Connection Points. Relationships are another place where God wants to meet us—not just when they are painful, but also when they are a blessing, or superficial, or detached, or nonexistent. Much more will be said about this in later chapters, but it's important for us to understand how much our relationships matter to God and how much we need Him if we're to glorify Him in them, especially in our families and workplace.

The other day my wife asked me to help her take care of some kids in our church so the parents could get away a few days. I'm all for her ministry, and I want to be a part of it. But this meant sacrificing my Sunday afternoon and evening (which I often enjoy as a time to relax after expending energy as a pastor over the previous six hours). And besides, it was Father's Day! So God and I had to have a little meeting. It wasn't exactly pretty, but it was real—and good. It happened because I used relationship challenges to drive me to *come* to Him.

Idle Connection Points. These are times in which our mind is free from tasks and relationships. Times like driving, standing in line at the grocery store or bank, walking, waking up, waiting in the doctor's office, or showering— even when we have some down time and our impulse is to channel surf in front of the TV or call a friend on the phone. Any time you don't *have* to think about something else can be used to meet with God, even for a few seconds.

One of my favorite times is driving. I am, admittedly, a talk-show and news kind of guy. So it's tempting to use that driving time to pursue my love of knowledge and information. But I generally keep the radio off for awhile until God and I have connected. I also have disciplined myself to drive at the speed limit (rather than my preferred five-eight miles per hour over!) in order to meet with God. (This was prompted by reading John Ortberg's chapter on "Slowing Down" in his book, *The Life You've Always Wanted*.) Instead of my heart wanting to get some place quickly, I am training it to enjoy God. Even those dreaded 25-miles-per-hour zones down country roads have become a welcome time with God. (I do add five miles per hour if someone's on my tail, but this is out of love, of course—and not wanting their wrath upon me!)

Reading is also a time for me to *come* to God. So a family member may find me in the lounge chair, footrest extended, head back, and eyes closed, with my book on my lap. They don't know exactly *what* I'm doing in this position, though the odds are about ninety percent that I'm meeting with God— and the other ten percent I'm enjoying a different kind of meditation!

If the purpose of my life is to glorify God, then I will look for ways to *come* to Him as often as possible because it also means coming to love and joy.

It's now time for us to turn our attention to the *content* of our meeting with God. We've joyfully answered the knocking door. There He stands before us. Now what?

> *"And pray in the Spirit on all occasions with* all kinds of
> prayers and requests" [emphasis mine] *(Ephesians 6:18).*

Let's look at some of those "all kinds" of prayers. A balanced relationship
with God will mean using them all, not just the ones *we* like.

Come to Glorify God

This is the big picture. It's what all the following *comings* are all about—
and sometimes we need to talk to God directly about it. The "Oh God" prayer
at the end of the previous chapter is one of those "big picture" prayers. It focuses our heart so that all the other things we come to God about are primarily
about Him and not primarily about us. We just get to be the deposit and reflection of His glory—which is pretty amazing!

So say it many times, "Glorify Yourself in me!" Let the thought arise from
your soul throughout your day like incense to Him. "Not to us, but to Your
name be glory!" It's the most important cry that can pour from your soul.
"God, I want to know and show your greatness in my life no matter what I
encounter today." It doesn't get more basic than that.

Come to Listen

Someone has said, God must be trying to tell us something by giving us one
mouth and two ears. At least it works as an object lesson. One of my favorite
passages in the Bible is from Isaiah 55:

> *"Come, all you who are thirsty, come to the waters; and you
> who have no money, come, buy and eat! Come, buy wine and
> milk without money and without cost. Why spend money on
> what is not bread, and your labor on what does not satisfy?*
> Listen, listen to me, and eat what is good, and your soul will
> delight in the richest of fare [emphasis mine]. *Give ear and
> come to me; hear me, that your soul may live" (Isaiah 55:1-3).*

Again we see God's invitation to happiness and satisfaction—"the richest
of fare." It's what God uses to motivate us to come to Him. It's not bad to come
to God to be happy! But notice that we won't enter into this reality unless we
first "listen." Isaiah uses the word twice to emphasize how important this is,
then he reiterates it with: "Give ear and come to me."

This isn't what we like to do. We would rather talk, despite the warning of
Ecclesiastes 5:1-2, "Guard your steps when you go to the house of God. Go

near to listen rather than to offer the sacrifice of fools, who do not know that they do wrong. Do not be quick with your mouth, do not be hasty in your heart to utter anything before God. God is in heaven and you are on earth, so let your words be few." When God bids us *come*, He doesn't have in mind a therapy chair where He just listens and we do all the talking. God has something to say to us. So "go near to listen."

Jesus says the same thing in Matthew 11:28-30:

> *"Come to me, all you who are weary and burdened, and I will give you rest. Take my yoke upon you and learn from me, for I am gentle and humble in heart, and you will find rest for your souls. For my yoke is easy and my burden is light."*

So when we are weary from parenting, burdened by financial pressures, or stressed by complicated relationships, we're to take His yoke upon us and learn from Him—and that requires listening.

Picture an oxen yoke—two large pieces of curved wood clamped together but with two openings for necks of oxen. Now picture Jesus' neck in one of those openings. His eyes meet yours and then His hands motion as an invitation for you to stick your neck into the other opening. The burden is still back there in the oxcart, but He's pulling *with* you—which makes the burden lighter.

But that's not all that's going on there. Part of this burden-lightening process is that He wants you to "learn" from Him. So when we bring our burdens to Him, it's not just a matter of God carrying them and seeing just "one set of footsteps on the beach instead of two." He's not carrying it for you, He's carrying it *with* you, and He's going to teach you how to carry heavy burdens with Him—like how to understand what makes it a burden in the first place, and how to rely on Him for specific loads.

Some time ago I was struggling with a hurt in my life. It was gnawing at me and robbing me of peace. As I met with God and shared my heart with Him, I placed myself under His instruction. And He taught me. I saw an old familiar sin pattern staring me in the face. As I confessed it, the burden was lifted and I was free again—free to feel peace and free to love.

"Be still, and know that I am God" (Psalm 46:10).

Being still is a prerequisite to knowing God. This means we must slow our spirits down long enough to be able to listen—both to God and to our own inner life. And this often means getting alone. Dallas Willard, in his book, *The Spirit of the Disciplines*, says that "Of all the disciplines of abstinence, solitude is generally the most fundamental in the beginning of the spiritual life, and it must be returned to again and again as that life develops."[5] Being alone and still are necessary if we're going to know God at the level he wants to be known.

So what might we hear when we *come* to listen to God? Plenty of our own thoughts, that's for sure! Most of these we *know* are our own—especially the ones about the football game later that day and what we need at the grocery store.

But on the other hand, if we are to do *all* to the glory of God, then God *does* care about the things our minds wander to! He cares about them probably not in the same way *we* often care about them, but He does have *something* to say to us in all situations—especially regarding the attitude of our heart towards them. (So that game and those groceries *will* have the voice of God surrounding them in some way!) This all means that God can even use *our* thoughts as ways to bring up a subject He would like to talk to us about.

There are, however, certain things we can expect God to say to us on a regular basis. We know these things because He has said them many times already—*in His Word*—which is the ultimate test of whether any "voice" is from God or just something out of our own brain.

Expect to hear God talk to you quite often about:

> • Reminders of His character. "I love you." "I am holy." "I am able." "My ways are not yours."

> • Exposures of your sin and how to address it. "Where did that attitude come from?" "You need to stay as far from that temptation as you can next time."

> • Whom and how to love. "She needs to hear a word of affirmation from you." "Give some money to help those missionaries."

These are the voices of God. He may, at times, speak very directly to you about certain issues you are facing in life (who to marry, what job to take, what church to attend, etc.), but these directions will always be in the context of this larger voice that has been speaking to generations through the Scriptures. As Jesus said, "The words I have spoken to you are spirit and they are life" (John 6:63).

So listen well, my friend. The quality of your life and the glory of God in you depend on it!

Come to Surrender

I believe this is one of the most important—and should be one of the most frequent—ways we *come* to God. Why? Because it is the surrendered, humbled heart that magnifies God's greatness, and it is this same heart God can bless. As Jesus said, "Blessed are the poor in spirit, for theirs is the kingdom of heaven. . . Blessed are the meek, for they will inherit the earth" (Matthew 5:3, 5). We will deal with this more fully in Chapter 7, but Jesus' words in Luke 9 show us how important this prayer of surrender is:

> *"If anyone would come after me, he must deny himself and take up his cross daily and follow me" (Luke 9:23).*

To follow Jesus is to surrender our wills, agendas, plans, desires, and life to God. It means coming into His presence with a "not my will, but yours be done" attitude, just as Jesus did in the Garden of Gethsemane (Luke 22:42).

If there's anything that can block the joy of God in us, it's an unsurrendered heart. Too much of me and not enough of Him will kill spiritual life.

I often find it helpful to bring particular situations that I'm facing, or will be facing, before God in this kind of prayer. I surrender the need to have my children be perfect, the desire to be praised in a public speaking setting, the longing to have more "stuff." It's a time of casting my cares upon the Lover of My Soul, often with outstretched hands as symbolic of my yieldedness to Him.

Often this prayer has very little, if any, words. But God looks at the heart, and the prayer of surrender is one of the sweetest daily prayers He hears. It understands our clay vessel status in the hands of the Master Potter and cries out, "Melt me, mold me, fill me, use me. Spirit of the Living God, fall fresh on me."

Come to Praise and Be Thankful

> *"Shout for joy to the LORD, all the earth. Worship the LORD with gladness; come before him with joyful songs. Know that the LORD is God. It is he who made us, and we are his; we are his people, the sheep of his pasture. Enter his gates with thanksgiving and his courts with praise; give thanks to him and praise his name" (Psalm 100:1-4).*

God loves an attitude of gratitude. Why? Because it glorifies Him! This may sound strange to us at first because it makes God sound somewhat conceited! But if the universe was created for Him, then it follows that His greatness is magnified when who He is and what He does is proclaimed. God says we are "the people I formed for myself that they may proclaim my praise" (Isaiah 43:21).

Psalm 100 said that praise and thanksgiving are entry points into His presence. It's one way we are to *come* to Him. This will mean gratitude for two kinds of things: Blessings resulting from the fact that we are His creation, and blessings resulting from the fact that we are His people.

Instead of just enjoying the pleasures of this life (like family, friends, games, music, gentle breezes, tulips, water, laughter, etc.) we must see them as ultimately coming to us as His creatures. These are not blessings we are given because we are His children by repentance and faith in Christ—they are blessings we enjoy because we are alive on Planet Earth!

One way we have kept this focus of praise alive in our family is by devoting periodic meal-time prayers to a letter of the alphabet and then spending time thanking God for things that start with that letter, including *why* we are grateful for them. This was also a good wisdom exercise for our children as they grew up. Even now, with our kids in their 20's, we still do this periodically. (That is, letter "B": "God thank you for balls that enable us to enjoy each other in games!")

But there is more. We must be people who speak as much about our salvation benefits as we do our creation benefits.

> *"Praise be to the God and Father of our Lord Jesus Christ,
> who has blessed us in the heavenly realms with every spiritual
> blessing in Christ" (Ephesians 1:3).*

The rest of Ephesians 1 details many of these blessings. Two additional lists are found in Psalms 103 and 145.

The 7 "F's" listed in Chapter 3 are categories I come back to over and over again in giving praise to God: Fellowship with God, forgiveness of sins, freedom from sin, fullness of life, family of God, flow of love to the world, and forever life. Each of these "spiritual blessings in Christ" has many specific praises associated with them that are unique to each one of us. They are part of the symphony that we offer to God echoing in the halls of heaven throughout our lives.

Know this: Minds that dwell on blessings are minds that resist complaining and worry and fear. They see God as He truly is—not through our self-centered lenses. They know that the past, the present, and the future are filled with His loving goodness.

One application of this call to praise is singing. When singable tunes are matched with inspiring words, they're like wings for our joy-filled soul to soar upon. The more God satisfies our deepest longings, the more praise is in our hearts and joy is its expression. Even monotone singers can make a joyful noise to God (though it might be loving to surrounding worshippers if they back off on the volume a bit)!

But as wonderful as musical praise is, it's not worship by itself. The rhythms, the enjoyable melodies, the harmonies, the instrumentations—all can become ends in themselves (and even distractions at times) to *coming* to God. If we come to sing for the mere joy of the music, we glorify the music, not God. If we are dependent on certain songs or certain well-played instruments for feelings of worship, then we have come to ourselves and a worship band—not to God.

It was this concern over music-based worship that led a British pastor to suggest that his church put the worship band and sound system away for a while and learn to worship without all the props. It wasn't easy at first, but God began to teach the church how to have a "Heart of Worship," which was the title of the song the church's worship pastor, Matt Redman, wrote at the end of their worship team "fast." It was then that he could say, "The songs of our hearts had caught up with the songs of our lips." These are some of the words he wrote:

> *"When the music fades, All is stripped away,*
> *And I simply come;*
> *Longing just to bring something that's of worth*
> *That will bless Your heart.*
> *I'll bring You more than a song,*
> *For a song in itself is not what You have required.*
> *You search much deeper within through the way things appear;*
> *You're looking into my heart.*
> *I'm coming back to the heart of worship.*
> *And it's all about You; It's all about You, Jesus."* [6]

Another means of coming to God in praise is by learning to rejoice in our trials. Why is this so important? Certainly not because evil, sin, and sickness come from God, but because our good and gracious and powerful God is able to turn lemons into lemonade, oysters into pearls, and coal into diamonds!

> *"Consider it pure joy, my brothers, whenever you face trials*
> *of many kinds, because you know that the testing of your faith*
> *develops perseverance. Perseverance must finish its work so*
> *that you may be mature and complete, not lacking anything"*
> *(James 1:2-4).*

"Pure joy!" So we thank God for our hardships, suffering, and weaknesses because we know He's up to something great in us—something that will ultimately glorify Him and satisfy us!

Come to Trust

Closely related to praise is trust. Trust is acknowledging the character and works of God for what He *will* do rather than for what He *has done*.

> *"Trust in the LORD with all your heart and lean not on your own understanding; in all your ways acknowledge him, and he will make your paths straight" (Proverbs 3:5-6).*

Behind most problems Christians face in life is a lack of "trusting in the Lord with all their heart." To trust God is to believe He is good to us now and tomorrow—without expecting any particular outcome or feelings other than that God in His holy love and power is there for us.

When Jesus told His disciples that He was soon going to leave them and return to His Father, they became distressed. What was His counsel? "Do not let your hearts be troubled. Trust in God; trust also in me" (John 14:1). Today it's common for people to tell their friends it's okay for them to be worried because they have a right to their own feelings. But Jesus moves us past our emotions to see a God who, when trusted, changes those emotions. As Jesus taught in Matthew 6, anxiety about tomorrow is inappropriate for disciples who know God cares for them.

Some of the most anxious people I know pray a lot. But they are people who haven't learned to trust. I've sometimes suggested to them, "For the next week don't ask God for anything. Your prayers have become more self-promoting than God-promoting and you've lost sight of God's love for you. Don't try to control the situation or try to fix anything. Just shift your confidence away from your petitions and into the arms of God."

Of course, it's not wrong to ask God for our needs, but it is wrong to neglect to trust Him. Over and over again the psalmists see trust as the antidote to their stress.

> *"When I am afraid, I will trust in you. In God, whose word I praise, in God I trust; I will not be afraid. What can mortal man do to me?" (Psalm 56:3-4).*

Think about it for a moment: What *can* mortal man do to me? Well, he can slander me, abuse me, criticize me, talk behind my back, tease me, take away my job, hit me—even kill me. Actually, that's quite a lot! In fact, people *did* most of those things to King David who wrote these words. But these words are rhetorical. People can't really do anything to us of significant harm because "If God is for us, who can be against us?" (Romans 8:31).

You see, there are two ways to trust God. The first is to trust God to remove the external source of our trouble. "Take away my health problem, transfer my boss to another position, straighten out my wife, and bring spiritual revival to my three-year-old!" This kind of trust looks to God to lighten the load, change the circumstance, remove the rub, and take the trial away. The problem is that God hasn't promised to do these things for us. He may do them but there are no guarantees.

The second kind of trust (and the most important kind of trust) expects God to reveal His goodness to us not by removing the trial but by giving us resources to face the trial in His loving presence. His goodness is experienced not primarily by relief but *by knowing God is working for His glory and my good*. It may include my character development, or benefit for others, or a deepening understanding of God's nature. Or it may include spiritual blessings that are in the future—even heaven!

To trust in God doesn't primarily mean that my kids won't have car accidents, or that I won't have a heart attack, or that when I stand to share a testimony in church I won't get a brain freeze and make a fool of myself. It primarily means that I believe God exists and will be good to me—even if that goodness can only be measured in spiritual and eternal categories.

When we come to God in trust, we believe that every fork in the road and every possible path ahead of us is bathed in God's loving presence. No action we take, no tragedy we face, and no hurt we experience can place us outside of God's love. It's imagining the "what ifs" of life and believing with confidence that *NOTHING* can separate us from the loving goodness of God—not even death (Romans 8:35-39).

To trust God also means that we *forsake* trusting in other things. In Israel's day one common trust was in their military. But God says that's a misplaced trust, "Some trust in chariots and some in horses, but we trust in the name of the LORD our God" (Psalm 20:7). We are warned about trusting in wealth and in ourselves (Psalm 49). We're even guilty of placing our trust in our spouse, our job, our kids, our government, and our church. But God alone is our trust. And it is to Him that we must come to place our trust, day in and day out.

So, in your stresses and distresses, are you resting in his promises to care for you, to make you holy, never leave you, and to be your life? Perhaps God wants less asking and more trust from you—and the opportunity to show you and others that he is, indeed, great. He *can* be trusted!

Come to Become

One of our most fundamental purposes in life is to become like Jesus, which we will unpack in greater detail in Chapter 7. Becoming like Jesus will involve heart, mind, speech, and deeds (or as the prayer at the end of the previous chapter says, "in all I want, think, say, and do.") I've noticed that becoming holy is not high on many people's prayer lists. Yet certainly our daily encounters with people and life are in desperate need of God's character.

Coming to God to become like Jesus will involve saying at least three things often to Him: *"I'm sorry," "Change me,"* and *"Okay."*

Confession: "I'm Sorry!"   To confess is to acknowledge to God that we have fallen short of one of His standards and we are sorry about it.

> *"If we confess our sins, he is faithful and just and will forgive us our sins and purify us from all unrighteousness"* (1 John 1:9).

Note that confession brings both forgiveness and purification. God is saying, "I forgive you, but I don't want you to stay the same!" He wants us to be holy.

Ideally, we should come to God at the point of sin—right there in the kitchen, right there in the car, right there on the basketball court. But sometimes distance is required and we come to God at a later time (maybe even at the end of the day) and allow Him to bring our sins to our mind and confess them to Him.

Some time ago Cathy and I had a difficult discussion about some matter. I felt I was right, and she felt she was right. In the minutes following our little collision of wills, I realized my heart was not where it should be. So I went to my bedroom to come to God. I knew I needed to be humbled, so I knelt by my bed and listened to God. I also told God why I was right! After about 10 minutes of going back and forth with Him, my sins of pride and self-justification had been revealed and confessed and I was able to return to Cathy with a more pure and humble heart.

Transformation: "Change Me!"   This completes the process of repentance. "I'm sorry" turns us *from sin*, and "Change me" turns us *to God*. This includes asking God to change us but it's much more. It's *coming* to God to receive all He has for us so that we can be changed. It's coming to Him for a renewed mind, a "godward" heart, and holy speech and behavior. It's spending time with Him in any way necessary for this total transformation to take place.

Obedience: "Okay." Obedience is doing what God says we should do. It says, "Okay, Lord, whatever you say." Obedience may follow specific instances of confessing a sin to God, or it may just be a result of listening to God—for example, hearing Him tell you to give money to a person in need.

Jesus says, "If you obey my commands, you will remain in my love" (John 15:10). If I want to have a love relationship with God, then I must obey Him. That's the way it works with God. Why? Because to obey God is to embrace the things that are on His heart. It's to be trained to know His love, His holiness—to know *Him!* Obedience isn't just an experience of submitting to God, it's pursuing a love-relationship with Him.

We come to God to become like Jesus, and that will mean frequent words of "Sorry," "Change me!" and "Okay." Each glorifies God.

Come to Ask (for His Kingdom)

We now come to the most commonly used expression of coming to God—the request. And from my observation, it's the least understood and inappropriately used expression of them all. The reason I say this is that typical requests are some of the most self-centered, self-glorifying experiences in the Christian life.

Consider these words from A. W. Tozer, a leader in the Christian and Missionary Alliance Church in the first half of the last century: "Many prayer meetings are being called these days. And no wonder, for the need is great. But if my observation is correct, much effort is wasted; very little comes from them. The reason is that motives are not sound. Too many praying persons seek to use prayer as a means to ends that are not wholly pure. Prayer is conceived to be little more than a technique for self-advancement, a heavenly method of achieving earthly success. . . The problem is self. Selfishness is never so exquisitely selfish as when it is on its knees."

Now this is a problem. If "asking prayer" is the most common way Christians tend to come to God and, if it is, in practice, predominantly selfish, then our communication with God has become quite twisted! We have forgotten that "not to us, O Lord, but to your name be the glory!"

Jesus makes this clear in the following verse:

> *"And I will do whatever you ask in my name, so that the Son may bring glory to the Father" (John 14:13).*

Here we have the purpose of prayer. Every request we make must ultimately be to "bring glory to the Father." Not our glory but His. Not our selfish pleasure but His righteous pleasure.

But, we ask, wouldn't God be glorified if every person we invited to church came and surrendered their lives to Christ? Wouldn't God be glorified if He answered every prayer of ours for healing? Wouldn't God be glorified if all the Christians in school would pray and get perfect scores in tests and if all Christians excelled in every sport because they prayed?

I played lacrosse in college, and during an indoor winter practice a big defenseman body-checked my 140-pound body and it hit the gym floor with a thud, breaking my collar bone. I figured this would be a great time for God to glorify Himself by healing me really quickly. I would be sure to give God all the glory.

So I asked. A number of times. (I had wonderful ideas for God!) "Unfortunately" He had the final say and it was "no." In fact, it took *longer* to heal than the doctor thought it would. (Along these same lines, I also thought it would be really cool if I was a star player on the team and I could give God glory for everything I would accomplish. God and I didn't connect on this one, either!)

So what's God up to? I believe our problem is that we typically conceive of God's glory as outward displays of power. We want the healings, the church numbers, the easy friendships, the compliant kids—the works! Certainly God has a track record of doing some amazing things throughout history.

But outward displays of power are not the only—or primary—ways in which God seeks glory. He is mostly concerned about inner power. Like bringing peace to a worrying mother. Self-control to a drug addict. Humility to an athlete. A heart of sacrificial love to a husband.

So not only do we often have a faulty understanding of power, but we have a faulty understanding of glory. It's not just God's power that shows Him to be great, but His other characteristics as well—like His love, holiness, truth, and justice. These all must be part of our prayer requests if we're going to know and show His greatness!

And here, again, we come face-to-face with the reality that God's glory is most displayed not when we are strong and in control but when we are weak and life is out of our control. So if we're going to pray for God's glory, we can't pray against all trials (Lord, give me a close parking place in this rain), for trials are opportunities for God to display His greatness in us.

Take the apostle Paul. He describes some near-death experiences and trials and then concludes,

> *"But this happened that we might not rely on ourselves but on God, who raises the dead" (2 Corinthians 1:9).*

And he accepts his "thorn in the flesh" (after asking for it to be removed three times!) so that "Christ's power may rest on me" (2 Corinthians 12:9). *Strong people have their own glory. Weak people know they need God's!*

What should we pray for when we come to God for His glory?

• Pray that *God will receive glory* in satisfying your needs anyway He chooses (2 Corinthians 9:8).

• Make your *spiritual needs a higher priority* in prayer than your physical needs (John 15:7-8; James 4:3).

• Pray for *renewed spiritual taste buds*—increasing dissatisfaction with worldly pleasures and a greater thirst for and joy in spiritual blessings (Isaiah 55:1-3).

• *Look behind every emotional need for a spiritual need* of trust, sanctification, and obedience (Psalm 37:1-11; James 4:1-10).

• *Don't pray to be released from all trials* because they're often necessary to reveal His glory in us (2 Corinthians 12:7-10).

• When burdened about physical needs (or other desires that He has not promised to satisfy here on this earth), *simply ask Him for help—but do so with undemanding humility and faith,* believing He *can* do it if He *chooses* to do it, but your greatest longing is for His will to be done (Luke 22:42; Daniel 3:17-18).

• Pray for the *spiritual needs of the church*, not just your own, because that is where He is most fully glorified to the world (Ephesians 3:20-21; Romans 15:5-6).

Learn to delight in the things God values most. This is a problem for many American Christians. We have been trained by our culture to feel we need certain medical care, a certain life expectancy, a certain financial security, and freedom. So we expect God to grant these, even though these things are *not* given to Christians living in most underdeveloped countries (and they don't even expect them from God!) We must learn to be content with what He has actually promised—and that may, at times, be very little in the physical realm (Philippians 4:11-12). Our greatest needs are spiritual.

We must identify the needs that God wants to satisfy apart from prayer. Prayer is not the only means by which God meets our needs. Some needs He meets through His created universe, like giving us rain, air, and food (Matthew 5:45; 6:25-26). Some needs He meets through the society we live in, using governments (Romans 13:4-6) and family relationships. Some needs He meets through the body of Christ (Acts 2:42-47). And some needs He meets through our fellowship with Him and our obedience (John 15:7).

So as we present our requests to God—for health concerns, spiritual conversions of friends, personal wisdom in decision-making, safety for our children, wisdom for government leaders, missionaries' success, etc.—we do so realizing that our prayers may not always be the means He is intending to use to accomplish His will on earth. To know the mind of God and His ways is not our full privilege. Prayer may or may not be necessary for God to accomplish His purposes in us and the world around us. But, since we never really know what His ways *are* tied to here on earth, it's wise to simply ask, for this we know: God delights in our humble, trusting participation in His rule.

The fact is, there is no power in prayer—the power is in God. Prayer may be useful for unleashing His power, but there also may be other unfulfilled criteria God is waiting for—like the holiness and motives of the one who asks (James 4:3; 5:16), or the desire to work something deeper in us through suffering. Or, as we saw earlier in this chapter, we must accept the reality of the groaning world we live in and that all things are not as they will be one day.

But the reality remains: some things will *only* come if prayer occurs. As James 4:2 says, "You do not have, because you do not ask God."

Come for Fellowship

To fellowship is to share something in common together. To fellowship with God is to share our common spiritual lives, with the expectation that in the end we will have known or shown God's greatness in the process.

I think the best way to describe this kind of *coming* is "hanging out with God." It's the kind of thing one does with a good friend where perhaps few words are shared but there is joy in being in each other's presence. The Old Testament word *meditate* is part of this. It's a mulling over, a self-reflecting, a serious consideration given to God and His ways.

Fellowshipping with God is both a mental and a heart exercise. It searches out truth and it searches our motives. We *come* to God to encounter Him at whatever level He or I may determine. It's like walking on the beach together with no one saying anything initially but knowing that either one may make an observation, ask a question, or share a concern. It's the Revelation 3:20 invitation He makes to us to "come in and eat" with us.

One of my favorite ways of meeting with God has freed me from the feeling of needing to talk when I'm with Him. I sit in a favorite chair or lay down for bed at night and just consciously come into His presence. No agenda. No lists. Just me and God and the assurance of His holy love. (And even if I drift off to sleep, who better to drift off into sleep with than Him?) Often my time with Him will move into one of the above *come* categories, but other times it may just be thinking about life together, letting Him make every thought holy to Him.

Recently I felt very emotionally dry and drained. I didn't feel like a great pastor or a great anything. As I turned my heart to Him, He reminded me of His grace for me. I just sat there and soaked in His love. It was sweet fellowship and enabled me to continue my day to His glory.

Some time ago I approached a friend I hadn't seen for some time. I extended my hand to shake his, but he reached right past and held out his arms to embrace me. That is God. We so often come to Him with a handshake—and He opens His arms wide.

Coming for fellowship is like the embrace. We hang out with God, not knowing what will happen next or who will initiate conversation or if we will just be there together with few words spoken. But this we know—His love will be reaching out to us in lavish proportions.

Keeping Love Alive—Parallels to Marriage

As we close this section on *coming* to God for His glory, it would be good for us to see that our relationship with God is a lot like our human relationships. We can easily get into relational ruts.

Take marriage as an example. A husband may be a poor listener and become caught up in his own self-centered world. He may have withdrawn from meaningful conversation with his wife or only give her enough responses to make it look like he's listening, when in reality he isn't.

Or a wife may rarely praise her husband and he feels all she does is ask for things and complain to him. Perhaps trust has been eroded, and neither one has made the effort to restore it. Perhaps fellowship is gone, and they rarely spend relaxed time together in expectant love.

You can see the many spiritual parallels. Just as a marriage needs communication adjustments (which always originate with a heart adjustment), so often does our relationship with God frequently need adjustments. We may be hurting in the trust department, or weak in coming to Him to be holy, or rarely hanging out with Him. We may realize that we're always asking Him to make us happy our way and that perhaps we should be listening more to what His agenda is for us—something that may involve more than prayer.

Though we want to avoid formulas that deaden love, we may also find that periodically going through these eight, healthy-communication ingredients as a checklist will guard imbalances or correct deficiencies.

An acronym that many have found helpful is ACTS: Adoration, Confession, Thanksgiving, and Supplication. But as I have implied in this chapter, this doesn't encompass the fullness of our love-relationship with God. So I played with the eight *come* patterns above, and fit them into the acronym "GLORIFY" (with a bit of massaging). If this is helpful, good. If not, ignore it. I'll let you figure out how they fit with the headings used above: G - Gratitude, L - Listen, O - Overcome, R - Rely on, I - Inquire, F - Fellowship, Y - Yield.

A way to summarize this teaching on *coming,* or prayer, is to describe it as *"conversing with God about love and His kingdom."* A slightly more expanded version would be, "Prayer is talking to and listening to God about His love for us and our love for Him, and about how He wants to rule on earth in us and through us." That about says it all.

In marital counseling it's common for couples to realize that some element has been missing from their relationship, and once that is restored, joy also is restored. You will most likely find that the same applies to you and God. So *come* to Him in the varied languages of love—not just what is love to you, but what is love to *Him.* If you do, you will glorify your God—and be satisfied in Him!

For Self-Reflection and Life Application

1. How do you deal with the fact that God is spirit and unseen? Is this a problem to you, and if so, what might you do or remember to address this?

2. Have you spent scheduled times alone with God? What have been the benefits of these times? What has worked best for you?

3. To what extent have you been successful in connecting with God on all occasions throughout your day? What has helped you and what has not? What insights from this chapter may help you *come* to God more frequently and more spontaneously?

4. What difference would it make in your life if you quickly and humbly *came* to God in all your emotionally needy moments?

5. What are some idle times in your life that you can use to *come* to God? What might hinder you from using these moments in this *coming*, God-glorifying way for the rest of your life?

6. In each of the following ways of coming to God, describe (a) the frequency of this kind of communication with God in your normal week, and (b) how coming to God this way can make Him great and satisfy your soul.

- Glorify

- Listen

- Surrender

- Praise

- Trust

- Become

- Ask (for His kingdom)

- Fellowship

7. Reflect on the section entitled "Come—To Trust." How might you incorporate trust in God more regularly in your own life?

8. What is one way your asking prayers might need to be changed to promote God's glory more than your own? Consider the variety of requests you make in a typical week and submit them to what you know of God's will and His heart for you.

9. What would it be like if God revealed Himself in visible and powerful ways every time we asked Him to?

10. Plan two *normal* days of your life (so it includes kids, work, etc.—whatever is normal for you) to consciously *come* to God at least 7 times throughout

the day, being especially aware of having a well-balanced relationship with Him by the end of the day. Reflect on the results of this when you have completed it. What do you want to do to make aspects of this a normal part of your daily living from this day on?

[1] Philip Yancey, *Reaching for the Invisible God,* Zondervan Publishing House, Grand Rapids, 2000, p. 101

[2] Ibid., p. 138.

[3] Anthony Bloom, *Beginning to Pray,* Paulist Press, Paramus 1970, p. 2.

[4] Gary Thomas, *Spiritual Pathways,* Zondervan Publishing House, Grand Rapids, 2000, p. 21f.

[5] Dallas Willard, *The Spirit of the Disciplines,* Harper & Row Publishers, San Francisco, 1988, p. 161.

[6] Matt Redman, *The Unquenchable Worshipper,* Regal Books, Ventura, 2001, pp. 102-4.

[7] Ole Hallesby, *Prayer*, Augsburg Publishing House, Minneapolis, 1959 ed., p. 12.

Chapter 6

Become—The Glory of Becoming Like Jesus

The man spent about a week in Kingcity, meeting with the people. They quickly became like brothers and sisters to him. And, of course, he spent time with the King. It was like starting life all over again. The joy he knew in the King's love for him was wonderful—so much so that he decided to leave Kingcity and bring his family back with him.

One of the questions he wanted answered during his last day there was the meaning of the spring. He learned that drinking from the King's spring water was, indeed, necessary for those in that land, and numerous springs existed throughout the nearby countryside as well as within Kingcity itself.

But he also learned that the spring and its healing powers were only part of the total gift the King offered. His real offer was Himself and His loving rule in them. One question still lingered in the man's mind: What about the people—like his family—who lived out in the villages? Were they safe from the death the boils brought?

He sought out an older gentleman who was known for his wisdom and knowledge of The Breath, *a book which had taken on a whole new meaning to him in light of his experience with the King's love. The gentleman showed him that drinking from the spring could not, by itself, save someone from the boils' death; rather, there must also be loving devotion to the King. That was the King's design from the beginning, but some people in the villages had oversimplified His good news and had ended up settling for far too little.*

"The King's ultimate goal," the older gentleman had explained, "is to create a people to love and a people to be like Him. He takes ordinary people like you and me and makes us into extraordinary people by recreating us with His heart!"

That's what the man had found. That encounter with the King in the park on his first day in Kingcity had changed his life. It was then that he had made his decision to submit fully to the love of the King, and to turn from his self-centered ways and to be transformed to be like Him.

He hadn't traveled more than a few hours out of Kingcity when he came across an old man alongside the road who seemed to be in some kind of distress. His clothes were dirty and worn, and his gray beard and hair looked like they had been neglected for weeks.

The man's natural instinct was to ignore the old man and continue walking on. He had learned long ago that it was better to mind one's own business and not get involved in other people's problems. Besides, he was eager to see his family and he didn't want any distractions.

Just as he was passing by the old man and intending not to make eye contact with him (for he knew that it was easier to stay detached if he didn't look him in the eye), the King's face suddenly appeared in his mind. Something stirred within him. His feet came to a stop a few paces past the "inconvenience." The man's body froze, as if caught in the midst of a great tug-of-war.

What was going on? This had never happened to him before. Into his mind flowed thoughts about the King's love for him, and the joys that came from that love. He felt his will slowly yielding to the will of the King, his previous objections weakening. Then in one final act of surrender, the man slowly turned to look into the eyes of that broken man who was sitting in the dirt beside the road. He never felt more out of control in all his life.

What You've Been Made For

You and I have been created to display the greatness of God through a love relationship with God and His Son, Jesus. This greatness, or glory, begins when we choose to *come* into His presence in response to His moment-by-moment daily invitations. Coming to Him is our first priority if we're to glorify God. It all starts with relationship. It all begins with our neediness and His provisions. It's all bathed in love—and He's the First Lover.

Now we come to our second word-handle that focuses the purpose of our lives on His glory. *Become.* This theme is found throughout the pages of Scripture, but this verse makes *becoming* explicit:

> *"God made him who had no sin to be sin for us, so that in him*
> *we might* become [emphasis mine] *the righteousness of God"*
> *(2 Corinthians 5:21).*

What does the apostle Paul mean here by "become the righteousness of God?" First of all he means that the One Man Jury transfers Christ's righteousness to us so that we are pronounced "Not guilty" in His court room. Instead of seeing our sins—which demand a "guilty" verdict—the Judge sees Christ's righteousness and acquits us. It's what the Bible calls "justification" and it puts us in a right relationship with God by His grace and through our faith, so that we are not condemned.

But there's more here—more than being *declared* righteous by the Judge. The context of verses 15-20 tells us this righteousness is also to be *experienced.* ". . . those who live should no longer live for themselves but for him who died for them and was raised again" (2 Corinthians 5:15). And we are "a new creation; the old has gone, the new has come" (2 Corinthians 5:17). The butterfly has replaced the caterpillar! We have been created for a Christ-like life.

Here's another text that speaks about our purpose of becoming like God:

> *"For those God foreknew he also predestined* to be con-
> formed to the likeness of his Son [emphasis mine], *that he
> might be the firstborn among many brothers" (Romans 8:29).*

Just in case we don't understand what it means to be righteous like God, God took the ultimate step of becoming human like us, and showing us what His righteousness actually looks like in human experience. *In Jesus.* Every teacher knows that this is the best way to teach—by demonstrating it (not just talking about it) and then saying to the student, "Okay, now you do it."

So we have been created to *become* like Jesus. This doesn't mean we have to wear sandals, be Jewish, remain single, or die at the age of thirty-three. What it means is that we are to take on His character.

That's what Jewish rabbis like Jesus expected from their disciples. Disciples didn't just spend time with their rabbi so they could recite his sayings backwards and forwards. They sought to become *like* him. And we are to become like *Jesus.*

One way to understand this concept is to ask the question, If Jesus was facing the same situation I am facing right now, how would He react? To *become* like Jesus is to live life through His eyes and with His heart. As Romans 8:29 says, we are to live like He is our "brother." Because we have the same father as Jesus, we should have similar "family features"—spiritual features.

People will often say to me, "I can see your father in you." Occasionally my wife will give a little laugh, and when I turn to her with a quizzical expression, she'll say, "That look you just made was just like your father." And so it is with us and Jesus—but the "look" is that of holy hearts.

Dallas Willard observes that "You are somebody's disciple."[1] Somebody (or a collection of somebodies) has shaped you in their mold, whether intentionally or unintentionally. As Christians, we make a choice that Jesus will be that primary somebody.

Now the point I most want to make is simply this: *We have been created to glorify God, and since becoming like Jesus glorifies God, the transformation of our lives into the character of Jesus should be a life passion.* Becoming like Jesus isn't just a *good* thing to pursue. It's a *necessary* thing to pursue. In fact, it's for this very reason that we exist! We have been "predestined" to this call-ing (Romans 8:29). It has been in the heart of God to make us like Himself from the very beginning of creation.

Think about it. What greater way can a person reveal the greatness of God than by becoming like Him? Is it not the greatest compliment we can give someone to say, "I want to be like you when I grow up?" What better way to *know* the glory of God than to have His character formed within us? What bet-ter way to *show* the glory of God to others than to display His very character to others through our lives?

This text is a good summary:

> *"For God, who said, "Let light shine out of darkness," made his light shine in our hearts to give us the light of the knowledge of the glory of God in the face of Christ" (2 Corinthians 4:6).*

When we encounter Jesus (i.e. see his "face"), God's life penetrates our hearts so that we *know* (experientially, not just intellectually) the glory of God!

When biblical writers speak of knowing God they are describing the kind of knowing that happens between a husband and wife, not the kind obtained from an Internet search. It's in a transforming encounter with Jesus that we say, "Yes, God is indeed great because I am experiencing His wonderful char-acter in my life!"

This is to be our heart cry. It's not optional to the follower of Jesus. From the time we wake in the morning until we hit the sack at night, our day is to be motivated by becoming like Jesus. It's why we're here. It's how God will be glorified. It's what "Jesus is my Lord" means. And it's how we find our greatest joy!

"God, I want to become like Jesus!"

The Glory-Robber

Okay. It's time for a reality check. All is not at peace on the planet of humans (and I doubt I need to tell you that)! There is an enemy loose among us. It may surprise you that I'm not referring to Satan (more on him a little later). I'm talking about sin.

In the Bible *sin* means to fall short of God's moral standard for living. Both the Hebrew word *chata* and the Greek word *hamartia* (both translated "sin" in our Bibles) mean "to miss the mark," as an arrow would miss its target. Sin is the violation of the holy nature of God. Or, as Romans 3:23 says, "All have sinned and fall short of the glory of God."

Sin is essentially placing self over God. (The "i" in the middle of the English word "sin" can serve as a reminder to us.) When "I" becomes the center of our world rather than God, we sin. Isaiah 53:6 says it this way: "We all, like sheep, have gone astray, each of us has turned to his own way; and the LORD has laid on him [the Messiah] the iniquity of us all." Sin is going our way instead of God's. It's removing God from His rightful place of authority and life.

For this reason, some have called the essence of sin *pride* (another word with "I" in the middle of it!), since pride essentially exalts self above God. Others see sin as essentially *unbelief* in God, since every time we fail to believe (or place our trust in) God we are trusting in ourselves. Romans 14:23 says, "everything that does not come from faith is sin." All of these go back to the primary problem of not placing God's glory (His greatness and worth) first in our lives.

In light of this, we might define *sin* this way: "Sin is anything that opposes the character and will of God."

How do we know what His character and will are? To begin with, Romans 2 says that God has placed His moral standards in each person's conscience. Every person knows without being told that to kill one another is wrong, and to lie and steal is wrong—though admittedly every culture (including our own) has had a tendency to distort these basic laws, sometimes quite severely!

So we shouldn't be surprised to realize that the conscience can be a tricky standard. Our parents and culture can dull them significantly, and we're capable of amazing rationalizations to satisfy our sinful desires. "It's okay to steal from a rich person if what I'm taking is not very significant." Or "It's okay to have sex with my boyfriend because we're really in love." Or "It's okay to lie if the truth would embarrass me." And on it goes.

This is why God gave people a more objective way of knowing His will for them. He gave them His Law. It was on Mount Sinai that God wrote the most basic of these laws on stone and gave them to Israel through Moses. We know this as the Ten Commandments.

Then Jesus came. And the Law came into focus even more sharply—not with more detailed rules, but with *less* rules! (This is not what we might have expected!) His life, teachings, and person "fulfilled" the law (Matthew 5:17). In Him was no sin (1 John 3:5). So the character and will of God became clearer than ever. Do you want to know what is right and good and pleasing to God? Listen to Jesus. Watch Jesus. Follow Jesus. Sin is going in the opposite direction.

Putting the Devil in His Place

You may be wondering why I have put sin—and not Satan—in the role of primary "glory robber?" There's no doubt that Scripture sees this fallen created being as our foe. Jesus says Satan is the "ruler of this world" (John 12:31) and John says that "the whole world is under the control of the evil one" (1 John 5:19). There is, indeed, a struggle going on, and it's "not [just] against flesh and blood, but against the rulers, against the authorities, against the powers of this dark world and against the spiritual forces of evil in the heavenly realms" (Ephesians 6:12). This is no minor opposition!

But here's the good news. Though his authority is significant and his schemes are clever, he no longer has control over Christians! His power has been severely limited—disarmed—since Jesus "triumphed" over him at the Cross (Colossians 2:15).

Yes, we still need to be careful. Satan has enough power to undermine our relationship with God. He's a "roaring lion looking for someone to devour" (1 Peter 5:8) and full of schemes. But the Scriptures teach us that even this level of attack is not to be feared if we are clothed with the essential counter-attacking weapons of truth, holiness, and faith. These three are the core of the spiritual armor we are to wear at all times (Ephesians 6:10-18).

According to Scripture, Satan's primary weapons against us are lies, afflictions, and our sinful nature in which he gets a "foothold" to tempt and deceive us (Ephesians 4:27). This means that Satan may *use* our sin against us, but he does not *cause* us to sin. One of the major teachings in the Bible is that *sin* is our master (Romans 6:6 is just one of many examples) and it is primarily from *sin* that we need to be set free. (Note that in Acts 8:21-23 Peter identifies Simon the sorcerer's problem as "your heart is not right before God" and that he is "captive to sin," not demonic control. And Ephesians 2:1-3 says that Satan is at work in "those who are disobedient.")

One of the unfortunate results of placing blame primarily on the Devil for our problems is that we subtly shift responsibility for our actions from us to him. Instead of looking inside *us* for the cause of our moodiness, or why we get frustrated with our children, or why there's so much conflict on the church board, there is a tendency to tell the Devil to "be gone in the name of Jesus" or some similar warfare strategy without facing our real enemy—sin. Or we feel like we're doing such great things for God that "the enemy is attacking me," resulting in passive delight rather than self-examination and repentance.

But we would do well to consider the instruction of James:

> *"Submit yourselves, then, to God. Resist the devil, and he will flee from you. Come near to God and he will come near to you. Wash your hands, you sinners, and purify your hearts you doubleminded" (James 4:7-8).*

This is how we resist the Devil—by submitting to and drawing near to God with a pure heart. The closer we get to Him, the *less* we will need to worry about Satan. We don't need to talk to Satan (something believers are never taught to do in Scripture). But we *do* need to talk a lot with God! If we deal with our hearts, we will then also be dealing with the Evil One.

It's a Matter of the Heart

There seems to be a tendency among Christians to want to legislate sin. We want to know exactly when we've stepped over the line—usually so we can get as close to it as possible without really *sinning!* This begins at quite early ages.

A few years ago, I was taking care of someone's child who loved jumping on our couch. He would start by climbing over the back. So I told him, "Josiah, please don't climb over the couch." So what did Josiah do? He went behind the couch and jumped up on the back, with one leg over the back and one leg behind it—and his eyes locked on mine!

But, of course, we adults are pretty good at pushing the limits, too. So if we can make up rules that define *the line*, then we can push them really close—so we don't sin, of course!

This has resulted in all sorts of lines. Some measure hemlines and hair lengths. Others ban certain modern day conveniences. One common line in some churches is to ban all alcohol, despite the fact that Jesus made gallons of the stuff at a wedding and Psalm 104:15 (NRSV) says that God made "wine to gladden the human heart!"

Many Christian young adults have placed the line at sexual intercourse so that they are able to explore sensuality fully and freely—without crossing the line, of course.

One particularly challenging environment is the Christian school and college world. Here administrators are constantly walking a fine line between the holiness standards of past generations and the standards of the current generation. Legislating Christian behaviors for all people and all generations can be tricky business.

It's not that laws are bad or that sin is indefinable. Jesus specifically told His Jewish followers to obey the law God gave to Israel. But He ruffled feathers when He approached it from a direction they didn't expect.

Picture the scene in Matthew 15. Some religious leaders approached Jesus with a criticism—His disciples weren't washing their hands before they ate. No, they weren't obsessive clean-freaks! These men believed that when Jews came in social contact with spiritually "dirty" non-Jews, this made them unholy. So as a sign of their desire to be holy, they had developed a rule: If you were in public settings with Gentiles, you needed to wash your hands before the next time you ate.

But Jesus surprises them. He admonishes them saying "their hearts are far from me" and "their teachings are but rules taught by men" (Matthew 15:8-9). (Perhaps Jesus was thinking about human rules like "No running in the sanctuary" or "Pray with your eyes closed" or "Don't wear jeans to church"!)

Then He addresses the root of their problem—which is the root of my problem and yours:

> *"But what comes out of the mouth proceeds from the heart,*
> *and this is what defiles" (Matthew 15:18 NRSV).*

It's not socializing with Gentiles that makes someone dirty before God. *It's what's going on in a person's heart.*

This is not new with Jesus' coming. God had revealed this throughout the Old Testament. For example, God's description of people on earth just before Noah was that "every inclination of the thoughts of his heart was only evil all the time" (Genesis 6:5). Through the prophet Jeremiah, God said, "The heart is deceitful above all things and beyond cure. Who can understand it? I the Lord search the heart and examine the mind, to reward a man according to his conduct" (Jeremiah 17:9-10).

The biblical writers use the word *heart* to describe the center of the inner life. Just as the organ called the heart is the center of our blood system, and thus the source of our physical life, so the word *heart* is used to describe the center and source of our inner life. That's why God says,

> *"Above all else, guard your heart, for it is the wellspring of*
> *life" (Proverbs 4:23).*

The Bible doesn't make strong distinctions between such words as *heart*, *mind*, and *soul*; yet, it's clear from the way they are used that they're not always interchangeable either. For the purposes of this book, I'm going to emphasize the heart's desire component and the mind's belief component, though there are biblical overlaps. Both of these are essential to why a person does what he or she does. And I think these partial distinctions will assist us in focusing our understanding on what God is seeking to do in us for the glory of His name.

When Jesus speaks about the heart being the source of what comes from our mouths (or of what's done in our deeds), He's including what we want, what we long for, what drives us, and what motivates us to say and do the things we say and do. (Further biblical texts referring to the heart in this sense are Matthew 22:37; Acts 13:22; Romans 1:24; and 1 Corinthians 4:5.)

Having just completed writing the above paragraph, my wife Cathy called me downstairs for some strawberry ice cream covered with homemade, rhubarb sauce. I knew it was a love gift to me. We sat out on our rear deck sharing conversation for a short time. During the course of it, I made a gentle, but firm, criticism of something she said. She didn't respond. We moved on to other topics and soon finished our conversation. I returned to continue writing. But God's Spirit showed me my heart. Behind my gentle words to Cathy was a self-focused, impatient, and insensitive heart. I had crushed her spirit with words that had not been necessary at the time. I had sinned against my wife and against God.

If I was a Pharisee in Jesus' day, I would justify myself with, "But I didn't raise my voice or threaten her" or "I didn't use sarcasm." And my favorite rationalization of the heart, "I spoke the truth!" And Jesus would put me in my place as He did the Pharisees.

What we must see clearly is that if we're to glorify God by becoming like Jesus, we must become like Jesus *in our heart!* We must *want* what Jesus wants. And fundamentally we must want to know the greatness of God in the inner places of our being. We must want to love God and love people. That's the orientation of the heart God desires.

Jesus says a good tree bears good fruit, and a bad tree bears bad fruit. So, as counselor Paul Tripp says, the biblical order is "root to fruit." If we want godly fruit, we must pay attention to what is going on in our roots, which either feeds life or death to the rest of our being.

The glory of a transformed heart is a thing of beauty. To will only what God wills, to delight in what God delights in, to weep over what God weeps over—this is to know and show very great and very deep eternal things. It is, simply, to glorify God and be satisfied in Him.

Four Common Root Sins of the Heart

There are many ways to see the heart, but I've found it helpful to divide them into four groups. Though there's some overlap, these four categories allow us to get a mental and verbal handle on what is going on in the inner world of our soul. (Appendix B, "Spiritual Transformation Goals," provides additional self-reflection questions for each of these four root sins to help people identify some major targets. It also offers multiple, biblical passages for further personal reflection.)

Pride. Pride is desiring attention and self-worth apart from God and His purposes. It hates being wrong, being criticized or failing. It craves approval, power, control, respect, and praise. And it's quick to criticize, judge, and put down others.

> *"In his pride the wicked does not seek him; in all his thoughts there is no room for God" (Psalm 10:4).*

Fear, anxiety, and worry. Fear and worry desire comfort and peace more than God and His care. They hate insecurity, uncertainty, disapproval, and death. They crave safety, lack of conflict, good health, approval, and being in control.

> *"Do not be anxious about anything, but in everything, by prayer and petition, with thanksgiving, present your requests to God. And the peace of God, which transcends all understanding, will guard your hearts and your minds in Christ Jesus" (Philippians 4:6-7).*

Self-centeredness. Self-centeredness desires my energies to be spent on "me" rather than God and loving others. It resists loving others when there is nothing in it for themselves and lacks sensitivity to the feelings and needs of others. It craves love, success, and popularity. It often shows itself in irritation, anger, and impatience.

> *"Do nothing out of selfish ambition or vain conceit, but in humility consider others better than yourselves. Each of you should look not only to your own interests, but also to the interests of others" (Philippians 2:3-4).*

Pleasure-seeking apart from God. As we saw in Chapter 3, God wants us happy! Pleasure is His invention and it's a good thing! But pleasure outside God's holiness and love are distortions of His design (chapter 12 will expand on this further). It craves sexual pleasure, chemically-induced feelings, entertainment, competition, and whatever money can by. It hates self-control, delayed gratification, and losing at anything.

> *"'Everything is permissible for me'—but not everything is beneficial. 'Everything is permissible for me'—but I will not be mastered by anything" (1 Corinthians 6:12).*

As I have counseled people regarding their problems and have looked at my *own* problems, I consistently see these primary root issues of the heart behind them. Perhaps one will stand out to you personally, or you may feel that several (or all) are significantly active within you.

One of the most heart-searching lists of sins in the Bible is found in 2 Timothy.

> *"But mark this: There will be terrible times in the last days* [Note: The "last days" began with the coming of Jesus and continue until his return]. *People will be lovers of themselves, lovers of money, boastful, proud, abusive, disobedient to their parents, ungrateful, unholy, without love, unforgiving, slanderous, without self-control, brutal, not lovers of the good, treacherous, rash, conceited, lovers of pleasure rather than lovers of God—having a form of godliness but denying its power. Have nothing to do with them"* (2 Timothy 3:1-5).

Over half of these sins are *explicitly* heart-centered, dealing with distorted desires; the others *imply* a heart problem. God is concerned about our affections. And that's why the core issue to becoming like Jesus is to pledge allegiance only to Him.

An Example of Heart-Based Becoming: Dealing With Anger

Let's see how this heart-centered change is applied in a particular area like anger. It's common to hear people speak about "managing" anger. Hit a pillow or scream into it. Work out your aggression in the gym. Count to ten. Take medication. The goal is to control your anger so at least it doesn't hurt someone.

When Jesus taught His Sermon on the Mount, recorded in Matthew chapters 5-7, one of the primary points He was making was that righteous behavior is not just about actions. God is more concerned with the heart. For example, Jesus says that sin is not just the act of adultery, it's even *desiring* a sexual encounter outside of marriage. And sin is not just committing murder, it's even being angry (Matthew 5:21-30).

James expands on this:

> *"What causes fights and quarrels among you? Don't they come from your desires that battle within you? You want something but don't get it. You kill and covet, but you cannot have what you want. You quarrel and fight. You do not have, because you do not ask God"* (James 4:1-2).

There are two causes of anger mentioned in this text: not getting what we want, and not asking God for what we want. The first cause of anger—not getting what we want—is a problem of making a desire into a demand, thinking we *must* have a particular thing to be happy/content/fulfilled/etc. For example, we may demand respect from a child or a driver on the road, or we may demand perfection from our team, or we may demand hot food from a restaurant waiter. If we don't get what we want, we get angry.

The second cause of anger is a problem of not going to *God* for our real needs. Instead, we go to someone (or something) else. If only we had gone to God—either to have Him satisfy our hearts or to have Him correct any misdirected desires in the first place—we wouldn't have gotten angry.

Both of these are a heart problem. Both require heart surgery. Jeremiah says the same thing James (and Jesus) is saying when he describes "two sins" of the people, though Jeremiah makes his analysis in the reverse order of James. First, he says, people haven't fed their soul from God; and second, they have tried to feed it from something else (Jeremiah 2:13). Sin is a misdirection of the heart.

Once when my son Brian was in high school, he and I were sitting at the kitchen table discussing the realities of his day. He shared about an experience that had made him a little frustrated. I took this as a teachable moment and explained to him that often even irritations or frustrations are signs that our soul is not content in God and that we are looking elsewhere for satisfaction. So these milder forms of anger are still anger—in the heart. Before any mean word, or harsh tone or dumping-to-a-friend can take place, anger has already begun. Brian's response was classic—and humble: "Wow, you've just doubled my sins!"

Today people speak of "anger management" as if to say, It's okay if you get upset. That's normal. Just don't do anything that will hurt anyone. But Jesus, James, and Jeremiah would say, "You've missed the point." Or more specifically, "You've missed God's heart."

Occasionally I will be convicted of a sarcastic statement I've made to Cathy. Sarcasm can often be a mild form of anger—dressed up in the truth. I may want something from her (like respect, love, perfection, pleasure, etc.) and when I don't get it, sarcasm can be a means of expressing it to her without being direct. If I reflect on this later and think I may have hurt her because of it, I'll often go to her and confess it and express sorrow for the effect it had on her. Sometimes she'll say "thank you" because it did, indeed, hurt her. Other times she'll say, "Oh, I didn't even think anything about it! That didn't bother me at all."

Now I have to admit, in those situations when she's not offended, it's tempting to feel that I'm off the hook! But God doesn't allow me that luxury. Perhaps my comment didn't hurt her, but I still know that my heart had pursued self-glory. I had wanted something and had not gotten it, and I was not content without it. I hadn't gone to God first.

Of course, there is a place for righteous anger in the Bible. God gets angry and so did Jesus. Their anger, like ours, was also the result of not getting their way. But there's a slight difference here! Their anger was motivated by desires for the glory and will of *God*. And this is often *not* like ours.

So, yes, strive to have only righteous, God-glorifying anger (and as Ephesians 4:26 says, "In your anger do not sin"), but let's be honest—most of our anger tends to be heavily weighted in the sin category! It's all about *me*! And that's where the sin begins.

Further Biblical Ways to Understand Your Heart

I want to drive this home by using a few other biblical ways of seeing what God wants us to *become*. It's important that we understand how deep this transformation is intended to be. This is no "throw a coat of paint on that ugly pea green wall" project. If sin is anything that opposes the character and will of God, then becoming like God will often mean ripping out the wallboard and studs behind it because some of that ugly green stuff is mold and it's been eating away at the wall for many years! Change must go deeper—to the heart.

Be Holy. To be holy is to be set apart—to be like God. It's to take on His goodness and moral perfection. At the core of holiness is not a set of rules, but God's heart. To be holy is to love what God loves and to hate what God hates. It's to desire what God desires.

The apostle Peter puts it this way:

> *"As obedient children, do not conform to the evil desires you had when you lived in ignorance. But just as he who called you is holy, so be holy in all you do; for it is written: 'Be holy, because I am holy'" (1 Peter 1:14-16).*

Notice that the desires themselves are evil, not just acting upon them. And evil desires make us unholy. That's why Jesus tells His followers that it's the "pure in heart" who will see God (Matthew 5:8).

The word *holy* is often used in our worship songs, but how many people sing about God's holiness with the longing to be holy like He is? How many want the purity of the heart of God for themselves?

Here is a prayer for this kind of holiness: "God, create in me a clean heart, that the longings of my soul in my everyday activities will be the same as your holy longings, my desires your holy desires, so that my actions will conform to your holy will."

Trust God. ". . . and everything that does not come from faith is sin" (Romans 14:23).

When Israel failed to trust God's promise to give them the land of Canaan, they sinned for their lack of faith. When Peter took his eyes off Jesus while walking on the water—he, too, sinned. Lack of faith is sin because it's a heart response based on fear and self rather than on God.

Trust is ultimately about the heart. It shifts us from self-reliance to God-reliance, from humanism and pop psychology to surrendering to the Designer of the human soul.

> *"May the God of hope fill you with all joy and peace as you trust in him" (Romans 15:13).*

Trusting in God enables us to not be afraid of what people can do to us (Psalm 56:11)—like firing us, embarrassing us, being critical of us, or defeating us in a game. Trusting in God means we "have no fear of bad news" (Psalm 112:7)—like a stock market crash, a terrorist strike, a cancer report, or the death of a loved one. With Isaiah we say, "You will keep in perfect peace him whose mind is steadfast, because he trusts in you" (Isaiah 26:3). Some level of concern is appropriate, of course, because it motivates us to be responsible and take care of our lives. But fear, anxiety, and pride are gone when trust is present.

An active, conscious, reliance on the teachings of Jesus, and His work on the cross, and in His resurrected power to be with us and change us, is the opposite of unbelief and self-reliance. Trust will change us to become like Jesus.

Turn from Idols. Related to the sin of distrust is the sin of idolatry. An *idol* is anything that competes with our devotion to God. It may be a favorite sport team, money in the bank, or even a child or spouse. It may be our home, our own beauty, or the food in our kitchen cupboard.

Whenever we seek satisfaction from any person, value, or thing apart from God and the goodness He offers, we make that source an idol. It is God and God alone in whom we must place our primary trust and our affection (Psalm 62).

God tells Israel not to set up "idols in their hearts" (Ezekiel 14:3-8). It's not the thing itself that's the problem. It's what it does to the heart. If it rules us and demands our affection it's an idol. Jesus says we can serve only one Master—God.

Of course, money isn't bad—but if it rules you, it has become an idol. Sex isn't bad—but if it captures your heart more than God, it's an idol. Power isn't bad—but if you need it to feel important, it's an idol.

John puts it this way, using "desire" in place of "idol":

> *"My little children, I am writing these things to you so that*
> *you may not sin. . . . Do not love the world or the things in the*
> *world. The love of the Father is not in those who love the*
> *world; for all that is in the world—the desire of the flesh, the*
> *desire of the eyes, the pride in riches—comes not from the*
> *Father but from the world" (1 John 2:1, 15-16 NRSV).*

God has given us many different ways to see how our lives don't conform to righteousness and the character of Jesus. Whether it's deviation from God's holy standards, a lack of trust in Him, or the erection of idols in our heart, the issue is the same. Our fundamental longings are opposing the heart and will of God.

Asking the "Why?" Questions

From my experience, our culture has raised generations of nonreflective people. And sadly, the church is no exception. Christians seem to rarely pause to ask themselves, "Why do I say the things I say? Why do I feel what I feel? Why do I do the things I do?"

Perhaps it's because we think we already *know* why—it's the *people* and *circumstances* in our lives that make us say and do these things! So we say things like, "He makes me frustrated." Or "I worry when she's late." We blame our actions on our parents, our spouse, our kids, our genes, our government, our childhood experiences—even the weather.

Now, of course, these are often contributing factors. But according to the Bible, they're not the whole story. At most, they may *trigger* our actions, but they aren't the real *cause*.

Why do you get quiet during conflict? Why do you work so hard at work? Why is it so important for you to look good? Why do you lose your patience, or sulk when you don't get your own way? Why do you snap at your children—or spouse? Why? God has an answer. And it's written all over the pages of His Word.

If I cherish "sin in my *heart*" the Lord will not listen to me (Psalm 66:18). When I place God's "word in my *heart*" I won't sin against God (Psalm 119:11). My prayer is to be "Search me, O God, and know my *heart*; test me and know my anxious thoughts" (Psalm 139:23).

David asked good questions—and he gave spiritually truthful answers!

> *"Why are you downcast, O my soul? Why so disturbed with-*
> *in me? Put your hope in God, for I will yet praise him, My*
> *Savior and my God" (Psalm 42:5-6).*

As followers of Jesus Christ, we must stop making simplistic connections between events "out there" and our own actions. We must take on the mind of Christ and see our lives as inhabitants in a spiritual universe where God and our hearts are engaged in a relational drama. And every word and action is an expression of this—either from the presence of the rule of God in us or its absence.

When someone comes to see me in my office with a problem, I usually have two options about how to help them (and I sometimes share these with them). I can offer them practical advice (wisdom) to make their lives work better . . . or I can offer them God. Generally I seek to do both. So if a man is struggling with a rebellious teenage son, I may offer him advice about how to respect his son, how to understand his son, and how to establish behavioral limits on his son without crushing his son's spirit. But I will have failed him if I don't offer him rivers of living water.

If I don't nourish people's minds and hearts with God, it's like putting a band-aid on a deep gash. It may stop the bleeding for awhile, but the wound is still there—and there's a good chance it could be infected. Deeper troubles likely lie ahead.

Think about it this way. If someone likes to play in the ocean surf, but they find that they're frequently being drawn out into deep water and are desperately trying to stay alive, how can I best help him—give him little blow-up floaties for his arms, or teach him how to swim? The best way to help people cope with life's people and circumstances is to teach them to live with their hearts in God. It will equip them for all of life; it will lead them to joy; and it's why they were created in the first place!

The truth of the matter is this: The reason we say what we say and do what we do is because our hearts have been shaped to seek happiness in someone or something. Either it's in God or another source. We must teach ourselves to ask good and hard questions (which we'll look at in Chapter 7) and not be afraid of them. And we must teach our souls to find these answers in God.

No More Blame-shifting—I'm Responsible!

This brings us to an important conclusion. I am responsible for my words and actions. I can't blame my father or mother. I can't blame my temperament or personality. I especially can't blame the "triggers" or "button-pushers" in my life. Every external event that I experience is filtered through my heart and what comes out is a function of my heart, not the event.

So if I feel frustrated when I hit a wall of bumper-to-bumper traffic, it's not the traffic that's making me frustrated—it's my strong desire to be productive with my time, or my strong desire to not upset someone who's waiting for me, or my strong desire to experience the pleasurable event I was heading towards. I'm responsible for my desires and for finding my primary satisfaction in God.

Amy Carmichael was a single British missionary to India where she served for 55 continuous years, rescuing children from temple prostitution and giving them an alternative life in her community. Her last 20 years were confined to her house after a fall into a deep pit. In her little book *If*, she describes the power of Calvary love—the love of Jesus for us. One of her many wonderful "If. . ." statements is: "If a sudden jar can cause me to speak an impatient, unloving word, then I know nothing of Calvary love. . . (For a cup brimful of sweet water cannot spill even one drop of bitter water, however suddenly it is jolted.)"[22]

So if someone kicks over *your* bucket (sending a critical word or an unloving statement your way), what kind of water (words, emotions, actions) will come out? It all depends what was in your bucket (heart) in the first place. If you were filled with self, self will come out. If you were filled with God, peace and love will come out. And you're responsible for which it is—at all times.

Occasionally I'll hear someone describe their friend's decision to act irresponsibly (drinking, sexual activity, etc.) as their choice and that they're responsible for it. I agree—and I don't. Yes, choice was involved, but often not where people think. Most (if not all) behavioral choices are really the results of choices of heart and mind made long before a choice of behavior. So in that sense they really aren't free to choose right behavior because their beliefs and values have already significantly enslaved them.

What we *want* and what we *believe* will significantly shape our actions. So alcoholism starts at the heart. Perfectionism starts at the heart. The need for approval starts at the heart. Anger, worry, workaholism, lying, pornography, anorexia, greed—all start in the heart. They may have other factors at work as well, but our battle is fundamentally about the heart. It's there that God wants to make us holy.

A New Way of Seeing—and Expecting

This may be new territory for you. Or it may be reinforcing what you already know. Either way it's a new way of seeing things compared to how the world (and many Christians) view their lives.

Years ago I was at a meeting of various leaders in my church to discuss a particular issue. During the meeting I became frustrated with the way a person there was portraying the elder board. I felt it was uninformed and hurtful.

I expressed my opinions in what I thought was a controlled way. Later, one of my fellow elders told me I had looked angry. I knew I was definitely frustrated with that person, but I didn't think I was angry! I rationalized that I was just passionate and intense; and after all, can't a pastor be a little human, too? But his words echoed in my mind for some time.

I began to see that my heart had not been surrendered to God. My response was more self-centered than compassionate. From that experience, I came to the conclusion that I must never let my spiritual guard down in a meeting—or *anywhere!* I must *always* walk with God with a humble heart. I must *always* speak with a heart of love. Being merely human isn't an option. I am a child of God, a disciple of Jesus, indwelt by the Spirit. No matter what anyone says or does in a church meeting, or in my home, or anyplace else, I never want to speak apart from God's heart and rule in me. I must always be satisfied in God. *Why would I want anything else?*

I invite you to catch this vision—a vision of Christ being formed in you. The promise of the new covenant in Jeremiah is that God will put his law "in their minds and write it on their hearts" (Jeremiah 31:33). In fact, I think there is reason to believe that this is the primary new thing Jesus brought to us that wasn't available in the old covenant. This is not cosmetic surgery designed to only look good to the people around you. This is life-changing reality, from the inside out.

The truth is, as lovers and followers of Jesus, the Spirit of God has been given to us so that we can actually *want* to and actually *do* God's will! It's in our minds and hearts. It's there—waiting for you and me to let it be the dominant reality in our lives.

Can you imagine a life where God's heart rules yours? Where your knocked-over bucket is always spilling out peace, joy, and love? God says it's your inheritance. Now. It's what you've been predestined for. And it *is* going to require some effort.

For Self-Reflection and Life Application

1. Reflect on the statement, *"We have been created to glorify God, and since becoming like Jesus glorifies God, the transformation of our lives into the character of Jesus should be a life passion."* What parts of this statement stir something within you—whether positive, negative, or questioning? And why?

2. How might it change your life to think about becoming like Jesus as soon as you wake up in the morning and to keep this thought recurring throughout your day?

3. What do you think about the definition of *sin* being "anything that opposes the character and will of God?" What does this say about the kind of relationship we might expect with Him?

4. In what ways have you (or people you've known) put too much blame on Satan—so much that they failed to identify sin in their lives that may have been contributing to their problems?

5. What religious/church rules have you experienced in your past or present that either have no foundation in God's heart, or if they do, have replaced the deeper matter of motivation and desire?

6. Consider various sins of word or deed, and for each one try to identify what motivation or desire could be behind it that is displeasing to God (i.e. that opposes His character and will).

7. Identify which of the four "root sins" listed is most prominent in your own life, and share two or three ways you observe it in your daily life.

8. What might you do to put Proverbs 4:23 into practice in your life: "Above all else, guard your heart, for it is the wellspring of life?"

9. How do you see anger (including irritation and frustration) in your life? In what ways do you see the truth of James 4:1-3 and Jeremiah 2:13 in your anger—that you've made a *desire* for happiness into a *demand*, and that you didn't go to *God* for your real needs.

10. What are some examples in which people fail to trust in God for satisfaction and instead put their primary trust in idols? What are some idols that you personally must guard your heart against?

11. Reflect on the last 2 hours of your life and consider why you said, did, and felt the things you did. What difference might there have been in some of these if you had God as the center of your desires?

12. Imagine your life controlled by God, such that your character is substantially the character of Jesus. Picture your heart responding to daily stresses and trigger events with God's heart. Role-play these scenes in your mind and delight in them. And let their beauty stir you to want them to be a reality for you—for the glory of God and your joy!

[1] Dallas Willard, *The Divine Conspiracy: Rediscovering Our Hidden Life in God*, HarperCollins Publishers, New York, 1998, p. 271.
[2] Amy Carmichael, *If*, Christian Literature Crusade, Fort Washington, 1938, p. 46.

Chapter 7

Become—Intentional Steps For Life Transformation

The inconvenience looked up at the man from his roadside position. Their eyes locked. It was as though a force was compelling the man, yet he was aware of his own yielding to that force as well. The King's face before him was inspiring his surrender.

For as long as he could remember, the man had battled fears in his soul. Fear of failure. Fear of rejection and inadequacies. Fear of not being in control. Fear had often held him back from doing many things he knew he could (or should) be doing. He figured this was just the way he was. Other people had their problems; he had his. Nobody was perfect.

But then came that woman on the road. And Kingcity. And the King. He knew that life would never be the same again. And the more he spent time with the King, the more he saw that his old life was incompatible with His. So as he looked into the old man's eyes, he felt a freedom to risk, knowing that the King of love would be with him.

"What's your name?" the man asked. "Do you have family in the area? How can I best help you?" The old man answered his questions and the man found himself sitting down beside him, treating the inconvenience as if he was a long-lost friend.

The man gave him some of his food and the few remaining coins he had on him. But in the end, the greatest gifts he gave the old man were dignity and conversation and a parting embrace. In return, the man had been given the gift of peace—first by the King, and secondly by the old man's friendship and gratitude. Two men—not one—had been touched alongside that road.

As he returned to his journey, the man thought about what had just happened. It was exciting—a little scary but still exciting. Soon he was lost in thought about his life—and that inevitably took his mind to his father. He could feel the resentment that normally accompanied these thoughts rising within. Scenes replayed in his mind. Words echoed in his ears. And he felt the wounds to his soul all over again.

Eventually he sensed the presence of the King breaking through into his mind. (How long he had been trying to get through the man didn't know, but he knew the King wanted to meet with him.) He walked off the road to the shade of a maple tree and sat down. Within a few minutes his heart was humbly listening to the Lover of his Soul.

He recalled the King's words in The Breath, *"I am your light and your salvation—whom shall you fear? I am the stronghold of your life—of whom shall you be afraid?" But he* was *afraid. He was afraid of confrontation. Afraid of being criticized. Afraid of never being able to get his dad's approval.*

"What do you want me to do?" the man asked the King. There was no audible voice; silence fell upon their meeting. And there, in the quiet, the man surrendered his heart, again, to the King, just as he had when he stopped in his tracks with the old man a few hours ago. The fog in his heart slowly began to lift, and he gradually began to see his dad from the King's perspective. His eyes moistened and he pledged to the King not to be ruled by fear but by trust and love.

As he continued his walk home, the man and the King had numerous conversations, some of them joyful, others quite sobering. And with each step closer to his house, he knew he was not out of the woods—not by a long shot.

So Where's the Change?

Statistics about Christians aren't too encouraging. Poll after poll says that professing Christians don't live a whole lot differently than professing non-Christians. How can that be—especially in light of what God says happens in the person who follows Jesus?

Take, for example, Romans 8:

> *"You, however, are controlled not by the sinful nature but by the Spirit, if the Spirit of God lives in you. . . . For if you live according to the sinful nature, you will die; but if by the Spirit you put to death the misdeeds of the body, you will live, because those who are led by the Spirit of God are sons of God" (Romans 8:9, 13-14).*

So two things are going on in the Christian: (1) The Spirit is in ultimate control of us, not sin; and (2) We must continue to consciously give the Spirit control ("put to death the misdeeds of the body").

This text and others in the New Testament[1], show a two-fold work necessary to make us like Jesus—God's work and ours. In response to our initial and on-going surrender to Jesus, the Spirit acts to transform our lives to be like His. It is, after all, one of God's primary reasons for saving us. And according to passages like 1 John 2:4, 3:6, and 4:8, if a person *doesn't* show evidence of increasing holiness, there's reason to doubt whether they really are Christians in the first place.

So why *don't* people change? To be frank, some don't want to. They like their lives the way they are. There are others, however, who expect God to change them with little effort on their part. They hope that by going to church, reading their Bibles, praying, and having faith, change will just happen. Still others don't change beyond certain levels because they actually don't know *how*.

In the pages that follow I want to lay out a clear, biblical process of change—a process that emphasizes the need for heart change above all. It is an *intentional* process, requiring specific steps towards spiritual transformation, for the glory of God and our joy.

Steps and Leaps

Most lasting change doesn't happen quickly. It takes time. The layers of sinful heart attitudes, unbiblical thinking, and ungodly deeds imbedded in our beings were built over years of repetition, so they aren't going to go away without a fight. Time-consuming battles will need to be fought, one small victory at a time.

> *"And we, who with unveiled faces all reflect the Lord's glory, are being transformed into his likeness with ever-increasing glory, which comes from the Lord, who is the Spirit"* *(2 Corinthians 3:18).*

When Moses came off the mountain after meeting with God, his face glowed with God's glory. But he didn't want the people to know it was starting to fade. So he put a veil over his face. Unlike Moses, *we* experience "ever-increasing" glory! We're "being transformed." Becoming like Jesus takes time[2], *but the process is certain.* It is happening.

Many have discovered that change is often dramatically sped up through fresh encounters with God that involve deep brokenness and surrender, like the kind Isaiah had in Isaiah 6 when he saw the supreme glory and holiness of God and his own unworthiness and pride. John Wesley noted this leap of dramatic change in most every victorious Christian he knew.

I've walked in loving trust with Jesus since childhood. But it wasn't until my early twenties that God began to convict me of a spiritual holdout in my heart—I didn't want to serve Him overseas. (I recall that Africa was at the top of my "don't-send-me-there" list!) It took that God-passionate house church I mentioned earlier to teach me new things about joy in God and free my heart to be able to surrender this part of my life to Him. Returning from worship one night, I knelt down in the middle of my apartment, with tears in my eyes and hands raised to Him, and I ended the tug of war. Gratefully I lost—and it was the beginning of many such encounters with God, encounters that continue to free my heart to become fully like Jesus, not just in small steps but, at times, in large victorious leaps.

We shouldn't resign ourselves to a process of becoming like Jesus that takes a lifetime in every area of our lives. We should expect that the holy God is powerfully at work within the hearts and minds He lovingly rules. Change should be substantial and visible, both by steps and leaps. It is normal Christianity.

The Foundation of Jesus and Coming

Change isn't first about us—it's about God and *His* pleasure. If we resolve to change primarily so our marriage can avoid divorce or so we can primarily stop making people mad at us or so we can primarily live a healthier lifestyle, then we have missed something very fundamental.

Counselor and psychologist Larry Crabb offers the following critique: "Helping people feel loved and worthwhile has become the central mission of the church. We are learning not to worship God in self-denial and costly service, but to embrace our inner child, heal our emotions, overcome addictions, lift our depressions, improve our self-images, establish self-preserving boundaries, substitute self-love for self-hatred, and replace shame with an affirming acceptance of who we are. . . . We have become committed to relieving the pain behind our problems rather than using the pain to wrestle more passionately with the character and purposes of God. *Feeling better* has become more important than *finding God.* And worse, we assume that people who find God always feel better."[3]

I see this all too often. There's more self-effort than heart-change, more trying to live by biblical principles of morality than living in God.

The apostle Paul warns us:

> *"See to it that no one takes you captive through hollow and deceptive philosophy, which depends on human tradition and the basic principles of this world rather than on Christ"* *(Colossians 2:8).*

"Human tradition and the basic principles of this world" actually do work at some level. You don't need to be a follower of Jesus to have nice kids, success at your job, and a comfortable retirement account. But it's those who *depend on Christ* that know God's life—who know *real* life.

John Bunyan lived in England in the 1600s. Before coming to Christ for salvation, he was frequently plagued by fears, habitual swearing, and depression. Even after his conversion, they persisted. What finally set him free—and enabled him to later write one of the all-time best-sellers, *Pilgrims' Progress*, from jail—was a living relationship with Christ. In his words: "Oh! Christ! Christ! There was nothing but Christ before my eyes. . . . It was glorious to me to see his exultation, and the worth . . . of all his benefits. . . . For if he and I were one, then his righteousness was mine, his merits mine, his victory also mine." And when facing a deep testing, his heart would cry out, "I must go to Jesus."[4]

What does this look like in practice? It means we consciously look daily to Jesus to feed us, forgive us, free us, and fill us. Or to put it another way, we must *consciously and deliberately* live in Christ, for Christ, and through Christ. And if we live this way, we *will* begin to change.

Some time ago we had a laptop computer that was giving us fits. I spent hours and hours with computer techs on the phone from India (whose accents would challenge me greatly), then I sent it off to California (twice), spending $300 to fix it—only to have the same problem when it returned. (If your hard drive has crashed, or your three-hour writing project has mysteriously vanished into nothingness, you probably can relate!) "I must go to Jesus" was my cry throughout this ordeal—not primarily so my computer would be fixed, but so that my spirit would be fixed—to become like Jesus. I needed His heart to be alive in me. Before I could *become*, I had to *come*.

Choosing Between Relief From Suffering and Jesus

Picture your two-year-old throwing a temper tantrum on the floor, or someone pulling out in front of you forcing you to slam on your brakes to avoid meeting his rear bumper. We may not like to hear this, but one of the best indicators of whether *becoming* is a priority goal in our life is to look at the way we respond to experiences like these.

When these happen, what do we want *most*—relief or God? Comfort or character growth? What *do* we want? To what or to whom do we most turn? Can we respond and say, "Thank you, God, for an opportunity to become like You right now?"

That's what Paul teaches us to do:

> *"Not only so, but we also rejoice in our sufferings, because we know that suffering produces perseverance; perseverance, character; and character, hope" (Romans 5:3—4).*

"You mean I'm supposed to be *glad* when stuff like that happens in my life?" Yes—not because you like to suffer, but because you know it can develop the character of Jesus in you. Isn't it interesting that many of the very things we complain about in life are actually opportunities to *get* what our soul really wants—to become more like Jesus?

Think about it: If you could get a salary raise on your job and not grow more like Jesus as a result, *or* get a salary cut and become more like Jesus, which would you choose? What does your answer say about the goals of your life? Is becoming like Jesus a priority in your life or is it something you pursue when it's merely convenient or when it's forced on you?

If we're serious about glorifying God through *coming* and *becoming*, we must have a radical reinterpretation about difficulties and disappointments in our lives. They are not obstacles to our goals in life—they are actually aids to it. Pressure and heat are what make diamonds.

Five Intentional Pursuits to Become Like Jesus

I'd like to outline a process of spiritual transformation that I believe is biblical and effective. For those who commit themselves to pursuing these following five realities, there will be much reward. Godly change will happen.

Dallas Willard says, "you lead people to become disciples of Jesus by *ravishing them* with a vision of life in the kingdom of the heavens in the fellowship of Jesus."[5] I've sought to do this in prior chapters, as have many other helpful authors. The rest of this chapter is for those who *want* to become like Jesus but don't know how to get there.

If you desire to be a follower of Jesus, if you are excited about the glory of God in you, if you are eager to know the spiritual joy that satisfies your longings in God, then I invite you to read on.

Become Through Surrender

I pray that these five elements—surrender, insight, repentance, grace, and perseverance—will help bring you closer to your heart's desire. If I had to say which of these five is the most critical for God to change us and make us holy, I would probably say it's *surrender*. Or more specifically, death. Jesus says that a seed can't produce life until it first falls to the ground and dies (John 12:24). The path to life passes through death. Always. It's the only road around.

But what does this mean? In the verses that follow in John 12, Jesus talks about the "man who hates his life" and who "follows me." Elsewhere He says,

> *"If anyone would come after me, he must* deny himself and take up his cross daily and follow me [emphasis mine]. *For whoever wants to save his life will lose it, but whoever loses his life for me will save it"* *(Luke 9:23-24).*

To take up a cross in Jesus' day was a metaphor for walking to your crucifixion. It was a metaphor for death, for dying to self—such as selfish ambitions, self-promotion, self-rule.

> *"I have been crucified with Christ and I no longer live, but Christ lives in me. The life I live in the body, I live by faith in the Son of God, who loved me and gave himself for me"* *(Galatians 2:20).*

Notice that there is a past tense to this death ("I *have been* crucified with Christ") and an on-going daily sense to this death ("take up his cross *daily*"and "*live* by faith"). So we are continually renewing the choice we made the first time we believed in Jesus. It's like marriage. Vows are made once, then lived out every day. It's why Romans 12:1 says, "offer your bodies as living sacrifices" to God. Each day we lay ourselves on the altar and die to "self." (See also Romans 6:11-13 and 8:9-16.)

So there is an initial death, and there is a daily death. There's also a situational death. This is the surrender that takes place in the face of a particular sin or temptation. It's saying, I am crucified with Christ *right now* as I face this person, these emotions, and this situation. A single, sincere prayer in the morning won't cut it. God calls us to a daily and situational dying—so he can live in us at every moment.

But our surrender isn't just from something (self)—it's surrender to someone. We surrender to God and that means surrendering to life! We forsake so we can embrace. There *is* life after death.

Jeanne Guyon lived in France in the 17th century. At the age of 16, her mother forced her to marry a wealthy man 22 years older than she was and it was a very unhappy marriage. But Jeanne's deep spiritual conversion at age 20 gave her the ability to endure it. When her husband died nine years later, she began writing and speaking about an intimate, personal relationship with Jesus Christ. It was a message that was not popular with her Catholic church and as a result she spent many years in prison, including four in the Bastille.

But her writings spread throughout France and eventually the world, and today she's regarded as one of the most influential women in all of church history. Her most famous book was titled *Short and Easy Method of Prayer,* which today is entitled, *Experiencing the Depths of Jesus Christ.* She says, "I have written this book with a desire that you might wholly give yourself to God. . . Oh if only once we could be convinced of God's goodness towards his children and of His desire to reveal Himself to them! We would no longer seek our own selfish desires."[6] Her message was that surrender brought intimacy with God. "Surrender your freedom into His hands. Yield to the Lord His right to do with you as He pleases." "Abandonment is the key to the inward spiritual life. . . Abandonment is practiced by *continually* losing your own will in the will of God. . . Abandonment must reach a point where you stand in complete indifference to yourself. . . . Abandonment is being satisfied with the present moment, no matter what that moment contains."[8]

This is the teaching of Scripture and the experience of Christians throughout the ages. Death must precede life. Absolute surrender must occur before the issues of our hearts and the habits of our bodies will be conformed to Jesus. As Andrew Murray says, "If our hearts are willing for that, there is no end to what God will do for us, and to the blessing God will bestow."[9]

What is this going to look like in your life—and mine? I believe it will essentially involve two things: a surrender of all the desires of our hearts to God—both in principle and in specifics—and a commitment to the pursuit of one desire—the glory of God in us.

This is seen in George Mueller's life, the man who ran an orphanage for 300 children without ever asking for money. At the age of 24, four years after his conversion, he experienced "...an entire and full surrender of my heart. I gave myself fully to the Lord. Honor, pleasure, money, my physical powers, my mental powers, all was laid down at the feet of Jesus, and I became a great lover of the Word of God. I found my all in God."[10] Later he would say, "There was a day I died to George Muller, his opinions, preferences, tastes and will."[11]

One of my daily deaths is the desire to feel happy based on circumstances. I used to hate it when Cathy and I were emotionally distant. I used to resent it when a church problem took away my joy in ministry. Why? Because I craved circumstantial happiness. I wanted to feel good. But I've learned that my greatest joy is often waiting for me in disappointments. And I can't get there unless I travel the road of sorrow that leads me to a God who wants to satisfy my soul with His love, truth, and purposes. So I have died—or rather, am dying—to the need for circumstantial happiness, which has helped me to interact with my wife and people with a heart of peace rather than anxiety.

Amy Carmichael writes about the power of Calvary love—the love of Jesus for us: "If I hold on to choices of any kind, just because they are my choice; if I give any room to my private likes and dislikes, then I know nothing of Calvary love." . . . "if there be a secret 'but' in my prayer, 'Anything but *that*

Lord,' then I know nothing of Calvary Love." . . . "If I refuse to be a corn of wheat that falls into the ground and dies (and 'is separated from all in which it lived before'), then I know nothing of Calvary love." . . . "If I covet any place on earth but the dust at the foot of the cross, then I know nothing of Calvary love."[12] How captured is your heart by Calvary love?

In her booklet about brokenness, Nancy DeMoss, says, "In God's economy, the way up is down. You and I will never meet God in revival until we first meet him in brokenness."[13] She gives three characteristics of brokenness, and I've written a corresponding prayer after each. May it be the prayer of your heart.

> 1. Brokenness is a shattering of my self-will. *"Your will, Lord, not mine."*

> 2. Brokenness is the stripping of self-reliance. *"Your resources, Lord, not mine."*

> 3. Brokenness is the softening of the soil of my heart. *"Your voice, Lord, not others."*

This surrender must become as natural as breathing if we're going to know the joyful satisfaction of becoming fully like Jesus. We must die to live.

Become Through Insight

I was a staff pastor at a Christian camp one summer and Cathy and I felt we needed to speak to a girl on staff about her immodest clothing. I explained to her how men are wired, how girls are often tempted to find self-worth from their clothes and from men, and how God desires purity of mind and heart in His people. The light went on inside her. She was a young Christian and nobody had ever told her these things before. But truth opened her eyes. She had been given insight and her dress changed immediately.

One of the greatest barriers to becoming like Jesus is our shallowness of insight into what is real around us. Our culture distorts the truth ("Your body is your own to do with as you please"). Our sinful hearts distort the truth ("If I only had more money I'd be happy"). Ephesians 2:1-3 describes our enemies as threefold—the world, our sinful nature, and the Devil—but in the end, we really don't need to know exactly which is to blame when we sin. The weapons we must fight with are the same for every foe, as the spiritual armor of Ephesians 6 teaches. And one of those weapons is truth, illustrated by the "belt of truth" and the "sword of the Spirit which is the word of God."

In John, Jesus makes this powerful promise:

> *"You will know the truth, and the truth will set you free" (John 8:32).*

Free from what? In verse 34 Jesus says, "Everyone who sins is slave to sin." So *truth sets us free from sin*. This means, then, that our sin must in some way be tied to what we believe and what we think. Sin darkens our understanding (Ephesians 4:18) so that we don't see clearly.

For example, when a wife makes a critical comment to her husband and he pulls back in self-pity and allows his love to grow cold for a time, he needs to examine both the "thoughts and attitudes of the heart" (Hebrews 4:12). Something is wrong in the way he's viewing God and himself and life. He's not seeing clearly. And when a woman feels she must find personal worth by being loved by a man, even if that means not confronting him about his verbal abuse, pornography habit, and relational neglect, it's not only her desires that must be purified but also her thoughts. She doesn't see the truth about love, about personal worth, and about a God who wants her trust.

We must open our eyes to how sin has infected the values and beliefs of the world we live in, for those values subtly deceive us.

> *"The weapons we fight with are not the weapons of the world. On the contrary, they have divine power to demolish strongholds. We demolish arguments and every pretension that sets itself up against the knowledge of God, and we* take *captive every thought to make it obedient to Christ"* [emphasis mine] *(2 Corinthians 10:4-5).*

Many worldly values have taken root in our lives as strongholds. They need to be critiqued and replaced by the truth of Christ. Our minds must be renewed so we don't conform to the patterns of this world (Romans 12:2).

God does this through (1) showing us who He really is, (2) showing us who we really are, and (3) showing us what life is really all about. As we unpack these three in the section that follows, listen for what God might be showing you personally. These truths are not lists to remember, but aids for personal victory over sinful patterns of living. Be looking for those that speak specifically to you.

Insight About God

All too often we make God in our own image—or we forget Him completely. A major part of the "truth that will set us free" is the truth about God. But distortions abound. People give God the characteristics of their earthly fathers who may have been demanding and stern and emotionally distant. They pick up muddled thinking from preachers who speak only of God's love—or only of His moral standards. Sadly, many make conclusions about God from observing professing Christians and conclude, "If *they* represent God, I want nothing to do with them."

Here are five affirmations about God that will equip you to *become* like Jesus:

1. God is passionate about *His glory* (greatness, worth, etc.)—and so must I be. We need to share God's passion for His own glory whenever we are facing the temptation to promote our own glory.

2. God is *loving and good*—and no person or event can thwart His acting for my best interest. We must believe this when we want to complain about our day, when we find ourselves worrying about how well we will perform in some situation, or when we struggle with what our friends think about us. Living in complete confidence of Romans 8:28 is totally life-changing, "And we know that in all things God works for the good of those who love him, who have been called according to his purpose." Meditating on this multiple times during our day is a powerful tool for change.

3. God is *holy*—and He is my moral standard. We aren't free to determine what right and wrong are. They are rooted for all time in the character of God Himself. Applications may change, but the principles never do. So if we find ourselves justifying our behavior with thoughts like, *At least I'm not as bad as so-and-so,* or *I don't want to be different from my friends,* then we must bow in surrender before our holy God and regain our sight.

4. God is *grace*—so He forgives me, accepts me, and helps me without my earning these blessings. We need this truth about God if we have a perfectionist streak in us and we tend to put higher expectations on ourselves (or others) than God Himself does. Perhaps we have a poor self-image, or we think we need to perform for God to love us, or we find ourselves struggling with the same sin over and over again. We must drench ourselves in God's grace!

5. God is *powerful*—and He is able to do in my life what I cannot do on my own. We must embrace the power of God if we feel we'll never be able to change the way we are, and if we're trying to change by sheer will power (or even by sheer prayer power). God's power can transform habits, attitudes, and beliefs in such a way that we will be able to endure great discouragement and pain—because God is at work in us, transforming us into His likeness.

Truth by itself frees no one. In fact, knowledge by itself often *hinders* spiritual insight because the "wise" have lost their childlike heart (Luke 10:21). But truth, humbly seen and wisely applied to our real issues, is transforming.

Consider this passage that has encouraged and focused many disciples of Jesus:

> *"His divine power has given us* everything we need for life and godliness through our knowledge of him [emphasis mine] *who called us by his own glory and goodness. Through these he has given us his very great and precious* promises [emphasis mine]*, so that through them you may participate in the divine nature and escape the corruption in the world caused by evil desires" (2 Peter 1:3-4).*

There is nothing more powerful than trusting in God for all He *truly* is for us! Which of the above are you most inclined to lose sight of and need to affirm in your own daily life?

Insight About Ourselves

"I don't recall my dad ever saying anything positive to me my whole life," a middle-aged woman told me with tears. "No matter how well I excelled, it was never good enough."

These kind of stories are everywhere. People learn from parents, spouses, teachers, coaches, and society in general that they are "no good," "unlovable," "stupid," or "a failure." They learn that they must be beautiful, talented, in shape, fun, articulate, smart, athletic, and successful to feel good about themselves. From an early age, their parents are eager to instill self-worth based on all these things—which has resulted in busy, frantic lifestyles that have produced insecure, competitive, and relationally shallow children. God offers another way.

Listen to who you *really* are—and believe it!

1. I am made in the *image of God* to glorify Him—and to fall short of His glory is sin.

2. I am *body and soul* and my behaviors are almost always caused by my heart and mind.

3. I am a *disciple of Jesus* and my life will be blessed when I follow Him wholeheartedly.

4. I am a *child of God* by faith in Jesus, and His Father-love anchors my soul like nothing else.

5. I am a *new creation*, indwelt by the Holy Spirit, and this true identity is emerging every day as I yield to it.

6. I am a *part of a spiritual community*—the church—and must both receive from and give to those relationships in meaningful ways.

According to God you aren't primarily a father, mother, child, carpenter, pastor, computer programmer, teacher, or musician. You are not what people say you are. You are not even what you *think* other people say you are. You are who *God* says you are!

So which of these six do *you* most need to remember to counteract the false self-beliefs you've picked up along the way? I encourage you to repeat them when you face challenging situations—regardless of how you may feel at the time.

The key to seeing ourselves as God sees us is recognizing *our heart* (related to #2 above), especially how the four primary root sins of the heart described in the previous chapter show themselves in us: pride, fear/anxiety/worry, self-centeredness, and earthly pleasure apart from God. We must see our sin as God sees it—and name it—then see where that root sin has produced bad fruit in the various relationships and behaviors of our lives. (Appendix B, "Spiritual Transformation Goals," can assist this insight process in each of these four roots.) But remember, sin is like poison ivy—the roots must be destroyed to kill it.

The following questions are condensed from David Powlison's list of 33 to help a person see his or her heart more clearly.[14]

- To whom or what do I usually turn when I experience something negative in my life (like anger, fear, stress, or anxiety)?

• Who or what controls me (such that my beliefs, choices, and actions are determined largely by these sources)?

• Where do I find refuge, safety, comfort, escape, pleasure, or security? . . .What or whom do I really trust?

• In whom or in what do I place my hopes for happiness?

• Whom do I feel I must please?

Determine which of these are most helpful to you in gaining insight into the dark places of your own soul so God's truth about you can permeate your life.

Insight About Life

What's my purpose in life? Why do I get up in the morning? In the midst of the options paraded in front of us from childhood (make money, raise a family, buy a nice house, be successful, etc.), what does *God* say life is all about?

Pastor Rick Warren's book, *The Purpose Driven Life*, tackled these questions in a way that made it a bestseller. The summary of the book, and perhaps the most quoted phrase in the book, appears in the first line: "It's not about you."[15] That is, indeed, where it must start.

The author of Ecclesiastes had wealth, cities, and women. "I denied myself nothing my eyes desired; I refused my heart no pleasure" (Ecclesiastes 2:10). In the end, however, he concluded everything was meaningless—until he reflected more deeply. He concluded, "Now all has been heard; here is the conclusion of the matter: Fear God and keep his commandments, for this is the whole duty of man" (Ecclesiastes 12:13). He finally saw life from God's point of view.

The following truths about life, based on the structure of this book, are God's reasons for why you should get up in the morning, and they help make sense out of your pain and discouragement.

1. I am made for *God's glory*—which both humbles me and exalts me.

2. I am made to be *satisfied in Him* and to find pleasure in creative *work* done for God.

3. I am made for a love relationship with God *(Come)*.

4. I am made to be transformed into the image of Jesus *(Become)*.

5. I am made to compassionately act in the best interests of others *(Love)*.

I regularly remind myself of these five truths (as well as a few of the prior insights dealing with God and myself) when I'm lacking joy or peace in my life.

Think of the 16 insights listed in the prior three sections as spiritual tools. When you walk down an aisle filled with kitchen or hardware tools, you look for those you need to do a particular job. It's the same with these. Identify those truths that God most wants to use in your life to overcome a particular sin that is prominent in your life right now. Even living in just one of these can help shift you from self-occupied desires to God-occupied ones—and move you closer to becoming like Jesus.

Windows to Get Insight

Imagine you're taking a test. The questions are hard and you don't know the answers. But there's another room where the answers are posted on the walls. Four windows give visual access to the room, and each gives a slightly different view of the walls.

That's the way it is with God's truth. I invite you to use each window below. Together they will help you see your life as you *currently* live it, and also how your life is *meant* to be lived.

> • The window of quiet, humble reflection with God (Psalm 139:23-24). *Come* to Him and listen. Just you and God. Nothing else. No Bible, no daily devotional, no worship music. Come in quietness. Surrendered. Longing to be changed. Reflect on what has been going on in your life and ask God to speak to you and show you truth, whether old or new.

> • The window of God's Word and biblically-based books (Hebrews 4:12). Read slowly, for insight and life-change (as you're doing with this book!) When something speaks to you, put the book down and meet with God about it. Mull on it. Dog-ear the page, highlight it, or make a note in the back of the book. Decide how it's going to make a difference in the next 24 hours.

> • The window of your emotions (Psalm 32:3-5; James 4:1). These are like warning lights on the console of a car. And they

should be heeded! (I felt quite foolish when I ran out of gas about five miles from home some time ago with the warning light glowing yellow!) Emotions are signals given to us by God. They aren't all warning lights of something bad going on inside but they often are. So when anger, frustration, worry, depression, fear, insecurity, or impatience flash your light, it's time to check what you're thinking and wanting. (One example of this is found in Appendix C, "A Prayer Seeking Freedom From Depression.")

• The window of relationships (Galatians 6:1). This is definitely one of the most painful windows to use, but it's probably one of the most effective if you'll listen. You may be blinded to how you affect people, but "Wounds from a friend can be trusted" (Proverbs 27:6)—especially those from your spouse and children. If you don't know what they feel when you're around them, ask them! Humbly and sincerely. Pray that they will love you enough to be honest.

A Personal Story

Probably about 15 years ago I became aware of some serious pride issues in my heart. Actually, there were hints of pride all through my childhood and early years of marriage, but they became more noticeable as I got married, had kids, became a church leader—and grew closer to God. I saw that my anger at my young children was really pride in not getting the respect I wanted. It was pride that caused me to need to correct my wife's food preparation patterns in the kitchen and correct her imprecise details when she told stories to our friends. I saw my pride when I'd be quick to defend my point of view at a church board meeting or in informal conversations, and I saw it when I felt the need to give my children "helpful advice" after their athletic games.

But change is happening. I'm growing "from glory to glory" and I'm getting much better at seeing what's going on in my heart—though sometimes it's a few minutes (or hours/days) later than I wish. Knowing my root sins, however, has enabled me to prepare my heart in advance of common ambushes to my spirit. It's increased my longing to find joy and peace in God alone, so when my "bucket is tipped over," I know what kind of water will come out. Insight isn't the only tool God uses in my life to form Christ in me, but it's a major one.

Become Through Repentance

When we have insight and realize we need to change—whether that change is a heart matter or a particular behavior—repentance must immediately follow. Repentance isn't only necessary at the beginning of the Christian life (Acts 2:38), it's necessary throughout the Christian life as we face daily sin.

There are three basic elements to repentance, and each of these is necessary for true biblical repentance to occur.

1. *Confession.* This basically says, "I sinned; I did it." It's owning up to the reality of sin. It's saying the same thing about our behavior and heart that God says about it. And it's spoken to all who were hurt by it. So first of all we say it to God, because every sin affects Him. And if the sin hurts someone else, the confession must be given to them as well.

> *"If we confess our sins, he is faithful and just and will forgive us our sins and purify us from all unrighteousness" (1 John 1:9).*

> *"Therefore confess your sins to each other and pray for each other so that you may be healed" (James 5:16).*

The longer we walk with God, we can expect to see more and more deeply into why we do what we do and why we say what we say and why we feel what we feel. It's one of those ironies of the Christian life: the closer we get to God the more we overcome sin—and the more we see new layers of sin we hadn't seen before.

2. *Sorrow.* This is saying, "I sinned, and I'm sad about it. "Godly sorrow brings repentance that leads to salvation and leaves no regret. . ." (2 Corinthians 7:10). Human sorrow is self-centered, but godly sorrow is God-centered and other-centered. It understands God and the people around us who are affected by our sin and it feels their pain. *Human* sorrow is sad because we got caught, we got embarrassed, or we're afraid of punishment. But *godly* sorrow knows our sin keeps us from the fullness of God's life in us and we grieve over this temporary loss.

3. *Change.* Without some degree of change, there's no repentance. You can admit your sin and feel sorry about your sin—yet still stay trapped in your sin. You can take off the dirty clothes but fail to put on the clean ones

(Ephesians 4:22-24). John the Baptist knew this when he told people, "Produce fruit in keeping with repentance" (Matthew 3:8). And when King David committed adultery and murder, he cried out to God to be changed—in the regions of his heart: "Create in me a pure heart, O God, and renew a steadfast spirit within me" (Psalm 51:7).

Another repentance couplet that I've found particularly helpful is:

"Hate what is evil; cling to what is good" (Romans 12:9).

To *hate* evil is to think about all the ways a particular behavior or attitude causes damage to yourself and others—what it does to your relationship with God, to your witness for Him, to the people it hurts, to your job and church ministry, to your peace, to the glory of God. This isn't just stopping something because it's wrong—it's stopping it because you see its ugliness and you want to have nothing to do with it! This has motivated me to stay far from many sins.

But it doesn't stop there. "Cling to what is good." *Love* it! Learn to see why God's righteousness is so wonderful and attractive. If you find yourself thinking that one of God's commandments *isn't* for your good, then you've been duped! The fact is, it's *good* to tell the truth. It's *good* to reserve sexual gratification for marriage. It's *good* to return hurt with love. It's *good* to have a submissive spirit. It's *good* to not covet people's stuff. *It's good!*

I like John Piper's description of this: "Pursue repentance through your pleasure."[16] What he means is that the more we understand the pleasure we have in God, the more we'll want to be set free from sin. That's why becoming like Jesus is a battle for our heart. Always. And that's where repentance must happen, even if it's seven times a day (as Jesus implies in Luke 17:4)!

Regularly practice repentance, especially with those around you. For example, "Frank, I was impatient with you because of my self-centeredness (confession) and I'm very sorry. I realize how my words hurt you (sorrow). I'm going to try to be more loving and humble the next time we have a disagreement (change)."

Repentance must be relentless and regular. Here are some further practical ways you can put repentance to work in your life:

• Cultivate a desire for God's holiness so that He is more attractive to your soul than sin is.

• Repent of any misplaced trust, that is trusting in yourself or others instead of God.

• Repent at all levels: heart (desires), beliefs (thoughts), and behavior (words and deeds).

• Repent often and deeply in your relationships with people—especially family members.

• Meditate on classic repentance passages like Psalm 51, James 4:1-10, and Revelation 3:15-20.

Becoming Through Grace

These steps of surrender, insight, and repentance are things *we* are to do. But they lack power and sustaining quality without the work of God. And that is what grace is.

As we saw earlier, grace is "God's loving acceptance and help given to me in my need without my earning it." The aspect of grace that we particularly need in order to become like Jesus is the "help" part. Here is His promise to us:

> *"And God is able to make all grace abound to you, so that in all things at all times, having all that you need, you will abound in every good work" (2 Corinthians 9:8).*

God will enable us to abound in *every good work*—and that includes the attitude and motive with which we *do* the work, not just the work itself. That means you really can correct your child without raising your voice. You really can play sports without needing to win. You really can talk with friends without gossiping about others. You can because God's grace is alive in you and you have "all that you need." You are satisfied in God!

Picture yourself in a room with many electrical slide switches on the ceiling. These switches turn on power to various items around the room that need electricity to run—a microwave, a TV, a computer, a few lamps, etc. Each item needs different levels of power to operate well. Some smaller items only need one switch on, and that switch may only need to be slid halfway, while other larger items (like the microwave) need several switches, and each needs to be slid fully on to supply enough power.

This is how God's grace works. For example, some people may only need to tap small portions of God's grace to forgive someone for saying something unkind to them, but those same persons may need large portions of God's grace to not complain about their job.

The switch metaphor communicates several things: First, God's grace is waiting and available. Second, His grace requires our operation. *We* must slide

them "ON." Third, there are varying degrees of "ON" and there are combinations of grace (switches) necessary to handle particularly heavy struggles.

In John 15 Jesus uses a vine and branch metaphor to describe this process
of grace-giving:

> *"I am the vine; you are the branches. If a man remains in me
> and I in him, he will bear much fruit; apart from me you can
> do nothing" (John 15:5).*

Jesus essentially says He gives people what they need to bear fruit. They
only need to stay vitally connected to Him. That is God's way to become like
Jesus.

A. W. Tozer describes the process this way: "From all this we learn that faith
is not a once-done act, but a continuous gaze of the heart at the Triune God. . . .
a habit of soul is forming which will become after a while a sort of spiritual
reflex requiring no more conscious effort on our part."[17] And Dallas Willard:
"The effect of standing before God by welcoming him before us will. . . be the
transformation of our entire life. . . . In doing that, I am constantly nourished by
the Holy Spirit in ways far beyond my own efforts or understanding."[18]

Grace empowers us to do what we would normally not be able to do by ourselves. Some grace comes to us *directly* from God in response to our going
directly to Him. This includes practices such as praise and worship, confession of sin, asking according to Jesus' will, listening in solitude and silence,
secretly serving others, and fasting from food or other habitual practices.

Other grace is more *indirect* and God uses a person or object as His means
of grace to us. This includes such practices as Scripture-reading, Christian fellowship, teaching, literature, Christian recording artists, and creation.

Some have called these seeking-grace actions "spiritual disciplines"
because they are things *we do in faith* in order for *God to do* what He wants
to do in and through us. The most important thing to know about spiritual
disciplines is that they are designed to nourish our spiritual life and facilitate
spiritual transformation—so that "Christ is formed in you" (Galatians 4:19).

Unfortunately, many Christians tend to rely on a few means of grace (like
weekly sermons, singing, and once-daily prayer) to carry all the weight of
spiritual transformation. And to make matters worse, they are often practiced
poorly (a lack of surrender, insight, or repentance), or are chosen for ease and
not according to what they most need.

For example, a person who tends to express his frustration with words that
hurt others would benefit from the discipline of silence, all the while staying
connected to the Vine for nourishment. The person who has a hard time being

submissive may need to engage in the discipline of service to those in authority—again, staying intimately connected to God.

So what can we expect to find when we go to God for grace? Fundamentally, three things: truth, love, and strength and each are unlocked through *faith*. Faith is the simple reliance on God that the grace of His *specific truths* and His *specific love* and His *specific strength* for each situation we face is, indeed, real.

If we're going to have victory over the sinful strongholds in our lives, we're going to need to avail ourselves of all the grace we can get. I'm amazed at how many Christians believe that prayer is all they need. No discipline. No change of mind or heart. Just sincerely asking God.

But the Bible makes it clear that change must be waged on multiple fronts with multiple resources (including prayer). And it's going to require work! Not the work of willpower, but the work of staying relationally connected to God for grace. Our fight is for grace, not certain behaviors. We fight to stay thirsty for God, not primarily for discipline. "True repentance must be preceded by falling in love with the all-satisfying God."[19] Our greatest motivator to say no to sin is an awakened taste for pleasure in God Himself!

> *"For the grace of God that brings salvation has appeared to all men. It teaches us to say "No" to ungodliness and worldly passions, and to live self-controlled, upright and godly lives in this present age" (Titus 2:11-12).*

We can't become like Jesus without His loving grace.

Perseverance

Life is hard—and discouraging at times. To persevere is to commit to the continual practice of the prior four elements of *surrender, insight, repentance,* and *grace*. Perseverance means taking the same sin and repeatedly revisiting these four change ingredients at new and deeper levels. Or it's revisiting these four with different sin issues. To persevere is to refuse to stop until spiritual transformation is found.

Probably the most powerful text on perseverance is the beginning verses of Hebrews 12:

> *"Therefore, since we are surrounded by such a great cloud of witnesses, let us throw off everything that hinders and the sin that so easily entangles, and let us run with perseverance the*

> *race marked out for us. Let us fix our eyes on Jesus, the*
> *author and perfecter of our faith, who for the joy set before*
> *him endured the cross, scorning its shame, and sat down at*
> *the right hand of the throne of God. Consider him who*
> *endured such opposition from sinful men, so that you will not*
> *grow weary and lose heart" (Hebrews 12:1-3).*

Picture an amphitheater where runners are in a race. As they run they look up into the stands and see thousands of men and women who have gone before them—people from all walks of life and every nation and race, people who have run the race successfully and affirm that it can be done by the power of God. They see people like Abraham and Peter, Martin Luther and Mother Teresa, maybe even some of your relatives or people in your church.

These people inspire us, because the race we run is hard. Difficult experiences from our childhood, difficult family situations, economic pressures, and racial prejudices—all must be overcome. Our sins so easily entangle us as well and sometimes cause us to falter in our faith.

But we must persevere. How? By "fixing our eyes on Jesus"—not our circumstances or our past or what people do to us or say about us, but on Jesus—and all who He is for us. He's the one who began our journey and He's the one who will complete it. And not only that, He's our most inspiring witness up there in the stadium! He, too, faced trials—even dying on a cross—and He, too, had to persevere. Like Jesus, we persevere "for the joy set before" us. We *will* overcome.

I know some of you are facing huge battles in your life. Chronic depression. Sexual addictions. Deep relationship hurts. Chemical dependencies. These will likely take extensive and sustained spiritual effort for you to experience substantial freedom—more spiritual effort than you've ever known. But each day is a new day in God.

Thomas Carlyle spent two years writing a book about the French Revolution. On the day he finished it, he gave the manuscript to a colleague, John Stuart Mill, to read and critique. It was before copy machines were invented so it was his only copy. Unbelievably, Mill's servant accidentally used the manuscript for kindling to start a fire. Two years of work were lost; thousands of long, lonely hours wasted. Carlyle fell into a deep depression.

Then one day while walking the city streets, he noticed a stone wall being constructed—one brick at a time. As he stared at that wall, hope was born. He realized that if he wrote one page at a time, one day at a time, he could write the book again. And he did.

Perseverance is refusing to allow failure and discouragement to rule us. It's saying we will pick ourselves up off the ground (by God's grace), and we will cast ourselves into the loving arms of God, from whom all mercies flow and from whom all power flows. We will continue to cooperate with the work of God in our hearts, for His glory and our joy, one step at a time.

Some Practical Becoming Strategies

There's much to digest in this chapter and the preceding one—if you're reading for pure knowledge. However, if you're reading to *become* like Jesus, it's likely God has just a few things for you to know and apply right now. The following practical strategies can further assist you in making "every effort" and putting theory into practice. (See also 2 Peter 1:5; 3:14*).*

> *"Make* every effort [emphasis mine] *to live in peace with all men and to be holy; without holiness no one will see the Lord" (Hebrews 12:14).*

• *Imagine* what life would be like if these principles were implemented in a specific sin area of your life. Picture the people or circumstances that prompt you to sin, then imagine responding with God-oriented desires and Christ-captured thoughts. Imagine the change in your feelings and in your reactions. Imagine the peace, the positive effect on you and people around you. Imagine what life would be like lived this way. And imagine it often.

• *Anticipate* the events that trigger your sin-responses ahead of time, and prepare your heart to meet them. Resolve to get your heart ready so that when you come home from work and greet your family or meet that difficult client or attend that meeting or walk past that aisle in the store, you'll be prepared. You won't be caught off guard. No ambushes. Anticipate your temptations and meet with God to be ready.

• *Prepare a Temptation Plan* so when you're facing a temptation to lust, yell, run, eat, covet, lie, spend, worry, etc., you implement a two-or three-point plan to keep yourself from sin. It may be reciting a biblical verse or a specific truth in your mind; it may be physically going somewhere to flee the temptation and meet with God; it may be recalling the snares of evil. But have a plan *before* you face the temptation—not while you're staring at it.

• *Confront* your weakness in a deliberate, head-on worship encounter in order to teach your soul how to delight in what is truly good. First, spend time in private worship with God by meditating on the goodness of His ways and the harm of evil and by delighting in His truth and love. Then, satisfied in God, deliberately go *near* to the place of temptation (but not into the place of temptation) and see the temptation in its true colors—evil and worthless. You might type in an internet site but not hit "Enter," or stand in front of an open refrigerator, or drive by your favorite bar. By bathing the doorway to temptation in God's presence, you are teaching your soul that God is better. God is stronger! (Psalm 62:11-12).

• *Declare war* on your sin. All-out war. It's time to get angry and ruthless over this oppressive enemy. Eliminate everything in your life (within reason) that is diverting your attention from God and His grace. Turn off the TV. Stop reading the newspaper. Turn off the car radio. In their place put on Christ, spiritual disciplines, and frequent God-connections throughout the day that begin training your mind, heart, and body to live in holiness and joy! It's the way serious athletes and soldiers train—can't disciples of Jesus train to deal with life-dominating sin? (1 Corinthians 9:25-27).

• *Team-up* with some same-gender friends and meet weekly (or more) to openly discuss your specific sin. Ask them to encourage you, pray for you, ask you hard questions, call you daily—whatever it takes to stay focused on God's life in you. One tool I've developed is the "Discipleship Partners" card that guides 2-3 people of the same gender to meet with God and receive His grace through reflecting on 50 key biblical chapters, reflecting on directed spiritual questions, and praying for one another. (See Appendix D "Discipleship Partners Card.")

Becoming like Jesus will not just happen. It requires deliberate and specific steps. God is waiting for you.

For Self-Reflection and Life Application

1. What, if anything, do you connect with in the opening parable?

2. As you reflect on some of the professing Christians you know, why do you think many are not changing to be conformed to the character of Jesus?

3. Reflect on Larry Crabb's statement, "Feeling better has become more important than finding God." What is the danger of this, and what difference

would it make in your own life if your pursuit of becoming like Jesus was a higher priority than relief?

4. What (in light of a particular sin situation you are facing) do you believe God wants you to surrender to Him?

5. In *each* of the three areas of needed insight (about God, ourselves, and life), share a lie (or distortion) and it's corresponding truth that you must apply more fully in your own pursuit of the character of Jesus.

6. Share an example of how both the window of *emotion* and the window of *relationships* have provided you insights into your sin, especially at the level of the heart.

7. What is something from the section on repentance that you can personally benefit from?

8. What have been the most effective means of God's grace into your life (such that they contribute significantly to God's power to help you change), and what is one means of grace that you believe you would benefit more from?

9. In what ways have you perhaps given up or put a particular sin on the back burner because of discouragement? What might perseverance look like to you?

10. Which one of the five ending strategies might be of assistance to you and why?

[1] Philippians 2:12-13; 1 Thessalonians 5:16-24; John 14:4-5; Colossians 1:22-23.
[2] Also Philippians 1:6; Hebrews 10:14.
[3] Larry Crabb, *Finding God*, Zondervan Publishing House, Grand Rapids, 1993, pp. 17-18.
[4] V. Raymond Edman, *They Found the Secret*, Zondervan Publishing House, Grand Rapids, 1984, p. 37.
[5] Dallas Willard, *The Divine Conspiracy: Rediscovering Our Hidden Life In God*, HarperSanFrancisco, San Francisco, 1998), p. 305.
[6] Jeanne Guyon, *Experiencing the Depths of Jesus Christ,* SeedSowers Christian Books, Auburn, 1975, p. xi.
[7] Ibid., pp. 17-18.
[8] Ibid., pp. 33-37.
[9] Andrew Murray, *Absolute Surrender,* Moody Press, Chicago, p. 5.
[10] Roger Steer, *George M̧ller:Delighted in God,* Harold Shaw Publishers, Wheaton, edition 1979), p. 37.
[11] Ibid., p. 319.
[12] Amy Carmichael, *If ,* Christian Literature Crusade, Fort Washington, 1938, pp. 36, 57, 74, 77.
[13] Nancy Leigh DeMoss, *Brokenness–The Heart God Revives*, Moody Press, Chicago, 2002, p. 50.
[14] David Powlison, *Seeing With New Eyes*, P&R Publishing Company, Phillipsburg, 2003, p. 132f.
[15] Rick Warren, *The Purpose Driven Life,* Zondervan, Grand Rapids, 2002, p. 17.
[16] John Piper, *Brothers, We are Not Professionals*, Broadman & Holman Publishers, Nashville, 2002, p. 125.
[17] A. W. Tozer, *The Pursuit of God*, Tyndale House Publishers, Wheaton, Special Edition, pp. 90-91.
[18] Dallas Willard, *Renovation of the Heart*, Navpress, Colorado Springs, 2002, p. 109.
[19] Ibid., Piper, p. 124.

Chapter 8

Love—A Radical New Way of Relating to Others

"Daddy!" his children yelled as the man walked towards his house. He ran toward them and they ran towards him, colliding in hugs and kisses. It had been almost two weeks since his departure to Kingcity.

Soon his wife appeared. She was warm, but a bit cautious. It hadn't been easy to have her husband pack up and leave them, and she was more than a little uneasy about his spiritual quest. They had already been uprooted once when they left their homeland and moved to the village. She wasn't looking forward to more change.

He decided not to talk about his time in Kingcity just yet, feeling that the atmosphere had to be just right. So he answered their questions with general descriptions like "It was a good trip" and "I'm glad I went."

His wife, however, wasn't hesitant to talk about her time while he was gone. The children had been fighting, foxes were chasing the chickens, there was a leak in the roof over their bed, the neighbor had fallen and broken her hip and needed help with her garden, and she didn't know how to make the latest land payment since his trip had left her short on cash.

The man began to feel his joy slipping away with every problem. Reality had returned like a March storm—and the winds were knocking his spirit all over the place. After about a half hour of listening to all the problems of the world (at least that's how it felt to him!), he felt like he was in a whirlpool, gradually being drawn deeper under the waters.

"I'm taking a walk," he told his wife sharply. With that he began walking down the road toward an area of cedar trees he often used for his woodcarving business. He picked up a small branch, found his carving knife in his pocket, and within minutes was transforming the plain piece of wood into the shape of a sparrow. It was one of the ways he had handled stress in the past—knowing it was much better than sticking around to argue with his wife.

"Why does she have to be this way?" he thought. "I was feeling so good from my time at Kingcity—and now this." It seemed to him that the women he met there were much more considerate, and he hadn't seen any nag their husbands like his wife did.

Just then a middle-aged woman he knew from the village walked up. She was a widow and he knew she appreciated conversations with others. He invited her to sit on a log nearby and she accepted.

She was easy to talk to and, before he knew it, they had chatted for over an hour and the bird he was whittling was mostly finished. "Thanks so much for the companionship," she smiled at the man. "You remind me a lot of my late husband. I'd love to talk again some time."

"Sure," he said. "I enjoyed it, too." And he had. As he watched her walk away, he noticed the beauty of her hair. At one point she glanced back and they exchanged waves. It felt good to be appreciated—a feeling he wasn't getting from his wife. His eyes followed the woman until she turned a bend in the path.

Feeling much better, he returned to add a few finishing cuts on the bird. "Done!" he said with satisfaction. He thought about the transformation the piece of wood had undergone. The sparrow was there in the wood all along— it just needed someone to come and remove what was not "sparrow."

Then it struck him. He was like that bird. And the King was shaping him. There was only one significant difference. The bird in the wood had no choice. He did. And ever since his wife had begun her complaining, his heart had become like hardwood that resisted the carver's work.

So there in the woods, just as when he passed that old man on the road, the man yielded his heart to the King afresh. This time it wasn't fear that the King had exposed, but his self-centeredness and lack of love—and his failure to seek out fellowship with the King when his spirit needed it.

The man got off the log, knelt down on the ground and lifted the whittled sparrow high up in the air. "Shape me like this sparrow. And keep me close to your loving knife."

Broken and filled, the man's heart became clear again. He saw the widow with the King's eyes. And he saw his wife with the King's eyes. Love filled his heart as he leaped from the ground and headed for his home. He had some business to do.

In the Beginning Was Love

From the beginning of time there were relationships—the eternal God, existing in some mysterious unity of Father, Son, and Spirit, sharing love before time began.

And out of this love that flowed from His very nature, God made humans in His image. They were created for His glory—created to reveal His excellent love. He would love them, with the desire that they would choose to love Him in return. He would take steps, of course, to invite their love, but He wouldn't force them. They would be free to choose.

The Scriptures are filled with variations on this theme of God's love. We hear it in terms like mercy, grace, everlasting kindness, forgiveness, salvation, redemption, goodness, and of course—love. The epic story of God's deliverance of Israel from Egypt and His commitment to love them with an everlasting love is an example of this love. "God is love," says John (1 John 4:16). He is. So He can't help but love.

Because of love He sent Jesus to earth. His coming, His teaching, His living, His death, and His resurrection are all about love. And now the church has the joy of living in that love.

I've chosen to speak of God's love at the beginning of this chapter, because if we're to take on the righteousness of God and become like Jesus, then certainly that must include His love! It will certainly be the most significant "family character trait" we have. Like Father—like son and daughter; like Master—like disciple.

> *"Be imitators of God, therefore, as dearly loved children and live a life of love, just as Christ loved us and gave himself up for us a fragrant offering and sacrifice to God" (Ephesians 5:1-2).*

And John moves it beyond command and says it's a simple reality of our new spiritual nature:

"Whoever does not love does not know God, because God is love." (1 John 4:8) God is love, so we love. It's just the way it is.

The Primacy of Love

We've already heard Jesus tell us that the greatest commandment is to love God with all our heart, soul, and mind. The reality is, if we don't get *that* commandment right, we won't do very well at the second. That's why coming was the first part of our living for His glory. Our relationship with God must precede and infuse our relationships with others.

But now it's time to hear the second greatest commandment:

> *"And the second is like it: 'Love your neighbor as yourself.' All the Law and the Prophets hang on these two commandments" (Matthew 22:39—40).*

Love God and love people. It's really not that complicated! And to underscore how really simple this is, Jesus tells us that all the laws He has given, and all the words spoken by the prophets, are about these two responses of the heart.

I've spent a number of weekends with a Christian residential community in New York State that has been sharing common property, goods, and funds for about 80 years. On one visit I asked them how they handle all the complexities of living this way, such as who decides what flowers to plant outside the communal apartments. Their response to this (and many of my questions) was simply, "Our only rule is love."

As I reflect back on that conversation, I wonder if I appeared more like a Pharisee than Jesus, wanting to make rules instead of living in the spiritual reality of love. (You six people divide the total square footage by six, and make sure that everyone gets equal sun and shade and that no flowers block your neighbor's flowers as seen from the walkway—unless, of course, you get special permission from the "Gardens Committee.") Perhaps my response showed how foreign this kind of love was to me at the time.

It's a fascinating exercise to apply Jesus' teaching about love to all our laws and rules. (See Romans 13:8-10.) Do they measure up to this test of love? The words "Is it loving?" should echo through our homes and churches because this criteria is the foundation of God's heart!

Perhaps there's no more clear priority given to love than in Paul's "love chapter:"

> *"If I speak in the tongues of men and of angels, but have not love, I am only a resounding gong or a clanging cymbal. If I have the gift of prophecy and can fathom all mysteries and all knowledge, and if I have a faith that can move mountains, but have not love, I am nothing. If I give all I possess to the poor and surrender my body to the flames, but have not love, I gain nothing"* *(1 Corinthians 13:1-3).*

So no matter how spiritual you look (you eloquent pastors, worship leaders, and proclaimers of God's will), no matter how biblically knowledgeable you are (you Sunday School teachers, Bible students, and well-read Christians), and no matter how impressive your good deeds are (you nursery workers, tithers, and church handymen), if you don't have love, you're nothing. Nothing! Because it's all about love.

A Lesson With a Basin and a Towel

"But that isn't fair," the child objects as a parent offers her brother a slightly bigger piece of cake. "Park there!" the wife commands, as her husband bites his lip to avoid saying what he's thinking. "I haven't spoken to my sister in ten years," a man says matter-of-factly, rehearsing his personality conflict with her and some hurtful conversation that took place many years ago. "Good news!" the boy announces to his high school teammates excitedly. "Their star player just fractured his ankle and he won't be able to play in tomorrow's game against us!"

These reactions may be normal in today's culture, but they should be abnormal for citizens of the kingdom of God. Just before Jesus returned to His Father, He left us with a picture that turns our culture upside down.

> *"Jesus . . . got up from the meal, took off his outer clothing, and wrapped a towel around his waist. After that, he poured water into a basin and began to wash his disciples' feet, drying them with the towel that was wrapped around him. . . Now that I, your Lord and Teacher, have washed your feet, you also should wash one another's feet. I have set you an example that you should do as I have done for you." . . . "A new command I give you: Love one another. As I have loved you, so you must love one another. By this all men will know that you are my disciples, if you love one another" (John 13:3-5, 14-15, 34-35).*

The command to love wasn't new to His disciples. Leviticus 19:18 already had told them to love their neighbors. So, then, what was so new about Jesus' command to love as he loved?

Consider what He had just done. He could have brought them a drink of water. Or He could have served them some fresh bread. But He chose to wash their feet—twenty-four dirty, sandled feet!

There are two things that made this act so distinctive and new. First, *it met their needs*. This wasn't a mere symbolic act. These men would have deeply appreciated this act—it would have touched their hearts, not just their feet.

The second was that it was *self-giving*. He gave of Himself by getting his own hands dirty with their dirt. He gave of Himself by doing what few people wanted to do. This was no job for the proud or the powerful. This was a job for a humble servant.

In my denomination, the Brethren in Christ Church, we practice foot washing—literally. At my particular church we gather for a shared meal and the Lord's Table on Maundy Thursday (when Jesus would have actually done this with His disciples), then we close the night with the men and boys in one room and the women and girls in another, gathered in circles around several basins and towels, reenacting Jesus simple command. It's not done out of literal obedience to Jesus' command to the Twelve that night, but as a reminder about the priority Jesus gave to love. (The word *maundy* is derived from the Latin, *maundatum*, which means "commandment," referring to the new commandment Jesus gave of loving as He loved). With Good Friday coming the next evening, Jesus' supreme example of love on the cross inspires our love for one another.

Foot washing is a moving experience. As we go around the circle we reinforce Jesus' command to love by sharing testimonies of love, challenges to love, and songs of faith that remind us Whose we are. After each foot washing, both individuals stand and embrace one another, a further expression of this love.

Occasionally I've had the opportunity to wash my sons' feet and have my feet be washed by them—both helpful reminders to each of us about what home life is to be like. A number of years ago I participated in a foot-washing service in Zambia, where the bare-footed men there provided a touch of biblical realism because the water was *very* dirty!

Recently my wife and I led a couples' retreat at which we closed our weekend by having spouses wash each other's feet. Tears came to Cathy's and my eyes as we watched tough young men and elderly couples gently wash their mate's feet, then embrace each other with tender and affectionate devotion. As I told them that morning, *"This* is glory of God stuff"—and it was.

Needed: A Biblical Definition

This brings us to the need for a definition of love. When I do pre-engagement and premarital counseling for couples, the first homework assignment I give them is to explore the biblical meaning of the word *love*, including how they can apply each "love is. . ." phrase in 1 Corinthians 13:4-7 on a personal level.

The meaning of *love* must be clarified because it's such a common word in our culture and used with varied meanings. We love ice cream. We love our children. Couples fall in love and even make love. Common to these uses are feelings and self-gain.

It's primarily about how someone or something makes *us feel*. We "love" ice cream, baseball, and our spouses because they all make us feel good. (And if they don't, "love" is gone.) We benefit from them, and enjoy them. So when Cathy tells me "I love you" she's usually thinking things like, I enjoy watching you interact with our kids. Thanks for fixing stuff around the house. I enjoy hearing you preach. You make me feel special when you patiently listen to my frustrations.

These are all good and appropriate. There's nothing wrong with feeling good! But that is *not* the essence of biblical love. Consider that list of "Love is . . ." phrases in 1 Corinthians 13:

> *"Love is patient, love is kind. It does not envy, it does not boast, it is not proud. It is not rude, it is not self-seeking, it is not easily angered, it keeps no record of wrongs. Love does not delight in evil but rejoices with the truth. It always protects, always trusts, always hopes, always perseveres"* *(1 Corinthians 13:4-7).*

These descriptions of love emphasize acting—not feeling; giving—not getting. It's not how someone makes me feel, it's how *I act* for *their good*.

This doesn't mean biblical love has no feeling, it's just not sufficient. 1 Corinthians 13:3 says we can give all we possess to the poor but *still not have love!* Something more than action is required. That something more is what 1 Peter 1:22 talks about: ". . . love one another deeply, *from the heart* [emphasis mine]."

In light of all this I believe biblical *love* is best defined: "Love is compassionately acting in the best interests of another." We see this clearly in the way Jesus loved His disciples that night with the water and towel. In addition, the New Testament Greek word usually translated "love" is *agape*, not the friendship love of *phileo*, nor the sensual love of *eros*. It's self-giving, need-meeting love.

This simple definition of love doesn't seem too radical at first glance but it is. In fact, it will likely turn your life upside down if you embrace it. It's so radical because our natural tendency is to be more concerned about "me" than "you." And what's worse, even when we *do* have concerns about "you," they're often really about "me!"

For example, let's say Linda hears that Brenda is in the hospital. Linda visits her and takes some flowers. It's possible that Linda is solely acting with compassion in Brenda's best interests—knowing that she would be encouraged by a visit. It's *also* possible that Linda is visiting Brenda because she doesn't want Brenda to think she doesn't care about her; or she's visiting because Brenda sent *her* a card when she was sick a year ago and now feels the pressure to reciprocate; or she's visiting Brenda because it will make her feel good about herself—and she'll also be able to look good in the eyes of her family and friends who will most certainly hear about her visit to Brenda very soon. As you can see, the places of the heart can be deep waters!

When you wake up and greet that first family member in the morning are you conscious of love? When you walk into your church building do you think about love (rather than *your* expectations of how others should love *you*)? As you go through your day and encounter people at your job, your school, your team, your club, your neighborhood, or your grocery store is love a priority goal in your heart?

God has compassionately acted for our good. As his children, we will do the same for others.

So What Really Is In a Person's Best Interest?

If *love* is "compassionately acting in another's best interest," then the question follows, What *is* in their best interest?

When teaching a young child how to love, I've often found it helpful to ask them, "Does it make the other person happy?" The benefit of such a definition is that it encourages both the compassion part of love and the action part of love. It teaches a child to be concerned about another's feelings and then do something about it.

This question can be helpful for older children and adults as well, but it definitely has its limits. When a parent prohibits her child from playing near a busy street because it's in the child's best interest not to be struck by an oncoming car, this action may not make the child happy! As Hebrews 12:11 says, "No discipline seems pleasant at the time, but painful."

When my daughter Katie was in high school, she had to go to her good friend's parents and tell them about destructive behaviors their daughter was engaged in. It was a very difficult thing for Katie to do. She knew it would likely turn her friend against her, but we convinced her it was the loving thing to do. Initially the parents didn't believe Katie, which made it even more difficult, but when they finally did, Katie's fears were realized. Her friend shut her out, and even years later the relationship was strained. But she had "compassionately acted in her friend's best interest," even though it didn't make her happy at the time.

So what *is* in another's best interest? Without a doubt, *it's in everyone's best interest to encounter and know God.* John Piper puts it boldly: "If you don't point people to God for everlasting joy, you don't love. You waste your life."[11] To settle for lesser joys is to cheat them out of life that is truly life. We can't force God on anyone, but through our words and deeds, we can intentionally and sensitively guide them to the living water He offers—even if we can't make them drink.

Another way to think about the best interests of another person is to ask *"Is this person feeling loved?"* As we have seen, love can't be ruled by another person's feelings. But if we're only caught up in acting in the best interest of their *behavior* and not their *inner soul*, we may, for example, speak words that they need to hear, but we do it in a way that neglects to pay heed to how our words are heard by their *hearts*.

When my sons were about 12 years old, they were in a recreational basketball league. They were both known for their quickness and hustle on the court, both offensively and defensively. I enjoyed going to their games and I always tried to be a supportive dad, especially while the game was going on. No obnoxious, micro-controlling, yelling dad for me!

In this particular game, their team lost a close one. Both boys played their hearts out but also made a few mistakes that contributed to their loss (as, of course, other boys did as well). When we got to our car, they were both quiet. I said my usual encouraging words to them and then felt this might be a good time for some fatherly coaching. After I made a few gentle observations about ways they might be able to improve, the car became quiet. I glanced over at Jeff who was sitting in the passenger seat, and I saw tears coming down his cheeks.

"What's wrong?" I asked. I wasn't prepared for what he was going to say next. Through his tears, he spoke words I had never wanted my children to think—let alone say, "It seems I can never be good enough for you."

I remember driving out of the school parking lot that day in an awkward silence with my mind racing. To my credit I kept my mouth shut. To my discredit I was arguing with his statement in my mind because I didn't think it was true or fair. After several minutes of inner self-defense, I had to face the reality that my critical tendencies had been taking a toll on him—and his twin Brian as well.

By the time we arrived in our driveway five minutes later, I had been able to shift my thinking from "How could he think this about me?" to "How could I have been so careless as to hurt my sons' hearts?" Through moist eyes of my own, I told Jeff and Brian I was very, very sorry, and I would be more sensitive in the future.

Unfortunately, that wasn't the last time I tried to love someone without considering their heart. By the grace of God, I know I've come a long way since that incident 12 years ago. Paul's prayer for the church continues to be my prayer for myself:

> *"And this is my prayer: that your love may abound more and*
> *more in knowledge and depth of insight, so that you may be*
> *able to discern what is best and may be pure and blameless*
> *until the day of Christ" (Philippians 1:9-10).*

Love that grows in "depth of insight" is love that is both *tender* (so that they *feel* loved) and at times *tough* (it's good for them but may not make them initially happy). It's going to mean that I give attention to what is going on *inside* a person (their thoughts, feelings, and longings)—not just addressing the words and actions I hear and see.

Above all, to love is to ask the question in the first place: "How can I compassionately act in that person's best interest right now?" Does he need humor—or would humor be more about me than him? Does she need a listening ear with empathy—or a helpful word of advice?

We can't truly love without these kinds of questions going on in our minds. Without them, we'll too easily react in our automatic mode, which, sadly, is more about *my* control, *my* feelings, *my* happiness, and *my* self-interest than we would like to admit.

Coming and Becoming to Love

The hardest part of loving is moving out of our self-centered worlds into the world of another. We're so self-centered, so pre-occupied with our own desires. This is why the reorientation described in the preceding seven chapters is so necessary. We must be fully devoted disciples of Jesus, committed to the passionate pursuit of His glory in our lives. We must be regularly *coming* to this God of love for all He is for us, and *becoming* like Him in the depths of our being. *Then* this kind of love is possible.

To pursue love requires us to be desperate for God because we so quickly run out of emotional, spiritual and physical resources to act in this way towards others. Our *natural* love runs thin. As the wedding vows I use for couples say, "I pledge to love you as God's love is added to mine." Both our love and God's are needed—especially with people close to us.

It's tempting to want to run from love because of the emotional cost, the risk, or the time it will require. But as we cling to the Vine, we find the will and the way to love.

Four Faces of Love

I'd like to offer four general ways that love is taught in the Scriptures. Through these we'll learn not only how to love, but how God needs to change our hearts in the process to make us more like Jesus.

First, a word of caution. In Luke 6:31 Jesus says we are to "Do to others as you would have them do to you." This is a principle, not a rule. It works most of the time but not all the time. If we only treat people in ways *we* like to be treated, we'll fail to listen to the uniqueness of *others'* needs. These have sometimes been described as "love languages." In other words, the way *I* like to be loved may not be the same way *you* like to be loved.

I experienced this many years ago when a fellow elder in my church and I had a difference of opinion about something (the subject of which has long departed from my memory). He pulled away from me, which I interpreted as unwillingness to engage in dialog and seek unity. I, on the other hand, pursued him and experienced frustration with his lack of engagement. It wasn't until many months later that we understood what was happening (and apologized to one another). I wanted to be loved by engagement, dialog, and seeking mutual understanding. He wanted to be loved by having solitude and time for personal reflection. We were both giving each other what *we ourselves* wanted, not what the other person desired.

So love will mean getting out of our own world of likes and dislikes, introvert and extrovert, male and female, parent and child, and think, What is in *that* person's best interest, given their unique personhood? Merely *asking* that kind of question is at least 75% of the way toward love!

Deeds of Kindness and Mercy

> *"Love is kind" (1 Corinthians 13:4).*

> *"Be kind and compassionate to one another" (Ephesians 4:32).*

Deeds of kindness are those done to communicate care and affection, and deeds of mercy are those done in response to a person's need. They are often the beginning place of love. It's what we teach our children: "Suzie, share your dolls." "Jared, help Daddy pick out rocks in the garden." Kindness is one of those basic civilities in life.

Throughout the Scriptures God instructs us to care for those in need (Proverbs 19:17)—the poor, the orphans, the widows, the lepers. The Good Samaritan gave kindness to the man who was robbed and beaten. Kindness motivates us to help Christians in other countries who experience natural disasters (2 Corinthians 8:1-7).

Kindness is the loving communication, "I care about you," while mercy is the loving deed extended in a time of need. They often overlap. When we vacuum the living room even though it isn't "our job," when we stay after the church dinner to help clean up, or when we let our spouse use the shower first (and get the most hot water!), we are acting in loving kindness.

It's putting your arm around your child who just had a disappointing game—without saying a word—or giving a day to watch some friends' kids so they can have some much-needed time as a couple. It's smiling at that elderly lady waiting with you in the checkout line, asking how she's doing, or carrying her bags to her car, even if it means you have to make a second trip to come back for yours.

Deeds of kindness and mercy are unconditional—they are done without regard to whether we have been loved by this person in the past, or will be in the future. As Jesus says,

> *"If you love those who love you, what credit is that to you?*
> *Even 'sinners' love those who love them" (Luke 6:32).*

Of course, this will mean being careful that we don't lavish kindness on our own children and family members so much that we are unable to give time, energy, and resources to the needs of others. Love must be given freely without regard to how special or important a person is (James 2:1-9), though it certainly will start at home.

Acceptance, Understanding, and Forgiveness

This is the category of love that responds to people's weaknesses, limitations, and sins. It's the kind of love that would have an "Even though you . . ." in front if it. It looks at other people and sees the bad and the ugly, the stupidities and the sins, the irritations and the things that drive us crazy, and says, "I will still compassionately act in your best interest."

> *"Therefore, as God's chosen people, holy and dearly loved,*
> *clothe yourselves with compassion, kindness, humility, gen-*
> *tleness and patience. Bear with each other and forgive what-*
> *ever grievances you may have against one another. Forgive as*
> *the Lord forgave you. And over all these virtues put on love,*
> *which binds them all together in perfect unity" (Colossians*
> *3:12-14).*

Of course, this category of love is the hardest to practice with those close to us. We often see our family members, the people at church, and our co-workers at their worst (and of course, we're often at *our* worst in these places, too, which makes life harder for *them*).

Acceptance. To accept others in the New Testament sense is to welcome them. It means receiving someone into our lives without conditions, overlooking their quirks, differences, personality, limitations, and weaknesses.

Acceptance is needed when someone "presses your buttons," when they repeatedly keep hurting or disappointing you, or when they disagree with you or criticize a decision you've made. Acceptance is needed when your husband would rather watch football than fix the kitchen drawer that's been stuck for three months. Acceptance is needed when your pastor asks you if you're pregnant—and you're not! (Yes, I've done this. Twice! And I'm very blessed that both women accept me to this day.)

> *"Accept one another, then, just as Christ accepted you, in order to bring praise to God" (Romans 15:7).*

> *"A man's wisdom gives him patience; it is to his glory to overlook an offense" (Proverbs 19:11). (See also Ephesians 4:2; 1 Peter 4:8)*

Acceptance means not demanding in our hearts that people change or demanding that they live like we live or value what we value or believe what we believe. (Romans 14 is a great treatment of this problem.) It means disagreeing *in love*—not just tolerating people.

In Matthew 7 Jesus teaches us not to be judgmental. One reason is because we, too, have faults—often bigger than the ones we're pointing to in others. Try this exercise: Live a whole week without making critical comments about anyone to anyone—not about, or to, your family, coworkers, church, or friends! Practice acceptance with your speech—and let it train your heart in love.

Understanding. One of the most powerful tools we have in accepting (and forgiving) others is that of understanding one another. It becomes a gift to them, because the more we understand why people do what they do and say what they say, the more we see them with compassion. Sadly, this is not always an easy task.

We looked at this passage before, but now let's apply it to seeing someone *else's* heart:

> *"The purposes of a man's heart are deep waters, but a man of understanding draws them out" (Proverbs 20:5).*

Have you ever thought, Why in the world would he do such a stupid thing as that? Or I can't believe she said that! These kind of statements show we have more "deep waters" to explore, seeing other people's hearts with understanding.

Understanding means we're trying hard to walk a mile in someone else's moccasins. We try to imagine what it would be like to live with their body shape and skin color, their parents, their personality, their background, and their hurts.

I've found two questions helpful in assisting me to understand people better:

> • *"What is hard for him/her to do?"* Maybe it's hard for them to have a dirty countertop, make decisions, handle the finances, apologize, watch action movies, or share feelings. When we understand what's hard for someone, we gain compassion for them because we know that some things are hard for us to do as well.

> • *"What does he/she value?"* Maybe he values competition, a clean car, and physical touch. Maybe she values spontaneity, friends, and reading a good book. Perhaps your kids value bugs, your boss values punctuality, and your teen values music that you don't value! Of course, not every value may be a good value, but it nevertheless helps you know what makes them tick. And since our values (those things we feel are important to us) help shape our heart, this question gives insight into how to compassionately act in someone's best interest at a deep level.

If you're the kind of person who is quick to speak in certain settings (like myself), then it would be wise for you to excel in the ministry of understanding. Here are two reasons:

> *"A fool finds no pleasure in understanding but delights in airing his own opinions" (Proverbs 18:2).*

> *"He who answers before listening—that is his folly and his shame" (Proverbs 18:13).*

Learn to listen before speaking because listening increases understanding. Listen because it keeps your mouth shut for a bit—otherwise you may speak the words of a fool!

I've been challenged by one line in the Prayer of Saint Francis of Assisi, written over 700 years ago. "O Divine Master, grant that I may not so much seek to be consoled as to console; *to be understood, as to understand* [emphasis mine]; to be loved, as to love." An "Amen" rises within me, especially in those hardest of situations—when I believe I've been wronged.

Forgiveness. Forgiveness is practicing acceptance when we are sinned against.

> *"Be kind and compassionate to one another, forgiving each other, just as in Christ God forgave you" (Ephesians 4:32).*

Forgiveness in the Bible is both a judicial act (I will not punish you) and it's a relational act (I will not withdraw from you). As such, forgiveness means:

> • *A refusal to punish or get even.* Romans 12:17-19 is clear: God is the judge, not us. "Do not repay evil for evil. . . 'It is mine to avenge; I will repay' says the Lord."
>
> • *A refusal to rehearse the hurt in my mind, with the offender, or with others.* This doesn't mean we won't think about it occasionally. When God says, "I will remember their sins no more" in Jeremiah 31:34, it doesn't mean He has amnesia. It means He puts them in the past, not the present. He doesn't hold our sins against us. So likewise, we, too, must put the past behind us (1 Corinthians 13:5) and not relive the offense in our minds or verbally with others.
>
> • *A refusal to withdraw from the offender.* When someone sins against us, either by what they say or do, or by what they *don't* say or do, relational walls can grow up. But forgiveness pursues relationship, with the possible goal of eventual restoration (which would require the other person's participation as well.) Of course, continually being sinned against will limit the level of relationship we can have, but forgiveness will always seek a peaceful connection as much as possible (Romans 12:18).

Put yourself in Spencer Perkins' shoes. As a 13-year-old black child, living in the segregated South in 1966, he experienced constant humiliation and cruel jokes in an all-white public school. Every day was a living hell, and the teachers and faculty didn't stop it. In their eyes, he was just a "nigger." Once when he was 16, he visited his dad, John Perkins, in jail and found a bloodied face, a torn shirt, and a beaten body—complements of the prison guards just because he was black. Spencer's bitterness grew deep.

Then, several years later, he heard his dad preach on the necessity to love—including loving white folks. His dad's words were piercing: "I used to think that blacks were the only victims of racism. But when I saw the faces of those men in the jail, twisted by the hate of racism, I knew that they were victims, too—and I just couldn't hate back."

That day Spencer knew what he had to do. "If I was to be a follower of Christ, I would have to try to be like him—to keep on forgiving. This was hard for me to swallow, but I knew it was right."

What kind of wounds have you received from people that make their words or deeds feel like they happened yesterday? Forgiveness isn't easy. I know. There are several wounds in my past that have been very painful. When my mind revisits the pain of those events every now and then, I consciously walk through the love-principles I've written about here. No punishment. No rehearsal. No withdrawal. Understanding. And a deep joy in a satisfying God. At times forgiveness will be more a process than an event, but love means pursuing these things with as much grace as we have at the time.

Of course, forgiving others is a gift to us as well. When we *don't* forgive, we're accepting bondage to resentment and bitterness, joylessness in the relationship, and distance from God. But above all, to forgive is a bold affirmation of the grace we have each received from God in Christ, as Ephesians 4:32 affirms above. For the sake of His glory, we must not refuse it to others. In fact, if unforgiveness is a pattern of our heart, we can't receive forgiveness from God (Matthew 6:15).

Speech That Edifies

The book of Proverbs says that words can be as sweet as honey, or as nasty as a storm. And James likens the power of our words to a rudder on a ship—a small movement can have huge effects. He says it's like a spark that can cause a huge forest fire. Such potential for damage! Yet, as James continues, such potential for goodness as well (James 3:3-12).

Perhaps the clearest instruction on how to love with our words is this:

> *"Do not let any unwholesome talk come out of your mouths, but only what is helpful for building others up according to their needs, that it may benefit those who listen" (Ephesians 4:29).*

This is imparting life with our words—words that are constructive and beneficial to the ones who hear them, words motivated by love (compassionately acting in their best interest).

This is an awesome responsibility. The word *only* in this verse doesn't give us a lot of wiggle room! Do my words bring life to others—or do they suck life out of them? Are my words intentional about what is in the other person's best—or are they more consumed with my own image, cleverness, opinions, and feelings?

How often do our "reckless words pierce like a sword" (Proverbs 12:18) and then we realize that our mouths merely spoke what was in our hearts—and what was in our hearts should have been taken before God and cleaned up! I've had to apologize for my words more times than I'd like to remember. I've apologized to Cathy, my kids, my parents, my in-laws, my bosses, my church boards, numerous church members, and even to my congregation.

One of the graces God has been granting me over my lifetime is the ability to be slower to speak.

> *"Everyone should be quick to listen, slow to speak and slow to become angry" (James 1:19).*

There are good reasons why James advises this. While I'm shutting my mouth, I can find room in my heart to listen to the heart of the other person—and listen to the heart of God. It also cultivates humility in me as I address any pride that may want to promote my own opinions. Being slow to speak not only slows anger, but it instructs my heart in the ways of love rather than self.

People who are *quick* to talk (and easily stick a foot into their mouth), and people who are *slow* to talk (If I don't talk I won't get myself into trouble) can both do so out of lovelessness in their hearts, failing to speak words "according to the needs" of others.

Consider this often-used text:

> *". . . speaking the truth in love, we will in all things grow up into him who is the Head, that is, Christ" (Ephesians 4:15).*

This will, at times, require *addressing another's fault.* Numerous biblical texts speak of this responsibility of the Christian to *go* to another person in order to mend a relationship or to help a person who is caught in sin (Matthew 5:23-24; 18:15-16). It is also to be done "gently" (Galatians 6:1), and sensitively to the inner needs of the person's spirit, not just their needs of right beliefs or behaviors. Without this discerning love in our hearts, it's usually best for us to wait.

I prefer the term *address* because it emphasizes the mutuality of the exchange. In other words, when we go we should be open to listening as well as speaking. When two parties address a matter, they are both free to share concerns, hurts, and observations in an attempt to reach the goal, whether that goal is reconciliation of a relationship, requesting greater love from the other, or helping the person overcome a sin pattern in their life. But the process should be mutual.

It's mutual because we may go to another person and not have all the facts right—so we must listen. It's mutual because the other person may have something against *us* that we don't know about—so we must be humble and open to spiritual growth in the process. It's mutual because even though we are addressing *their* issue, we're also quite conscious of our own sins and failures—so we go with compassion and gentleness.

Recently a man in my church came into my office with a concern about me. He did it really well—and I told him so. He was humble. He was deeply loving. He addressed a matter with me, which also resulted in his leaving with a different perspective than when he came in. And I came away with a greater sensitivity to his concern—which I needed.

At its essence we go to address a matter in order to hear the mind and heart of God for us. As Dallas Willard says, "I never think simply of what I am going to do with you, to you, or for you. I think of what we, Jesus and I, are going to do with you, to you, and for you."[2]

Ephesians 4:15 said that this "truth in love" process is ultimately about our "growing up," taking on the character of our head, Christ. This is the way the church—and Christian families—are to speak to one another. As followers of Jesus, we must avoid the extreme of stuffing our hurts and simmering in silence in relational rifts. And we must likewise avoid the other extreme of dumping and unloading our frustrations and hurts on people without humility and love.

Jesus calls us to a revolution of love, where every word is carefully chosen to be life-giving, every utterance is God-glorifying, and words of affirmation, encouragement, appreciation, understanding—and even correction—flow from the lips of God's people everywhere they go. It can begin with you!

Honoring One Another

I'll never forget the time Scott, a former co-pastor of mine, turned to me in an elders' meeting and lovingly confronted me with the fact that he often didn't feel honored in our exchange of ideas during meetings. At first I didn't understand what he was talking about. I always was interested in the opinions of others. Even church papers I wrote were always passed before the other elders for their additions and corrections and I welcomed them.

But as I listened, I began to understand. Scott (and other elders as well) felt that I too quickly analyzed their ideas before spending time appreciating them. I was so quick to evaluate them (and be efficient in our meetings) that I failed to connect to their hearts. Ed, another elder, shared how his personality liked to dream without having to be practical right away. (I've realized that my wife is often like this as well. She loves to talk about her dream house—and I have to resist the urge to figure out how much it's going to cost and how much work I'm supposed to do on it! So now I just smile and listen and agree that it's a nice house!)

> *"Be devoted to one another in brotherly love. Honor one another above yourselves" (Romans 12:10).*
>
> *"Do nothing out of selfish ambition or vain conceit, but in humility consider others better than yourselves" (Philippians 2:3).*

To *honor* someone is to show them that you *value their opinions, their feelings, their abilities,* and *their personhood.* Here are some examples of honoring love:

- Listening intently and carefully (eye contact is part of this!)

- Asking questions of clarification to make sure you understand

- Demonstrating sensitivity to someone's current feelings

- Affirming someone for who they are and what they can do—and minimizing criticism (especially important in parenting and marriage)

- Speaking with a kind and gentle tone—without harshness, irritation or sarcasm

- Not calling people names or putting them down (a special concern among youth and in the sports world)

• Not teasing people about their faults, mistakes, inabilities, or physical features (unless it is clearly a loving act and received in love)

Honor is love because it's in the best interest of another person for them to experience the dignity they were given by God. When we disrespect people, we are disrespecting the creative and varied work of God. Honor avoids the trap of using people for our own ends, whether those ends are money, power, self-promotion, efficiency, or control. It's something we need to teach our children how to do as well.

To honor doesn't mean we have to agree with someone. It just means spending meaningful time in their world before we share ours—and then perhaps give them the last word! Even our facial language is an expression of honor. When we honor people, we love them—and God is glorified.

Even The People Who Hurt Us?

But what about people who hurt us? What about people who hurt us a lot—like that harsh or detached parent, or that ex-spouse, or that kid you knew in school who seemed to live to make life miserable for you? What about that thorn in your side at church, or that totally unreasonable boss at work? And then there are the grossly evil hurts, where men sexually violate women, and terrorists randomly kill, and governments "cleanse" neighborhoods because people are from the wrong tribe, and nations bomb other nations because of some long-held uneven score? What about all them?

> *"But I tell you who hear me:* Love your enemies [emphasis mine], *do good to those who hate you, bless those who curse you, pray for those who mistreat you" (Luke 6:27-28).*

> *"Bless those who persecute you; bless and do not curse. . . If it is possible, as far as it depends on you, live at peace with everyone. Do not take revenge, my friends, but leave room for God's wrath. . . If your enemy is hungry, feed him; if he is thirsty, give him something to drink. In doing this, you will heap burning coals on his head. Do not be overcome by evil, but* overcome evil with good" [emphasis mine] *(Romans 12:14, 18-21).*

It's amazing to me how followers of Jesus will spend more energy trying to find loopholes in these teachings than living by them. We have been so caught up in the pursuit of our "self-evident, inalienable rights" of "life, liberty, and the pursuit of happiness" that we have lost sight of the upside down values of the King we serve. There's a serious clash of values in these two kingdoms, and people who live in the shadow of a suffering Cross (in which we are to "follow in his steps" according to 1 Peter 2:21) must come to serious terms with this.

The pursuit of personal rights is an attempt to secure dignity through how people treat us. But the followers of Jesus know that their dignity is in the eyes of a loving God who we are to imitate in equally self-giving love—doing good to them, verbally blessing them, and praying for them. (See Appendix E, "Reflections and Scripture for When Relationships are Disappointing.")

So self-worth in our children can't be taught by encouraging them to retaliate against bullies and stand up for their rights. We can't shun people who wrong us, pulling out a long list of grievances to justify our anger and hurt. We must come to grips with how the followers of Jesus are to be loving representatives of the kingdom of God when nations war against one another, even if our nation is pursuing what appears to be a good cause.

Does the world see us as disciples of Jesus who are characterized by His beatitudes of "poor in spirit," "meek," "merciful," "pure in heart," and "peacemakers?" Do we rejoice when we suffer for living these ways, knowing that Jesus says we are blessed when we do? (Matthew 5:3-10). Or does nationalistic pride obscure love and the deeper spiritual purposes of God today?

Ghandi is said to have been impressed with the person and teachings of Jesus, especially on love. But he said he met few Christians who actually *lived* this way. When they are seen, it's one of the most powerful proclamations of the rule of God on earth there is. It's so glorious because to love in the face of hurt also requires *coming* and *becoming*. It's evidence that the God we serve is more awesome than anything the world has ever know. To love one's enemies is to love God more than life. It's absolutely glorious.

Live a Life of Love Today!

Let me ask you: What would stop you from living your life fully in love? What would stop you from looking at people—at all times—with eyes of love instead of seeing them as inconveniences, hindrances, irritations, challenges, and ends to your own means?

Of course, we need time for personal growth and refreshment and spiritual renewal. But love would be ready to be given to the people we come in contact with each day—as well as the people who may be out of our sight but still need an email, a phone call, a prayer, or a kind deed scheduled for another day.

"But what," you may ask, "about *me*? Who will act in *my* best interests?" God will. Not necessarily in the way you want or expect, or even in the timing you might expect, but God has pledged Himself to love you. Wait on Him. Trust Him. Give Him room to use people or not use people. He will compassionately act in your best interest. If you need a reminder, read His stirring commitment to you in Romans 8:28-39. *It's all true!*

Trusting in God's love doesn't mean you can't *ask* for love from another person (like a spouse, a child, or a co-worker). But you won't demand it. And you'll love them even if they can't (or don't) love you. You'll know that love will come from somewhere in God's time. He's promised it.

Here are two beginners' assignments on love (though if you've been a lover and follower of Jesus for very long, this should, by now, not be very hard to do).

(1) *Pick a person* to intentionally show love to at least once each day for a week (and don't pick the easiest person)! By now you should have a pretty good idea what love looks like. You may even want to consider asking each close family member, "How can I love you better?" or "How can I act more in your best interest?" Perhaps their answers will guide you in who and how to love.

(2) *Pick a normal day* in your life that you will consciously think about loving every person you meet. You may not even *act* in love towards everyone you see, but you will resolve before God to open your heart and words and hands to love them the best you can with the time and resources you have. "How can I compassionately act in that person's best interest right now?" That will be the question on your mind for 16 hours straight, as you go about your normal routines of life.

Are these too much to ask of a disciple of Jesus who has made Him Lord and Savior? Is this not what it means, in part, to deny yourself daily and take up your cross and follow Jesus?

Dallas Willard asks a probing question: "Is it then hard to do the things with which Jesus illustrates the kingdom heart of love? . . . It is very hard indeed if you have not been substantially transformed in the depths of your being, in the intricacies of your thoughts, feelings, assurances, and dispositions, in such a way that you are permeated with love. Once that happens, then it is not hard. What would be hard is to act the way you acted before."[3]

For Self-Reflection and Life Application

1. Reflect on how love is, according to Jesus, a summary of every law God has made. (Pick a few and try to demonstrate this truth in each case.) Consider the rules you or your church have made. How well do they stack up to the law of love?

2. How much have contemporary meanings of the word *love* replaced a biblical understanding in the way you use the word and think about the word? Why might this be dangerous?

3. If love is "compassionately acting in the best interests of another," evaluate how much you think about and respond to people's needs to (a) encounter and know God; and (b) feel loved (for the good of their soul).

4. Reflect on how your sense of inadequacy to love this way can actually work for the glory of God by making you hungry to *come* and *become*. Why is this so helpful? How does it show up in your life?

5. Share some examples of how people need to be loved uniquely—and not just as *you* want to be loved.

6. Consider practical ways you might love the people in your life through deeds of kindness and mercy.

7. Who in your life needs to be loved through acceptance and who needs to be loved through forgiveness? What is one practical step you can take with these people?

8. In your desire to understand people better and be less judgmental and critical of them, try to answer these two questions about one person: "What is hard for him/her to do?" "What does he/she value?"

9. Reflect on Ephesians 4:29 and evaluate the purpose of your words to people. What is one way you can take a step toward these "according to their need" goals?

10. Review the list of ways we can honor one another. How might you desire people to honor you more? Who needs greater honor from *you*, and how?

11. Why do you think we struggle so much with Jesus' command to love our enemies and do good to them?

12. Do one of the two love assignments: Either pick a person to love daily for a week, or pick a day to love everyone you meet. Write a personal reflection about your experience and share it with someone you are in a close spiritual relationship to.

---

[1] John Piper, *Don't Waste Your Life*, Crossway Books, Wheaton, 2003, p. 35.
[2] Dallas Willard, *The Divine Conspiracy,* HarperCollins Publishers, San Francisco, 1998, p. 236.
[3] Ibid., p. 183.

Chapter 9

Love—Taking It on the Road

With each step closer to his home—and his wife—the man gained courage and strength. He was setting the King always before him now. During the walk from his whittling spot in the woods, the King had helped him see that behind his wife's complaining about his absence were some legitimate concerns— concerns he was responsible to address. And even if she greeted him with a cold rejection, that wasn't his concern anymore. His heart was now surrendered to the King of Love and it was love he would give.

She was in the kitchen preparing for dinner when he found her. "Hi!" he said, hoping to get her attention. She turned to face him. Her eyes were distant. He knew it wouldn't be easy to touch her heart.

"Listen, I'm really sorry," he said. "I was pretty self-centered and not very loving. It must have been hard on you these past weeks. I want you to know that I'm going to work real hard to get us caught up, and I'll also spend some time with the kids so you can get a little break."

He paused. Did she believe him, or was his confession mere words to her? He couldn't tell from the expression on her face. He so much wanted her to forgive him on the spot and give him a hug, but he was willing to accept whatever little she could give him.

She sat down at the kitchen table and put her head in her hands. When she looked up again, her face was stained with tears. "Thanks," she said. It seemed sincere, though it was obvious that much more was going on inside. He sensed that he shouldn't press the matter any further. He walked over, placed his hand on her shoulder and kissed her gently on the forehead. She didn't move.

As he walked away, she called after him, "Dinner's in 15 minutes." He turned to face her. "Thanks," he smiled. He saw a softness in her face that wasn't there a few minutes ago. "Thanks," he said again, though this time it wasn't about the dinner.

The next days were more peaceful around their home. The man chose not to talk about his experiences in Kingcity and he kept his relationship with the King to himself—for now. He really didn't know what her level of commitment and love to the King was, beyond her gratitude for the spring. But he knew that what his wife and kids needed most was a man who lived with the King, not talked about Him. They needed love that touched their hearts in both the good and the bad of family life—especially in the bad.

The next morning he stopped at the bakery on his way to work. Their hot fresh cinnamon buns were wonderful! As the waiter brought him his order, he felt the King's presence and was immediately drawn to see this man with eyes of love. "So how are you today?" the man asked.

"Okay, I guess."

In the past, his fear and insecurities would have prevented him from pursuing this conversation any further, but love now ruled his heart and the man decided to give the waiter another opening to talk. "You sure?" he asked.

The waiter looked down at the table for a moment, then at the man. "No," he replied. "My teen son and I had a heated argument this morning. We both said some pretty nasty things to each other. I think I'm losing him." His voice wavered.

The man asked further questions to befriend the waiter. As he listened, he recalled talking with a family in Kingcity whose daughter had pulled away from them for a time. They seemed to have the King's wisdom in their response to her, so the man shared about their experience. The waiter was very grateful.

"Well, I better get going to work. If you'd like some encouragement, I'd be happy to meet for lunch some day," he offered. The waiter thanked him and returned to the counter. As the man got up to go, he paused a moment, smiled, and laid a generous tip by his empty coffee mug.

Compelled By the Glory of God and Delight

How do you see the world? When you see people in the checkout line at the grocery store or watch them driving down the highway, what goes through your mind? What goes through *God's* mind?

From the creation of the first people, through God's covenant with Abraham, through God's salvation mission by Jesus, God has loved the world. And He has invited (not coerced) the world to love Him in return. He "desires everyone to be saved and to come to the knowledge of the truth" (1 Timothy 2:4 NRSV; also 2 Peter 3:9).

God made people to love, and the fullest expression of His love (compassionately acting in their best interest) is that they would know His glory.

> *"Sing to the LORD, praise his name; proclaim his salvation day after day. Declare* his glory [emphasis mine] *among the nations, his marvelous deeds among all peoples. For* great is

> the LORD [emphasis mine] *and most worthy of praise; he is to be feared above all gods" (Psalm 96:2-4).*

Through His offered salvation and His marvelous deeds, God's ultimate goal is to be praised as great and respected among all people.

In his book, *Let the Nations be Glad!,* John Piper says, "Worship, therefore, is the fuel and goal in missions. It's the goal of missions because in missions we simply aim to bring the nations into a white-hot enjoyment of God's glory. *The goal of missions is the gladness of the peoples in the greatness of God* [my emphasis]."[1]

Since missions is about the glory of God, I'll want my neighbors to embrace the first commandment—to love God with "a white-hot enjoyment" of Him. I want them to become disciples of Jesus because, in that relationship with Him, God will be glorified—and they will be satisfied.

This is clear in Jesus' parting command and promise in Matthew 28:19-20 where He told His disciples to make obedient disciples of all nations. Then He left them with this promise: "And surely I am with you always, to the very end of the age." God is glorified when people follow Jesus and enjoy His presence forever!

Not only is God's glory the goal of missions, but in Piper's words it's "the fuel of missions. Passion for God in worship precedes the offer of God in preaching. You can't commend what you don't cherish. Missionaries will never call out, 'Let the nations be *glad!*' who cannot say from the heart, '*I* rejoice in the Lord. . . *I* will be glad and exult in thee, *I* will sing praise to thy name, O Most High.' Missions begins and ends in worship. . . When the flame of worship burns with the heat of God's true worth, the light of missions will shine to the remote peoples on earth."[2]

Evangelism is the exaltation of the worth of God to the world, and this starts with *our experience* of His worth and overflows to wanting *others* to know His worth. It's believing there's a treasure of great value in a field that is worth selling everything we have to go buy it (Matthew 13:44). For us to be happy in this great God is the beginning place for evangelism.

Moved by Love

Jesus came "to seek and to save what was lost" (Luke 19:10). Lost people are people who don't have eternal life. They are people who are separated from the kingdom, or rule, of God. As Dallas Willard says, "the ultimately lost person is the person who cannot want God. Who cannot want God to be God."[3] But before this ultimate condition sets in, lost people simply are separated from God. And as we saw in Chapter 1, some of these lost people don't even know they're lost.

Perhaps they believe their generally moral lives will be acceptable to God. Or perhaps they think believing Jesus died for their sins is all that's necessary. But without repentance and a surrender to the rule of God, they are still lost.

Zacchaeus was a rich Jewish tax collector—and he was lost. But after one night with Jesus, he gave away half his possessions to the poor and repaid four times all those he had cheated. As a result of his faith-based actions, Jesus said, "Today salvation has come to this house."

People must be saved not only from their lost wandering without the life of God in them, but they must also be saved from eternal lostness where they face the danger of being "punished with everlasting destruction and shut out from the presence of the Lord and from the majesty of his power" (2 Thessalonians 1:9). So people need help in finding life—both here and in the world to come.

The previous section applied the first commandment to evangelism—love God. Now we apply the second—love people. If I'm to compassionately act in the best interest of others, then I will obviously, *out of love*, want them to encounter God, the one who can give them all they need! Jesus said, "I am the bread of life. He who comes to me will never go hungry, and he who believes in me will never be thirsty" (John 6:35). This means I'll want them to know this Bread of Life, this Living Water, this Good Shepherd, this Forgiving Judge, this Eternal Friend.

Love offers "the Answer" to lost people. It says, "This works! I'll show you. Please try it!" It says, "This is true! Please trust Him." Love says to people near and far, "Taste and see that the LORD is good . . . those who seek the LORD lack no good thing" (Psalm 34:8,10). With this kind of good news to offer, love doesn't get any better than this!

So What Do We Tell Them?

So there you are, at your friend's house, and she turns to you and asks, "I'm really confused. What exactly *do* Christians believe?" What's your response?

The priority approach of many people throughout the years has been to give out information about Jesus. But interestingly, this rarely seems to be the approach Jesus used (we'll look more fully at this in the next section). Content often came after encounter.

But at some point, we need to talk about truth. Jesus and the apostles He commissioned (especially John, Peter, and Paul) spoke a lot about content. There *is* information that is to be shared. Hearts *and* minds must be touched with the good news. Also, people are only able to embrace the *fullness* of the Gospel to the extent they encounter *Jesus*! He is the way; He is the truth; He is the life. They need to meet *Him*, even if they take different routes to get there.

The Good News (Gospel) is really the subject of this entire book. Everything we have looked at so far is good news! But I believe we can benefit from trying to distill the major themes. Not everyone thinks in five-point outlines (Jesus probably didn't!), but outlines can assist us in our own understanding as well as equipping us to succinctly share answers to inquiring, lost people.

Some years ago I stepped back to try to get a birds'-eye view of the overall Good News message of the Bible from beginning to end. I looked for passages that tied it all together. The following texts stood out and I commend them to you for your reading: Deuteronomy 7:6-9, Isaiah 53:6, Luke 19:10, John 3:16, Acts 2:38-39, and Titus 2:11-14. The big picture I saw is this: *God, in love, is rescuing people from their sinfulness and restoring them to Himself.* So if you only have five seconds to share the Good News with someone, try that!

Of course, there's more. During my college years, I went to a retreat on the topic of evangelism. Each of us was asked to write out what we would tell someone if they asked us how they could have eternal life. There were two requirements, however. We couldn't use any "religious buzz-words" (it had to be clear to someone on the street), and after we were finished with our personal answers, we had to get into small groups and come up with a composite answer (hashing out our ideas about what *really* was necessary to have eternal life.) The experience was eye-opening, and it began a serious biblical quest to know what was essential and what wasn't.

I'd like to offer the following outline as a summary of the Gospel (what we might share with someone if we have more than five seconds). I believe anything much less than this will, for most people in our culture, be insufficient for them to make an informed response to God. This is especially true if people have heard nothing previously about Jesus or have seen or heard distortions of His message. This outline is ordered in a logical flow that can be shared naturally, and the beginning letters of P-P-P-R provide an aid to memory-deficient people like myself!

A Basic Outline of the Gospel

1. God has a **Purpose** for us. *We were created to have a loving relationship with Him and to know true happiness in that relationship* (Colossians 1:16; John 17:3; John 10:10; John 7:37-38; Psalm 16:11; 34:8-10).

2. But there's a **Problem**. *Sin separates us from God, both now and forever* (Romans 6:23; Isaiah 59:2; Romans 3:23; 2 Thessalonians 1:9; Hebrews 9:27). The letter "i" in sin reminds us that the primary problem is my self-centeredness. We face three major problems: We are *confused* about what is true and right, *guilty* because of our sin, and *rebellious* in our lives toward God

3. Thankfully, God made a **Provision**. *Jesus came to remove everything that separates us from God.* He came to rescue us—to save us (Romans 6:23; 2 Corinthians 5:20-21; 3:16-18; Ephesians 2:11-20; Acts 26:18; 1 Timothy 2:5; Isaiah 53:4-6).

> a. *For our confused lives He gave us His **truth** by His teaching* (John 7:16-17; Matthew 23:10).
>
> b. *For our sinful guilt He gave us **forgiveness** by His death* (1 Peter 2:24; 3:18; Titus 3:4-7; Hebrews 9:26-28).
>
> c. *For our self-centered rebellion He gave us His **leadership and righteousness** by His resurrection* (1 John 2:3-6; Romans 10:9; Luke 14:23; Titus 2:11-14; Galatians 5:22-26).

4. But we must **Respond**. *We must humbly receive God's gift of salvation.*

> a. *This involves **turning**—*confessing our sinfulness and turning to God's ways (Mark 1:15; Acts 2:38; 3:19; 26:20).
>
> b. *And **trusting**—*actively relying on Jesus as Teacher, Savior, Lord, Friend, all that He wants to be for us (John 1:12; Ephesians 2:8-9; Acts 20:21; Romans 10:9-10).

5. The Gospel brings the following **Benefits**:

> a. ***Fellowship* with God** (John 14:23; Galatians 4:6; Revelation 3:20; 1 Peter 3:18)
>
> b. ***Forgiveness* of sin** (Acts 2:38; Ephesians 1:7; Psalm 103:2-3, 10-12)
>
> c. ***Freedom* from sin** (John 8:32-36; Romans 6:6-7)
>
> d. ***Fullness* of life** (John 10:10; 7:37-39; Psalm 16:11; Colossians 2:9-10)
>
> e. ***Family* of God** (Galatians 3:26-28; 4:4-7; Mark 10:29-30; Ephesians 2:19-22)
>
> f. ***Flow of Love to the World*** (Genesis 12:3; Matthew 5:16; Romans 12:17-21)
>
> g. ***Forever-life*** (Revelation 21:1-5, 22; 1 Corinthians 15:35-53; 2 Peter 3:10-13)

This, of course, is the expanded version, with the content that most people in our western culture need to hear. If we were to keep reducing it for purposes of increasing simplicity for our own minds, perhaps the successive stages would look something like this:

> • We can be rescued from our sinfulness and restored to a right relationship with God through having an active trust in all that Jesus is for us—especially as our Lord and Savior. Or . . .

- God, in love, is rescuing people from their sinfulness and restoring them to Himself.

Or. . .

- Jesus loves you.

This is the Good News!

Learning From New Testament Strategies

When we read the New Testament, it's fascinating to observe the strategies Jesus and the early church use to proclaim the kingdom of God. For example, Jesus tells stories (parables) that He says are designed to communicate only to the spiritually hungry, while leaving the others confused (Matthew 13:13-15)—not exactly a great formula for church-growth in most eyes!

Can you imagine Jesus saying, "Listen, guys, I believe the Father wants us to have faith for 2000 converts this year. Since only about 16 came forward last weekend at Capernaum, I'd say we're slightly behind our goal and we need to ramp up our efforts a bit—maybe try some music and candles? Okay, let's go!"

It's not that Jesus had no strategies. It's just that there was no one thing He did all the time. Sometimes He sent the disciples out in teams of two and sometimes He did mass preaching. Sometimes He healed people, and sometimes He didn't. Sometimes He would have theological dialogs with intellectuals, and sometimes He spent time with people in their homes. And often He would spend time with the twelve apostles, training them for the time when He would no longer be with them.

But, if I had to identify one particular biblical evangelism strategy for ordinary followers of Jesus, it would be this: *Live who you are, and people will be drawn to God.*

In Mark 4:26-29 Jesus says the kingdom of God grows "all by itself," just like a seed of wheat sprouts and produces grain. It's simple biology. Living cells naturally reproduce. It's happening all throughout our bodies this very minute. And that's how the living church is to grow—through natural reproduction.

In Acts 1:8 Jesus tells His disciples that they will be His witnesses. Witnesses aren't primarily preachers—they're "experiencers." They observe something and tell others about what they saw and how it affected them. For example, if you tell people that rainbows are refractions of light caused by light passing through water droplets in the sky, you have proclaimed the truth about rainbows. But if you tell people that you saw a rainbow and that it was beautiful and brilliant and that it brightened your spirit when you saw it, you've *witnessed* a rainbow. So when the Samaritan woman encountered Jesus, we're told, "Many of the Samaritans from that town believed in him because of the woman's testimony" (John 4:39). Witnesses talk about life with Jesus.

I don't have a personal dramatic conversion story to share. But I *am* a witness to Jesus. His words have given me peace and wisdom. His power has softened my pride. His example has taught me how to love. His love has supported me in relational crises. And it's this witness to Jesus' reality that leads us to look at the following evangelistic strategies—none of which, by the way, are optional for the disciple of Jesus.

Meeting Felt Needs

Jesus touched people's hearts. And He often did it through touching their felt needs. He healed them. He showed them respect when others didn't. He physically touched people society wouldn't think of touching. These were all natural expressions of love.

When God touches people at the level of their *felt* needs, those people will be open to having their most *important* needs met—which is their need for a love-relationship with God and to glorify Him.

Jesus sets the stage for this kind of evangelism at the end of his Sermon on the Mount:

> *"Let your light shine before men, that they may see your good deeds and praise your Father in heaven" (Matthew 5:16).*

These good deeds include those that touch their hearts. Deeds like giving compliments and words of affirmation, listening to their hurts and offering wise counsel, or offering to take care of their children for a night. Deeds like helping a neighbor with a house project or inviting a coworker over for dinner with his/her family.

When we help people in their physical needs, emotional needs, and wisdom needs, we're preparing their hearts for the *rest* of the Gospel (because they just tasted *part* of it!).

Real Relationships—Open and Sometimes Messy

Jesus apparently spent most of His time with His disciples, training them for His departure. But He also had a reputation for hanging out with other types of folks as well. Some said of Him: "Here is a glutton and a drunkard, a friend of tax collectors and 'sinners'" (Matthew 11:19). So all of Jesus' friends weren't from the choir and deacon team! (Of course, if this is a description of *your* choir and deacon team, you have some people to witness to!)

There's something very powerful about friendships. We can laugh together and cry together, talk about similar interests, and genuinely enjoy each other's company. Friends share a level of trust and mutual care.

This means followers of Jesus have a unique opportunity to share the good news of Jesus with our unbelieving friends in several ways. First, we know their felt needs better than many do. Second, we can share about our spiritual lives freely and openly—the things we do at church, how God is changing us, etc. And third, we have opportunities to explore spiritual issues with our friends. *The Barna Report* presented statistics showing that "more than three times as many people come to faith through the personal witness of a friend than through hearing gospel preaching in a church."[4] That's why each of us is so important!

My wife Cathy is an inspiration to me in this. My personality type doesn't naturally seek out many friends. I'm content with a few (and she's my *best* friend). But Cathy seeks out and enjoys many friendships. Whether it's business contacts, neighbors, or women she meets in the 45-and-over Red Hat Society she started in our church, she lives out these three "friendship evangelism" characteristics. I love her heart—and many women have been drawn to Jesus because of her.

Of course, we're not talking about making friends *projects*. We're talking about being yourself as a God-glorifying, Christ-imitating, love-focused follower of Jesus. And this includes when we fail—either with a particular friendship or in other ways. To be a friend means we let people see the messy stuff. And we let them see the surrender, insight, repentance, grace and perseverance process that changes us as well! This means we give apologies to friends. And acceptance and forgiveness. We share our weaknesses but with hope. They're looking for a God that makes a difference in real life—not a fake one.

The staff at Willow Creek Community Church has identified six personal evangelism styles in the Bible that fit our different personality types.[5] The Invitational Style enjoys *inviting* people to events in which they may encounter God, like church, home Bible studies, Christian concerts, etc. The Interpersonal Style enjoys making meaningful *friendships* and being transparent in them. The Serving Style enjoys *helping* others as an expression of God's love. The Testimonial Style enjoys sharing their "before and after" *story* about their relationship with Christ. The Confrontational Style enjoys speaking persuasively and raising challenging *questions* to unbelievers. The Intellectual Style enjoys debating and presenting the *evidence* for the Christian message to others.

Of course, each of these has its strengths and cautions, and each must be sensitively used with different people. But your friend *does* need a Christ-like friend—and you qualify!

Experiencing Christians

And this brings up another way for people to hear the Gospel of Jesus—by watching *us*! Unfortunately this has its horror stories. My online discipleship students are required to ask unbelievers about their impressions of Jesus and Christians. Jesus usually comes out pretty high—Christians don't. Over and over again I hear someone tell me that the greatest hindrance to their coming to Christ was the actual lives of professing Christians! One person was told by a deli clerk that the worse shift for him was Sundays right after church. That was when he encountered the most mean and unfriendly people. This breaks my heart again and again. I can only imagine what it does to God's.

In Acts 26:17-18, God tells Paul that He is sending him to the Gentiles "to open their eyes and turn them from darkness to light, and from the power of Satan to God." This "opening eyes" process isn't accomplished just by preaching. It's accomplished by showing them spiritual reality lived out in front of them.

People need to see in us something better than what they have. We "open their eyes" because we are Jesus to them. That's why the church is called the "body of Christ." Through us they have the opportunity to encounter the glory of God. Really!

Let's look at some of the ways Scripture says we are the face of Jesus to the world:

• ***Through our Love.*** This is probably the most powerful light of all.

> *"A new command I give you: Love one another. As I have loved you, so you must love one another. By this all men will know that you are my disciples, if you love one another"* *(John 13:34-35).*

Love turns heads—both our love for unbelievers and our love for "one another." When believers replace shingled roofs for each other, refuse to gossip about one another, and bear one another's burdens through thick and thin—people notice. They see disciples of Jesus. And there's nothing more powerful than that.

As I write, one of the worst disasters ever to hit America has just taken place—Hurricane Katrina has wrought massive devastation along the Gulf coast. As Christians pour out financial and tangible love, the world will watch.

> *"And if you spend yourselves in behalf of the hungry and sat-isfy the needs of the oppressed, then* your light will rise in the darkness [emphasis mine], *and your night will become like the noonday" (Isaiah 58:10).*

Heads will turn to this kind of light. And eyes will be opened.

• ***Through Our Unity.*** Just before Jesus is taken away to be crucified, He prays for all those who will believe in Him:

> *"that all of them may be one, Father, just as you are in me and I am in you. May they also be in us so* that the world may believe [emphasis mine] *that you have sent me. . . May they be brought to complete unity to let the world know that you sent me and have loved them even as you have loved me" (John 17:21, 23).*

If we want the world to know that God really sent Jesus, then we must get along with our Christian brothers and sisters, whether they're in our own church or the church down the street. We can still disagree, but we must do so with respect because we experience unity with God! And eyes will be opened. (More about unity in Chapter 13.)

• ***Through our Worship.*** Another way the world can encounter God is through what happens in our church gatherings. 1 Corinthians 14:24-25 speaks about how the ministry of prophecy can cause a person to be con-victed of sin, such that he will "fall down and worship God, exclaiming, 'God is really among you!'" Prophecy here is the ministry of communi-cating God's truth to the present needs of people. In a church service it can take the form of Spirit-inspired preaching, Spirit-anointed singing, and Spirit-led testimonies or words spoken to all. I've seen this happen often in worship services as truth awakens people's minds and hearts. And eyes are opened.

• *Through Our Integrity.*

> *"Teach slaves to be subject to their masters in everything, to try to please them, not to talk back to them, and not to steal from them, but to show that they can be fully trusted, so that in every way they will make the teaching about God our Savior* attractive" [emphasis mine] *(Titus 2:9-10).*

Let's face it—some parts of the Gospel are hard to swallow for some people. They need to have a reason to believe beyond that "the Bible says so." When Christians live honest, respectful, honoring lives—*especially at their jobs, whether as boss or employee*—some will take notice and be impressed—impressed with their God. Eyes will be opened. (More about workplace integrity in Chapter 11.)

• *Through our Hope Amidst Persecution.*

> *"Who is going to harm you if you are eager to do good? But even if you should suffer for what is right, you are blessed. "Do not fear what they fear; do not be frightened." But in your hearts set apart Christ as Lord. Always be prepared to give an answer to* everyone *who asks you* [emphasis mine] *to give the reason for the hope that you have. But do this with gentleness and respect." (1 Peter 3:13-15).*

When they see us handle hardships with grace and lack of fear—like a difficult marriage, a difficult child, or even a difficult boss—they'll want to know what makes us tick. They'll want to know about "the hope that you have." And, if we're "prepared to give an answer," eyes will be opened.

• *Through Our Attitude in Trials.* If there's anytime people are watching,
it's when life is hard. A friend of ours, Kathy, recently lost her husband to a surprise heart attack. A year later she found herself in the emergency room of a hospital as her mother lay dying from a fall down the stairs at her church. In the midst of her own sorrow, Kathy turned to a disheveled unshaven man in the waiting room and asked, "What brings you here today?" He said he brought his 25-year-old son who was suicidal. Kathy's love probed further and it opened the door for him to share his own struggles. He was a recovering alcoholic and said he had nothing to live for. Kathy pulled out her mother's New Testament from her purse and shared

Jesus with him. Kathy's exuberant life motto has always been, "God is good!" She lives it daily, even in a hospital waiting room.

> *"Do everything without complaining or arguing, so that you may become blameless and pure, children of God without fault in a crooked and depraved generation, in which you shine like stars in the universe as* you hold out the word of life" [emphasis mine] *(Philippians 2:14-16)*.

We shine like stars and hold out life to others when we handle difficult people and circumstances with grace and acceptance. No complaining or arguing—not because we're afraid to speak up or because we want people to like us but because our hearts are connected to the Vine who feeds us with everything we need. We're genuinely content. Life can be very sad at times, but God glorifies Himself in spite of it and through it. In this way the world's eyes can be opened.

• *Through Our Transformation to Christ*. A final "encountering Christians" strategy God uses is allowing people to see us become like Jesus.

> *"Be diligent in these matters* [godly speech, love, faith and purity—vs. 12-14]*; give yourself wholly to them, so that everyone may see your progress. Watch your life and doctrine closely. Persevere in them, because if you do,* you will save both yourself and your hearers" [emphasis mine] *(1 Timothy 4:15-16)*.

"Everyone" is watching your progress (or lack of it)! If you're diligent in spiritual transformation to the character of Christ, then "you will save both yourself and your hearers." In other words, you will secure your salvation by your ongoing life in Christ, and *others* will enter the kingdom because of you! And their eyes will be opened!

One practical illustration of this is found in 1 Peter 3:1-2. Wives are told to have a submissive spirit toward their husbands, "so that, if any of them do not believe the word, they may be won over without words by the behavior of their wives, when they see the purity and reverence of your lives." This is "Evangelism 101" for family members. Do you want a family member to come to Jesus? Forget the religious rhetoric and church invitations for awhile—*live* Jesus!

As Ravi Zacharias has said, "We must learn to find the backdoor to people's hearts because the front door is heavily guarded."[6] The most powerful tool you have is your Christ-like character as it touches people's hearts. And it's what they long for.

The strategy is this: Christianity will spread naturally when the people of God live supernatural lives in the world—lives drenched in the presence of God. Heads will turn, eyes will open, and hearts will be captured by Jesus!

You Are Salt and Light

> *"You are the salt of the earth; but if salt has lost its taste, how can its saltiness be restored? It is no longer good for anything, but is thrown out and trampled under foot. You are the light of the world. A city built on a hill cannot be hid. No one after lighting a lamp puts it under the bushel basket, but on the lampstand, and it gives light to all in the house. In the same way, let your light shine before others, so that they may see your good works and give glory to your Father in heaven" (Matthew 5:13-16 NRSV).*

Salt flavors and preserves. Light illumines. Both of these metaphors talk about our distinctiveness in the world—for the good of the world. And the world sure could use something good!

Yes, God uses the institutions of governments and families to salt and brighten the world with some essential goodness, but both of these agencies are often highly conditioned by cultural values. The followers of Jesus, on the other hand, get their values directly from God, which means they are the best salt and light God has on earth!

What's so distinct about us? The "beatitudes" preceded the text above and they say it all: "meekness," "merciful," "pure hearts," "peacemaking." *That's* our salt and light. Of course, some won't find our influence a positive thing. In fact, we're their worst nightmare! But others will appreciate what we bring to society, and in the end they will "give glory" to God. So not only are *we* blessed by living with the values of the kingdom, but many in the world are blessed by us as well—just as God's covenant to Abraham promised (Genesis 12:3).

In the popular legends of King Arthur, his city of Camelot was a model of justice, love, and peace for all. I love the scene in the movie, *First Knight*, when Guinevere is escorted by Arthur over a ridge in the evening hours, and she sees Camelot for the first time, shimmering with thousands of lamps and breathtaking in beauty. *That* is us in a world of darkness! *We* are "a lamp" on a "lamp stand," giving light for all to see so that they may come to the Light.

Of course, we don't know how the early church would have practiced being salt and light in a democracy ruled by the "will of the people." Living in a land ruled by Caesar wouldn't have given them much access to government or institutional change. But Jesus clearly gives a priority to developing spiritual realities in His *followers*. Once immersed into *His* kingdom, these salt and light bearers will be marked by the distinctiveness of their King and His values will overflow into the world, first to draw people to Himself, and secondly, to influence the world with goodness.

With these images of salt and light in mind, we conclude several things:

- *We must permeate society.* We can't stay in the salt shaker. We can't hide our light behind church walls and fortress homes. We need to be out where decay is happening—where it's dark and where people are hurting. We can't play it safe all the time. Our feet and hands must get dirty.

- *We must be distinct from society.* A city on a hill requires a separate identity if it's going to offer an alternative way of living to the world. So we must maintain some sense of a collective witness, a gathered presence as God's lighthouse people. Our churches and our home groups and our families must reveal the light of the glory of God, and woe to us when we blend in so well that there's nothing of the glory of God to draw them to something better.

- *We must seek to persuade.* Not only do we radiate, but we must debate as well. God's wisdom can often be persuasive to the world if we don't rely primarily on Bible quoting (since most don't accept the Bible as authoritative) but on arguments based on their common good. Our reasons for being pro-life, believing in sexual abstinence before marriage, encouraging dialog between warring nations, and respecting the environment must be made in ways that make God's ways compelling to them.

A woman in my church shared recently how her decision not to gossip at work has slowed down the gossip chain. A youth coach's decision to be an encourager rather than a yeller on the field has made a difference with his players. A man's refusal to go to a strip club with his boss and business associates won admiration from a co-worker who wants to be faithful to *his* wife. This is salt and light stuff.

Some may be called to make a difference in particularly dark territories that affect many, many people—like the film industry, the inner city, third world countries, corporate business, or politics. The rewards may be few and far between at times, but being salt and light is not just about results, it's about being faithful to Jesus. To change culture is not our mandate. To be salt and light is. So whether we seek to penetrate the darkness of the music recording industry or the dimness of a Christmas office party, we must ask the question, "Is my fire melting the ice around me, or is the ice around me, putting out my fire?"

Connecting to Unbelievers Through Culture

Meet Issachar. He was one of Jacob's 12 sons. "The men of Issachar [referring to his descendents]…understood the times and knew what Israel should do" (1 Chronicles 12:32).

When you read the morning paper, watch TV, or walk through a mall, you are faced with your culture. You can't get away from it (unless you do some very drastic things like joining a monastery). Two questions arise: "Do you understand your culture?" and "How then shall you live?" These are the questions Issachar's descendents were good at answering.

These are important to answer if we're going to live faithfully as Jesus' disciples in the 21st century in our culture. And they are also important questions to answer if we're going to communicate the Gospel to the people around us.

I say "communicate" because we can't merely talk any way we want to and expect every person to understand what we're saying. The real question is whether they *understand* what we're saying. Do they get it? Do they really know what they may be rejecting?

Thom Rainer, author of the book, *The Unchurched Next Door*, recently interviewed unchurched people across the United States and found that four out of ten unchurched people are "highly receptive to what you say about Christ."[7] He also found that the majority of the unchurched people have never had anyone tell them how to become a Christian, and that they indicate they *want* to have a relationship with a Christian in whom they can see Christ, ask questions, and get better acquainted.

So if many people are receptive to the Gospel, the question remains, "Do they *hear* it?" Or are there cultural barriers we aren't adequately addressing? The apostle Paul summarizes this principle well: "I have become all things to all men so that by all possible means I might save some" (1 Corinthians 9:22).

The way Paul spoke to synagogue worshippers in Acts 13:16f, to the intellectuals and philosophers in Athens in Acts 17, and to King Agrippa in Acts 26 were all different. Each presentation was sensitive to each particular audience. There was no canned spiel.

So the burden is on *us* to communicate to *them*—not *their* responsibility to figure out what in the world *we're* trying to say! This will mean paying careful attention to several things:

• ***Words.*** If I ask a neighbor, "Do you believe in God?" he may say "yes"—but have a very different definition of what it means to *believe* or who/what *God* is. When we use words like *sin, salvation, getting saved, personal Savior, Lord, born again,* and *died for your sins,* we're speaking a foreign language to many (or most) people today. Even the word *Jesus* may not communicate clearly. This is why in recent years I've started using *turn* rather than *repent,* and *trust* rather than *believe* when I share the Gospel with someone. The truth hasn't changed, but our words sometimes must if we're going to communicate to today's people.

• ***Music.*** For many years the church had its own musical culture. Hymns from past centuries were standard, as if to say following Jesus meant singing "our" songs—which were very old songs. Fortunately this has changed in many churches, and people can hear a sound of relevance when they enter a church to explore God and faith.

• ***Media and Technology.*** This is a mixed bag. There is much good—and much bad—that is associated with TV, film, radio, and computers. But whole generations have been raised on Sesame Street, Nintendo, and blogging. Unless Christians speak this language, we will be seen as irrelevant and boring, and we will fail to use a language the world is using.

• ***What Opens Their Souls.*** One thing that opens people's souls to God is authentic, meaningful relationships (as noted earlier). Also, people today are interested not so much in what is true as what works. So rather than try to argue for absolute truth, it will often be better to show them that God's life through Jesus does, indeed, bring about success—for marriage, parenting, business, interpersonal conflicts, emotional health, and more. Also, people are making decisions more through a process than at a point in time. So the doorway to people's souls will often require repeated visits, with multiple spiritual touches and often through multiple people.

As Mark Mittelberg says, "We overlook the fact that our friends and neighbors live in a culture that is growing more secular and less Christian. We forget that they don't know what we know, value what we value, or trust what we trust."[8] That's why we must be like the sons of Issachar who know the times and know what we should do to reach lost people.

Telling Them!

But at some point, our non-Christian friends will need to know more than *experiencing* Jesus through you. They need to hear *about* Him! This may come through a preacher, a Bible, a Christian book, or through remembering what their grandmother told them years ago, but someone needs to share information about Jesus with them. (We will further consider the role the gathered church has in evangelism in Chapter 13.)

Romans 1 and 2 speak about the dual witnesses of creation and conscience, both of which are available to every person, which makes them "without excuse" before God. But to know the fullness of salvation and to have assurance of eternal life and to perhaps help them in their journey to Jesus if they don't yet believe, someone must tell them facts about Jesus.

> *"But how are they to call on one in whom they have not believed? And how are they to believe in one of whom they have never heard? And how are they to hear without someone to proclaim him?" (Romans 10:14, NRSV).*

This isn't just about missionaries. It's about you and me.

So we must become familiar with two things: *God's story* (as summarized in an earlier section of this chapter) and *our own story* (about how we came to know Jesus and the difference it has made). These form the basis of what we have to say.

Many people falter at the point of not knowing how to make transitions into spiritual conversations. The following are ways to make this shift:

- "What has been your religious or spiritual background?"

- "What do you think about Jesus? . . . Have you ever seriously considered His statements about Himself?. . . What if Jesus really *did* die to rescue you from your sins and rise from the dead. What difference would that make to you?"

- "What's really stopping you from loving and following Jesus? Is it head stuff? Heart stuff?"

- "Do you ever wish the story about Jesus were true?"

- "If you were to die tonight, what would you tell Jesus if He appeared to you and asked why He should let you into heaven?"

Behind it all is the communication about God's love to sinful people. It's good news that we should not hesitate to share, because it's the kind of news that every heart longs for.

Intentionally Going

> *"But you will receive power when the Holy Spirit comes on you; and you will be my witnesses in Jerusalem, and in all Judea and Samaria, and to the ends of the earth" (Acts 1:8).*

We are to go. We can't just ask people to come. We must go out into our communities and to friends, then go to the outlying regions and country, and then on to the distant lands. It will require resources (especially money) and time. It will mean saying good-byes, and not clinging too tightly to our families and friends. It will mean learning new languages and customs, eating strange foods and drinks, not insisting we carry our American standard of living with us, and not thinking that our way is necessarily better. And it will mean affirming Jesus' call in Luke 10:2, "'The harvest is plentiful, but the workers are few. Ask the Lord of the harvest, therefore, to send out workers into his harvest field.'" We must pray this knowing that the "worker" actually may be me.

Whether we go to the teens hanging out in the street by our house, to the urban poor in a nearby city, to a bowling league, or to a far-off land without electricity and indoor plumbing, it will often mean entering new cultures, sacrificial love, and a cost. Going always involves leaving something.

Is It Really a Sacrifice?

So what about this cost? What about the things we leave behind or the things we suffer when we take a loving heart on the road for the glory of God? Martyred missionary, Jim Elliot, wrote, "He is no fool who gives what he cannot keep to gain what he cannot lose."[9] I believe one of the greatest hindrances to our embracing the fullness of the glory of God in our lives is that we value what God doesn't, and we don't value what God does. This is no more clearly seen than in the matter of loving people to Christ.

David Livingstone was a pioneer missionary to Africa in the early 1800's. He once spoke these words to students at Cambridge University: "People talk of the sacrifice I have made in spending so much of my life in Africa. . . Is that a sacrifice which brings its own blest reward in healthful activity, the consciousness of doing good, peace of mind, and a bright hope of a glorious destiny hereafter?. . . Away with the word in such a view, and with such a thought!

It is emphatically no sacrifice. Say rather it is a privilege. Anxiety, sickness, suffering or danger, now and then, with a foregoing of the common conveniences and charities of this life, may make us pause, and cause the spirit to waver, and the soul to sink; but let this only be for a moment. All these are nothing compared with the glory which shall be revealed in and for us. I never made a sacrifice."[10]

On one level it *is* a sacrifice to give up the relational closeness of extended families and the conveniences and comforts of this life. But when we see reality from God's point of view, we can be sad about loss while still rejoicing in what is our gain, as Jesus describes the loss of family and the resulting "hundred times" gain "in this present age" (Mark 10:29-30). It is true: we can be "sorrowful, yet always rejoicing" (2 Corinthians 6:10).

Danger Ahead—Be On Your Guard! And Do Not Be Afraid!

We are left no option by Jesus. We're in the world and we must relate to the structures and people in this world—because of love and because we are salt and light in it. But make no mistake about it, this world is a dangerous place. Jesus warns His disciples,

> *"I am sending you out like sheep among wolves. Therefore be as shrewd as snakes and as innocent as doves" (Matthew 10:16).*

That's not an easy combination to pull off—shrewdness and innocence. But it's necessary out there. Be on your guard. And keep your heart soft.

It's a dangerous world because it's under the control of Satan (1 John 5:19), and the culture wants to fit us into its mold. James warns us bluntly, "keep oneself from being polluted by the world" (James 1:27). This is no walk in the park.

But the person who is *coming* to God and *becoming* like His Son will have the resources to resist these pulls, for "the one who is in you is greater than the one who is in the world" (1 John 4:4). And,

> *"Everyone born of God overcomes the world. This is the victory that has overcome the world, even our faith" (1 John 5:4).*
>
> *"For God did not give us a spirit of timidity, but a spirit of power, of love and of self-discipline. So do not be ashamed to testify about our Lord, or ashamed of me his prisoner. But join*

with me in suffering for the gospel, by the power of God, who
has saved us and called us to a holy life" (2 Timothy 1:7-9).[11]

It should be clear by now that this love-assault on the world for the glory of God and people's joy is not for the weak. But the truth is this: God is with us, and though He may not always protect us from every harm here on earth, He *will* keep those who believe in Him safe unto our eternal rest with Him. His Resurrection guarantees it.

So when fears come, and we feel weak for the task ahead, and people resist either our love or our message (and our God), we will return again to the "spirit of power, of love, and of self-discipline" that results from the coming and becoming process of our minds and hearts. We won't be ashamed, because we live for God's glory, not our own. We'll constantly drink deeply from the well of God's grace. We'll remember the foundations of our faith and rejoice in our salvation and be satisfied in our God. Because of these things, we will be able to love lost souls again and again out there in the world where dangerous things and disappointing things can (and will) happen. Then we will have the privilege of rejoicing with the angels when one person says "Yes" to Jesus and His life!

For Self-Reflection and Life Application

1. How does doing evangelism with the motivations of the glory of God, your delight, and love affect the way you see lost people?

2. In what way is the Gospel presented in this chapter different than what you have previously thought when you heard the word "Gospel?" (Is there anything new? Anything missing?) Are there any ways you might want to change it to be more biblically faithful?

3. Practice sharing the logical flow of Purpose/Problem/Provision/Response/Blessing with another Christian you know. (The details don't have to be exactly as outlined.)

4. What felt needs might you possibly meet in some of the lost people you know?

5. What do you find most challenging in the process of developing real and open relationships with non-Christians so that your faith is visible in meaningful ways to them?

6. Pick out several of the listed ways people might experience Jesus in you, and reflect on how clear your witness is in these areas. What do people *really* see in you?

7. In what ways might God be wanting to use you as salt and light in the world you live in?

8. What might you need to do better to communicate the Gospel to people in today's culture?

9. Reflect on a time when you tried to tell someone about God's love through Jesus. How did it go? What would you like to do differently (if anything) next time?

10. Reflect on how you think about sacrifice in light of the quote by David Livingstone. What would it take for you to say with him, "I never made a sacrifice"?

11. What is God saying to you about how you need to live in this dark and dangerous world?

---

[1] John Piper, *Let the Nations be Glad!: The Supremacy of God in Missions, 2nd Ed.*, Baker Academic, 2003, p. 17.

[2] Ibid., pp. 17-18.

[3] Dallas Willard, *Renovation of the Heart,* Navpress, Colorado Springs, 2002, p. 58.

[4] Mark Mittleberg, *Building a Contagious Church* , Zondervan Publishing Company, Grand Rapids, 2000, p. 70.

[5] Mark Mittleberg, Lee Strobel, and Bill Hybels, *Becoming a Contagious Christian,* Zondervan Publishing House, Grand Rapids, 1995.

[6] Ravi Zacharias, *Outreach Magazine, July/August 2005,* p. 108.

[7] Thom Rahner, *The Unchurched Next Door,* Zondervan Publishing Company, Grand Rapids, 2003, p. 46.

[8] Mark Mittleberg, *Building a Contagious Church*, Zondervan Publishing Company, Grand Rapids, 2000, p. 48.

[9] Elisabeth Elliot, *Shadow of the Almighty: The Life and Testament of Jim Elliot,* Harper and Brothers, New York 1958, p. 19.

[10] John Piper, *Desiring God: Meditations of a Christian Hedonist, Second Edition,* Multnomah Publishers, Inc., Sisters, 1996, p. 204.

[11] See also Proverbs 29:25, Romans 1:16, 8:31-39, and Acts 5:40-42.

PART THREE

How to Glorify God in Whatever You Do on Earth

The foundation has been laid—following Jesus to the glory of God with deep joy. The house has been built—*coming* to Him in all things, *becoming* like Jesus, and *loving* others through Him. Now it's time to spend some intentional time in a few of the rooms. We've already walked through most of these rooms along the way, taking a glance at how they've been furnished. But some of these areas of life are just too important for a drive-through analysis. We need to sit down awhile in each one—family, work, money, earthly pleasures, the church—and seriously consider how they should look when we live there in Him, for Him, and through Him. After all, we spend *a lot* of time in these rooms.

These aren't new laws to live by. These are merely practical applications of living in the heart of God—the heart that we have already seen throughout this study. It's what life looks like on earth when it's drenched in His life.

As always, it begins with our desires being submitted to God's desires. Yes, we submit because God says we should, and because it's the humble thing to do, and the right thing to do. But we also submit because we're convinced that coming to God, becoming like Jesus, and loving others is in our absolute best interest. This is how we will be most satisfied.

The chapters that follow touch on the basic landscape of most people's lives. Don't be overwhelmed by what you read. It really is more simple than it may at first appear. That's because living in the kingdom is more about a surrendered heart to God's heart than living a principled life.

Will it require work? Yes. Change? Absolutely. But even more so, these chapters are a further invitation to joy. I pray they will inspire you to live in the kingdom of His love, for this is the life the Spirit has come to give us—a life filled with the glory of God.

Chapter 10

The Family—Where Fruit is Enjoyed and Tested

Rain was falling as the man walked through the front door. An order dead-line had kept him longer than usual, so it was late by the time he arrived home. The children were playing board games, and his wife was washing the dishes. He greeted her with a kiss on the cheek, as she began to warm up his dinner.

Ever since his apology and his subsequent love-efforts, she had been open-ing up her heart to him more and more. And then, a couple days ago he was thrilled when she looked at him and said, "You know, I think you have fewer boils on your face and arms than you used to." He smiled. It was happening just like the King had said!

They caught up on the events of each other's day while he ate. On several occasions her complaints were more than he wanted, but he recalled passages from The Breath, *or experiences he had with the King, and they would help him renew his surrender to the King's greatness and love. He looked forward to the day when these things would be automatic to him—like they were for some of the people he had met in Kingcity. But for now it meant daily dying to his self-centered desires that were based on anything other than the King.*

"Oh, by the way," she said casually, "my mother will be coming to spend a week with us tomorrow. You know how much she loves the kids."

He looked at her in disbelieving shock. Words automatically flowed out of his heart and through his mouth—as all words do. And immediately words ricocheted back to him from his wife's heart. Soon he found himself sitting on a chair out on his porch, alone and fuming.

Why did she have to do this to him? She could be so insensitive at times! It always seemed she got her way when it came to her mother. This was his house, too, wasn't it?

He felt he had been loving so well—until now. Several minutes followed of heaping blame upon his wife for how he felt. Gradually his spirit became still, and in the quiet of the setting sun, he began turning his heart to the King, slowly but deliberately. Soon he was on a journey into the King's love for him, where truth for his mind and freedom for his heart ministered to his wounds. At length he was humbly heading to his wife—again.

He sorrowfully confessed his selfishness to her and she accepted it. Then, as he looked into her eyes, he was suddenly moved with compassion. "How are you doing?" he asked her gently. "I really want to know. How are you?"

She responded like a young lioness yearning to be released from a cage. Pent up feelings tumbled out, as the man listened with compassion and understanding. He didn't understand everything he heard, but he understood more than he ever did before. Some of it was hard to hear, but his heart received it with the King at his side.

The experience drained her, and when she was done, she thanked her husband for listening, then excused herself and went to bed early. When she was gone he realized that it was late and he needed to take initiative to get the kids to bed.

"Bedtime!" he shouted into the next room. There was no answer. He was about to go into the room to see what was going on when he stopped himself. He knew that his kids often resisted bedtime. And, in the past, he would usually be impatient with their procrastination and excuses. He knew he had to prepare his heart to respond to whatever he might encounter in the next few minutes. He had let himself be ambushed once today—he would not let it happen again. He was coming to the King.

Ichabod in the Home?

The ark of the covenant was a gold-covered box that was a symbol of God's presence with Israel. At one point during their history, the ark was captured from Israel in fierce battle, and the high priest's son Phinehas was among the dead. Hearing of these losses, his father Eli fell over and died. The deep sadness of these events prompted Phinehas' wife to name her newborn son "Ichabod" (1 Samuel 4:21). We saw earlier that *kabod* means "glory." *Ichabod* means "no glory."

I'm afraid that God would describe many Christian homes as "Ichabod." There's no evidence of divine greatness there—only a social institution that generally tries to be moral. His glory is gone, and "Ichabod" is written over their doorways.

One thing I have learned in my years as a pastor is that what you see on Sundays is often not what happens Monday through Saturday. Quiet men can become angry men. Sweet women can become controlling women. Pleasant teens can become shockingly disrespectful. It's what one would expect in the world. It's not what one would expect of a disciple of Jesus.

I'm not speaking here about perfection. I'm speaking about God's glory— the life of God that bathes the believer because "streams of living water will flow from within him" (John 7:38). (Okay, so you're not at the rapids stage yet—but there *are* streams! And disciples should at least be getting quite *wet!*)

Why is the Christian home—the place where God's glory should most be experienced—so often filled with self? Why do so few seem to thirst for God in the family setting?

Perhaps that's the problem. Thirst. Everybody's thirsting for something else. Or some*one* else. Home life is filled to the top with expectations of satisfaction. Respect me. Love me. Make me happy. It's this self-need that the social sciences have tapped into, often resulting in advice to leave the marriage because it's no longer meeting one's needs. At best, this kind of marriage is thirsting after one another—not thirsting after God.

In this chapter I want to paint a picture of something radical and wonderful—a picture of a God-centered home where the Lord Himself dwells among us and His glory shines. It's a picture of relationships where the prayer, "Your kingdom come, on earth as it is in heaven," becomes a reality because the loving, happy, peaceful rule of God has filled at least one person in the home (you?)—and maybe several.

The reality is that if we *can't imagine* it, it *probably won't happen.* So dream with me as you read the following pages, and begin to taste of family life as God meant it to be. It is within your grasp.

Honor Your Parents

It's likely that most every person reading this book has had at least one adult in his or her life who functioned as a parent to them—and likely two. Consider God's life-giving instructions to children of all ages, whether their parents live in the same home with them or not.

> *"Honor your father and your mother, as the LORD your God has commanded you, so that you may live long and that it may go well with you in the land the LORD your God is giving you" (Deuteronomy 5:16).*

To honor our parents is to show them that we value them. (Recall the treatment of honor in Chapter 8.) We owe our very existence to them. We owe them gratitude for feeding us, bathing us, holding us, and changing our dirty diapers. And most of our parents gave us food, clothing, shelter, health care, gifts, recreational opportunities, and "taxi service" to our events. Some were even able to help us financially with college, weddings, or homes.

Given the spiritual, intellectual, and emotional resources they had at the time, our parents gave our nurturing their best shot. They taught us, corrected us, disciplined us, played with us, listened to us—and yes, got some of it wrong. Sometimes terribly wrong.

But, remember, we weren't exactly perfect kids, either! Think about what we put them through along the way. We certainly didn't come with an owners manual for our particular model! We stretched and challenged them many times. In fact, we probably don't have a clue at all what went through their hearts in raising us. The fears, the anxieties, the sense of being a failure and wishing they could do it better, the frustrations of not being able to "fix" us or even understand us. They gave a lot.

Honor is partially given to someone because of the quality of that person's life. They *earn* our honor. Other honor, however, is given because of a person's position (president, teacher, coach, church leader, etc.). Our parents are due at least this positional honor and, in varying degrees, they're due the former earned honor.

I think about my Mother's unconditional love and acceptance of us kids, her tireless, uncomplaining homemaking, and her devoted heart to God. And I think of my Dad's financial stewardship, his initiatives for family times, and his godly wisdom in the home and our church. They are both due honor in special measure when I recall my high school years when my wavy hair grew over my ears (to their dismay) and some of my ideas started being different than theirs and my musical tastes grew outside the boundaries of gospel! There never was any doubt about their love for me, even though these things stretched our closeness at times.

How, exactly, do we honor our parents in practical ways? How do we show them that we value them, whether they are 40, 60, or 90 years old? Here are some ideas:

- Seek their advice and express gratitude for it, even if you don't agree with all of it.

- Express gratitude to them frequently for what they have given you.

- Intentionally spend time with them. Or call them on the phone and ask how they're doing. Reminisce about the good old days—and talk sparingly about the painful ones. At family get-togethers, be a blessing. Don't go looking for love, go dispensing it.

• Don't dwell on their character flaws or regularly complain to others about them. Forgive them for their failures and sins against you.

• When it's appropriate to share a negative growing-up experience with a friend, do it in a balanced and understanding way and in a tone that you would use if your parents were actually present.

• As they grow into older age don't control their lives (see Leviticus 19:32 for how to respectfully treat them). Give them the dignity of their choices (within reason) and, if their bodies or minds deteriorate, be willing to care for them like they cared for you in your younger years, even if it costs you some freedom.

When we honor our parents, God promises that "it will go well with us." Something else happens, too. We glorify God. In a day when adult children feel they have a right to financial and social independence, and don't want to be "burdened" by caring for their parents, the people of God can "shine like stars in the universe as you hold out the word of life" (Philippians 2:15-16) by the way they honor their aging parents.

Consider one last aspect about our relationship to our parents:

"A foolish son brings grief to his father and bitterness to the one who bore him" (Proverbs 17:25).

If there is anything you have said or done (or not said or done) that needs to be confessed to them because it hurt them, do it today. Sure, maybe you feel that he or she owes *you* an apology—and maybe they do. But that's not in your control. *Your* actions and attitudes are. And honor means confessing the sins you committed against them to them, even if it's the foolishness of elementary school or high school. Your confession will show them you value them and desire peace and love with them.

A man I know had not talked to his mother for over 10 years. The pain of her abuse to him fueled his sense of justice. He had even returned cards she sent to his young son. And then God touched him. He wrote her a letter of apology and forgiveness. And today that relationship is healing—to the glory of God.

Love Your Brothers and Sisters

> *"Better a dry crust with peace and quiet than a house full of feasting, with strife" (Proverbs 17:1).*

My brother Doug and I had our times of strife growing up. We never hit each other, but we certainly aggravated one another, especially with our words. I remember one time when he borrowed my scissors for the hundredth time (at least that's how it felt!) without asking and without returning them. I was so upset that I dumped his desk drawer out on his bed. Neither of us had the tools then to deal with our hearts, so we could be best friends one moment in the backyard running complicated football pass patterns, and the next we could be slinging words around like daggers. (Today we're just great friends!)

Of course, sibling conflict isn't new. The first sibling relationship on earth, Cain and Abel, ended up in a murder. Jacob and Esau spent many years hating each other (sadly fueled by their mother). And King David's sons were a mess, with Absalom trying to take the throne from his father and Solomon killing his brother Adonijah.

Okay, so it's not quite that bad in your family! But since Jesus says that anger in our heart is just as sinful as murder, we're not off the hook so easily. Often some deep wound inflicted by a sibling or some personality difference keeps brothers and sisters apart. So it's easy to rationalize in later years, "They haven't tried to contact me so why should I try to contact them?"

Cathy and I would often tell our teenage sons that the way they treated their sister would likely be the way they would treat their future wives someday. Overall, they did a pretty good job and so did she and they are close adult friends today. But love and respect among siblings doesn't usually come naturally. It takes work—even into adult years.

Those who follow Jesus and live for the glory of God will need to do some serious self-examination about the way they treat their brothers and sisters. They'll probably have to face some serious pride and self-centeredness that will need to be repented of, and they'll need to pursue the process of change, particularly regarding love.

Marriage: The Relationship Most Destined for Glory (and Often Most Distant From God)

And now we come to that most intimate of all relationships on the face of the earth—marriage. Here, in this voluntary union formed by vows of love before God and witnesses, we would expect to see great things. Instead, there is often great disillusionment.

Part of this disillusionment is fed by the romanticism of movies, novels, and music, which often describe marriage in idealistic terms. Cathy confesses to being a victim of this in her teen years, and it made it more difficult for her to handle her nagging disappointment that I wasn't her knight in shining armor. A great friend—but no knight! It nagged her all the way to her wedding day.

Another contributor to marital letdown is passion—feelings of being in love and the power of the sex drive. When these ideals begin to fade, couples realize that having a sustained, intimate, mutually enjoyable male/female relationship can be more illusive than first imagined.

We shouldn't be surprised when we think about it. The home environment is often the place where we feel we can just kick back and be ourselves. The problem, of course, is that our spouse is often thinking the same thing, which means that two self-centered people are living together, sharing money, kitchens, schedules, property, parents, a bed, and often children together. Sounds like a recipe for disaster!

Add to this our culture's preoccupation with pleasure, personal fulfillment, and rights and marriage becomes a very mutually self-centered and fragile relationship. Divorce numbers in the church at large bear this out. And those numbers don't even account for the many couples who live together in quiet (or not so quiet) pain and sadness or those couples who feel that their marriage is at least better than most and that's about as good as they can expect.

The very relationship that's supposed to express vows of love is the relationship that's often the most self-centered. "I would never speak to my boss like I speak to my wife," a man confesses. Ditto for the wife.

So why have Christians come to expect so much of marriage at the wedding and so little of marriage years later? The answer is often that both have taken their cues from sources other than God. The romantic idealism of the early years as well as the self-centered pessimism of the following years are both the result of expectations that have been wrenched from the life found in God. Instead of hearts satisfied in Him and a relationship in His Son, satisfaction is pursued in their partner. The results have not only been damaging to marriage but damaging to God's glory here on earth.

I recently went to a wedding where the well-intentioned groom made an impassioned pledge to his bride to "meet your needs." I winced. I hoped she wasn't going to hold him to it! Not only would he never be able to deliver on his promise (and God never meant him to deliver!) but if his wife did expect him to make good on it, she would be making him an idol—a substitute for God.

Donald Miller, in his book *Blue Like Jazz*, describes a conversation he had with a newly married friend. Don asked him if he was happy.

"I am very happy. . . But it isn't what I thought it would be. I thought to be married was to be known. And it is . . . but Danielle can only know me so much . . . Marriage is the most beautiful thing I have ever dreamed of, Don, but it isn't everything. . . I never thought after I got married there would still be something lacking. I always thought marriage, especially after I first met Danielle, would be the ultimate fulfillment. . . . But there are places in our lives that only God can go."[1]

He's right. And it was God's plan all along. Gary Thomas points to this vacuum of spirituality in marriage in his book, *Sacred Marriage*, "Christian spirituality has undeniably been focused on celibacy and a solitary pursuit of God. This emphasis needs to change."[2] Spouses need to hear God say, "Find life in me. Yes, sometimes I will use your spouse to bless you, but he or she has never been my only channel into your heart. I have many springs for you to drink from."

Recently, during a time of feeling distant from Cathy, it became clear to me that if my desire to be made happy by her is stronger than my desire to be made happy by God, I will *resent* feelings of disappointment with her because I'll blame her for my emotional condition. But, if I desire happiness in God above all, then I will *use* these feelings of distance to drive me *to* Him— *coming*, *becoming*, then *loving* (her!) through Him.

The Glory of God in Marriage's Design

According to Genesis, a relational God made two human beings "in his own image." Yet, they are slightly different, implying that God's glory is most clearly seen in the way they relate to each other. The prophet Malachi takes this further:

> "Has not the LORD made them one? In flesh and spirit they are his. And why one? Because he was seeking godly off-spring. So guard yourself in your spirit, and do not break faith with the wife of your youth" (Malachi 2:15).

Here, the purpose of being made one as husband and wife, in both body and in spirit, is that God is seeking "godly offspring"—people who by their *marital unity* reflect their *spiritual unity* with Him. Marriage is to point us, as couples, to our relationship with God.

Also, in Ephesians 5:23-33 Paul says our husband/wife relationship is to mirror the Christ/church relationship, the essence of which is mutual love, where the husband *initiates* love and the wife demonstrates *responsive* love. This description is not the only way husbands and wives are to relate (see the mutual submission of Ephesians 5:21), but it *is* to be part of the God-reality we know and show.

Cathy and I took a clue from this at our engagement over 30 years ago when we had "Psalm 34:3" inscribed in the inside of our wedding bands, which is, "Glorify the Lord with me; let us exalt his name together." God is up to more in marriage than social partnership and propagating the species. He's passionate about His glory!

A Spirituality for Marriage

"Whatever you do . . . do it all for the glory of God." Who can doubt that marriage is a significant part of the "whatever?" Christian couples must embrace this conviction not only as a couple, but as *individuals* who make up the couple. In other words, though God wants to be glorified in our *mutual* experience of marriage (when both partners are pursuing God together), God also wants to be glorified in our *individual* experience in marriage (which isn't dependent on how spiritual or godly a spouse is). The reality is that you and I can glorify God independently of what our spouse does or doesn't do.

As I shared this at a marriage retreat Cathy and I led, one woman confessed, "I've been frustrated that my husband isn't the spiritual leader I want him to be and I've blamed him for part of my deficient walk with God. Now I see that I'm able to glorify God even if he doesn't lead like I want him to. This is really freeing."

Or think about this advice from Jesus:

> *"If anyone comes to me and does not hate his father and mother, his* wife [emphasis mine] *and children, his brothers and sisters—yes, even his own life—he cannot be my disciple" (Luke 14:26).*

When was the last time you heard *that* verse from a marriage speaker? Of course, Jesus isn't telling us to literally hate our spouses. This isn't a call to love our spouses less, but to love Christ more. He is our first priority of love—in pleasing Him, having affection for Him, doing His will. Yes, there may be times when this means making decisions that will disappoint a spouse, but for the most part it will mean being transformed by Christ's love to be able to love our spouses even better. This is biblical marriage counseling at its best. It not only means placing God first in our own hearts, but encouraging our spouses to love God more than *us*.

Here are some implications of a God-centered marriage:

A God-Centered Husband or Wife Will Become Spiritually Mature, Especially in Love. Marriages are ideal settings in which to find God and be changed to be like Jesus. I'm regularly humbled before God in my marriage as my pride and self-centeredness are exposed. When Cathy makes a critical comment about my driving (always uncalled for, of course!), or when she comes home with a hairstyle that takes my breath away (not in a good way), my heart has often wanted to say words that have no basis in God and no basis in love. The process of surrender, insight, repentance and grace is a recurring path I walk because my overall goal in life is about my joy in God, not her (though I do desire and find much joy in her)!

If I pursue God (through this *come, become,* and *love* trilogy), I will be equipped to love my spouse more fully. I will wash dishes without being asked. I will affirm her strengths. I won't need to show her more efficient procedures in the kitchen or jump on her when she "drives" from the passenger seat. I will, as Jesus taught, wash her feet.

It goes the other way, too. When we love our spouse, God promises us His grace:

> *"Husbands, in the same way be considerate as you live with your wives, and treat them with respect as the weaker partner and as heirs with you of the gracious gift of life, so that nothing will hinder your prayers" (1 Peter 3:7).*

The bottom line is that loving God enables us to love our spouses more fully, and as we love our spouses, God responds with love to us. God-centered marriages make us holy.

A God-Centered Husband or Wife Will Resist Divorce. It follows, then, that this kind of person will resist divorce. Sadly, not all matters are in a given person's control, so he or she may not always be able to *prevent* divorce, but the follower of Jesus will resist it with all the energy available. Why? Because it hurts children. It's financially costly. It makes for awkward, extended family relationships in the future. But more than that, divorce means at least one partner has allowed self-centeredness to win in their heart—the loser was love. It means vows have been broken, and God's glory has been dimmed on earth.

But the follower of Jesus doesn't approach marriage like the world does. He or she knows that in this world "you will have trouble," that a happy marriage is not a guarantee in this life, and that our sacrificial love will not always be returned.

The disciple of Jesus also embraces God's perspective on divorce:

"I hate divorce," says the LORD God of Israel, . . . "So guard yourself in your spirit, and do not break faith" (Malachi 2:16).

Yes, God does give exceptions and allows marriage vows to be broken in certain situations, but his heart is always for the permanence of marriage as seen in Matthew 19:4-9. As far as it depends on us, we should pursue peace and love in our marriages, found not by withdrawing from the marriage but from knowing a God who can bring light into the darkest night.

A God-Centered Husband and Wife Will be a Light to Their Children.
Children raised in these homes (even if *one* spouse surrenders to the glorious rule of God) will see a great and desirable God. When children see God-reflecting parents they will be drawn to God's light (Isaiah 60:1-3) and will "taste and see that the Lord is good" (Psalm 34:8).

When husbands and wives are more passionate about God and His life in them than they are about sports, home decorating, entertainment, and having a standard of living that forces them to work excessive hours with little energy left for quiet reflection and meeting with God, then an entirely new spirit will pervade their homes. God will be in their midst.

A God-Centered Husband or Wife Softens Demands to Humble Desires.
We've already addressed this matter of needs and demands in Chapter 4, but it warrants a brief revisit here. There are two major tendencies in marriage—to demand or to detach. Demanding spouses place great expectations upon their spouses to meet their needs, and if these needs aren't substantially met, they'll complain, attack, or leverage ("If you don't... I won't...") until they see some results.

Other spouses detach. They're more passive and make few demands on their spouses, often because they don't feel they need their spouses for much, or because they've given up hope of getting what they want from them. So they pull away. It's safer that way, and they learn to find other outlets for their needs, which may either be beneficial (work, children, reading) or harmful (drinking, pornography, drugs).

God's solution is neither demanding nor detaching, but contented desires that are *humbly requested.* In other words, it's true that we may need our spouse to love us in certain ways in order to have an intimate, mutually-fulfilling marriage, but this, in itself, is not a basic need. It, too, must be only a desire. But—we *can* ask for it. We can ask for a certain cleanliness standard around the house, or a different sexual experience, or particular spending patterns.

Humble requests give our mate the opportunity to change and to show *specific* love. They don't erupt out of simmering frustration; they're delivered when our hearts are reasonably satisfied in God so that our spouse is free to choose to love or not. They are essentially *invitations* to love, spoken with the other's best interests in mind as well as our own (Philippians 2:4). We can ask. But if we're denied (either by outright refusal or by poor implementation), we will still fix our eyes on Jesus, and we will *still love.* As Larry Crabb says, in his spiritually enriching book, *The Marriage Builder,* "It is now possible for me to give to others out of my fullness rather than needing to receive from others out of my emptiness."[3]

Regular Practices of God-Glorifying Husbands and Wives

Consider these practices of husbands and wives who grasp these realities:

• Christian husbands and wives will find the balance between *overlooking* each other's sins and faults in love, and *addressing* them in love so that change might take place. Both are loving and marriages need both—with a heavy weight given to the grace of overlooking.

• Christian husbands and wives will frequently say, "I'm sorry" to their spouses. Wives, especially, have told me that they can't remember the last time their husbands have said those two words to them. That's a sign of a self-centered approach to marriage, not a God-centered one.

• Christian husbands and wives will let love teach them how to communicate well. Our culture speaks about "communication problems" and rightfully so. Serious breakdowns have occurred in the way couples speak and listen to each other. But, let's face it, Jesus wouldn't have talked about "communication problems." He would have talked about a *love* problem. When couples learn to *talk* with love-motives and *listen* with love-motives, they won't need to rely so much on techniques to communicate better. They'll lay their speech and words down at the Cross. (Ephesians 4:29).

• Christian husbands and wives will see sex as both an expression of their unity, and as a mutual dance formed by their *becoming* and *loving*. Proverbs 5 speaks in quite graphic terms about sexual love and summarizes it this way: "May your fountain be blessed, and may you rejoice in the wife of your youth." And the apostle Paul says,

"The wife's body does not belong to her alone but also to her husband. In the same way, the husband's body does not belong to him alone but also to his wife" (*1 Corinthians 7:4*).

I often smile at this "dance" of physical love, because both share ownership of one another's bodies. This creates a playful tension between mutual desire and surrender that places both persons in charge of what happens, with no one person in total control. Desires will be brought to God to be molded in love, while still acknowledging what can often be very strong sexual passions and preferences. And these can be quite different from one marriage to another.

The Bible describes this physical union as something that both *demonstrates* our soul-unity of one flesh as well as something that *encourages* our soul-unity when it may be faltering. It also *celebrates* the joy of sex, though it certainly doesn't treat it as the center of the relationship, nor does it elevate it to the place of worship that the American culture does.

• Christian husbands and wives will be partners together in life, living as teammates to accomplish their individual and joint assignments given by God. The concept of partnership is mentioned in Genesis 1:28, and Malachi 2:13-14 reveals God's displeasure towards broken faith with a partner. Each partner is to assist each other in using their abilities, temperaments, and time for the purposes of God, sometimes together and sometimes supporting one another to pursue each other's strengths.

A Vision Worth Pursuing

Mark was relatively new at our church and one day he called to ask for an appointment. His marriage of five years was on the verge of collapse. It was his second marriage and his wife Leta's fifth. Leta was ready to call it quits, mostly because of his anger and her suspicions of pornography. Mark wanted the marriage to work, so he came to get help—and for the first time confessed his twenty-plus year addiction to porn. Leta wasn't sure she even wanted the marriage to work. "I care about him, but I certainly don't love him, let alone like him." Her trust in him was shattered.

But Mark was broken. He took responsibility for his sins, and after a number of weeks meeting with me for counseling (surrendering, gaining insight, repenting, and receiving God's grace), a shift occurred in his heart. God became his ruler and lover. And his changed life began to soften Leta's hardened heart. The anger stopped. The arguments began to cease. Mutual respect returned. The pornography was repented of. Eventually Leta, too, made a full surrender of her heart to God (at times kicking and screaming because she knew the drastic changes God would want to do in her life as well!) Over the past several years, not only has God renewed their marriage, he has made it better than it ever was.

Do you recall the eight beatitudes of the kingdom of God in Matthew 5 that I paraphrased in Chapter 1? Consider what they look like in your marriage: Who do you *need* more—God or your spouse? Do your losses of emotional closeness, love, or respect make you *hungry for God*—or withdrawn and bitter? Do you humbly surrender to God's will for you in your marriage and *treasure His ways*—or do you listen more to friends who just want you "happy?" Do you *reach out* to your spouse when he/she is hurting—or try to fix him/her for your own emotional sake? Do you have a *pure heart*—or do you manipulate and use him/her for your own purposes? Do you *work for peace* and resolution of conflict—or do you withdraw or aggravate the situation? Do you *accept suffering* for doing what is right—or do you take the easy path and run from it?

This is God's vision for your marriage, and the person who lives this way is blessed—as well as anyone who lives with this person! May God's vision become your passion.

Parenting: Giving Our Children an Experience of God's Greatness

"Children are a gift from God." But there are days when we wish He'd take them back for awhile! I kept an irregular journal during our early parenting years, and one entry when Katie was six years old is typical: "Last night was very tearful (for Katie) and stressful (for Cathy and me). Katie had a long string of disrespectful statements to Cathy and later to me. They varied from 'I don't *want* to do arithmetic!' to 'But *why?*'" to 'That's not fair!' (Who teaches kids these things, anyway?) It culminated in 'I wish I didn't live here!' at the dinner table." Add younger, mischievous twin boys to the pot, stir it a bit, and we had some pretty spicy stew at times!

As always, the Bible gives mothers and fathers an inspiration to handle these sometimes wild and messy gifts!

> *"He* [John the Baptist] *will turn the hearts of the fathers to their children, and the hearts of the children to their fathers"*
> *(Malachi 4:6).*

> *"Her children arise and call her blessed; her husband also, and he praises her" (Proverbs 31:28).*

God's desire is that mothers and fathers will parent in such a way that compassionate love flows mutually between parent and child, resulting in eventual gratitude. How do we get there? As with everything we do, it starts in God. Kevin Huggins confesses this in his spiritually insightful book, *Parenting Adolescents*, "Our goal was to deepen love in our family. God's was to develop the kind of pure character that generates love."[4]

Needed: God-Glorifying, Self-Examining Parents

> *"He who fears the* Lord *has a secure fortress, and for his children it will be a refuge" (Proverbs 14:26).*

To fear God doesn't primarily mean to be afraid of Him (though being afraid isn't a bad thing if you happen to be ignoring Him). To fear God means to have a deep respect and awe of Him as He really is—both loving Father and holy Judge. It is to tremble at what life would be like without His love to us, and it is to have so much respect for Him that we want to please Him and delight in Him in all we do. When parents fear the Lord, we are told, their children will be protected from the attacks of the world and their foolish hearts. They will find a refuge in their home.

This requires a God-centered heart and a self-examining heart. Parents naturally would prefer to have their children change instead of changing *themselves*. But think about it. Why should we put the burden on them, given that they're still developing children and *we're the adults*? So when a shouting match happens, who's most to blame? Who will God hold most accountable? (As a side note, when God told the Israelites that all those under twenty years old would not be held responsible for their grumbling and disobedience in the desert, this should at least caution us against being too hard on our children for some of their early foolish actions!)

Becoming like Jesus is nowhere more important than in parenting, and this requires the courage and humility to take an inside look regarding our parenting responses. All too often our agendas are motivated by pride (Don't embarrass me in public! Don't argue with me!), power (I'm the boss! I must win!), or personal peace (I have a right to peace and quiet!). When parents see their own heart-sins and faulty thinking, they will be able to love their children with more pure hearts, and they will also have more compassion for their children's sin struggles as well.

Parent, You're Responsible!

Parent, you are significantly responsible for how your children turn out. (I say significantly because Ezekiel 18 says that good parents can have rebellious children and the parents aren't always to blame.) Proverbs 22:6 says parents can shape their behavior—but it won't happen without being intentional, especially in today's culture.

Certainly, part of this training responsibility is to *protect* our children from negative influences in the world, just as God instructed Israel when they entered the Promised Land. But even more than that, God used *teaching*. It is summarized in the "Shema," which means "hear" in Hebrew and it's the first word of Deuteronomy 6:4.

> *"Hear, O Israel: The LORD our God, the LORD is one. Love the LORD your God with all your heart and with all your soul and with all your strength. These commandments that I give you today are to be upon your hearts. Impress them on your children. Talk about them when you sit at home and when you walk along the road, when you lie down and when you get up" (Deuteronomy 6:4-7).*

We are to intentionally nurture our children's minds and hearts in the ways of God. It's a daily and deliberate duty for every parent, as Paul says in Ephesians 6:

> *"Fathers, do not exasperate your children; instead, bring them up in the training and instruction of the Lord" (Ephesians 6:4).*

We can't relinquish this responsibility for our children to daycares, schools, or even churches. It's our responsibility to raise them—especially spiritually. We may, and often should, choose to have other adults participate in the raising of our children, but God places a significant responsibility upon the parents.

And this means *both* parents, as much as possible. Both mothers and fathers should be capable of implementing all the principles in this chapter alone. Yes, together is ideal, but both need to be equipped to parent effectively. Both need to be tender. Both need to be tough. Both need to be powered by love. There's no passing the buck in godly parenting.

In Hebrews 12, God uses the metaphor of child-training to show how He trains us in the spiritual realm. We can learn a lot from this portion as parents.

Train and Nurture Your Children With Love!

Parenting is challenging work! Our children don't think like we think or feel like we feel. They have different personalities than we do (sometimes very different). They're constantly changing developmentally so that just when we think we know how to relate to them, they've changed! They're being influenced by people (for good and for bad) who can't always be controlled (including us, their parents). Their hearts are "foolish" according to Proverbs 22:15. If we add to that our busy life-styles and a marriage that may, at times, be experiencing less than God's design, parenting can be a very tough job.

In the New Testament, the word often translated "discipline" is the Greek word *paideia* which means "to instruct, often by using punishment to discourage negative behavior."[5] At its core is the principle of arriving at a specific goal. So we might say, *training* is "lovingly and respectfully directing the mind, character, attitudes, and actions of a child in God's ways, by instruction, admonishment, consequences, and example."

• *Training should be preceded by and motivated by love for the child, not self interest.* Our model is God: "the Lord disciplines those he loves" (Hebrews 12:6). To compassionately act in their best interests means we must look past the tears, past the attitudes and defiance, and past the problems at school, to see what their *real needs* are. What's good for their sense of self-worth, their emotional well-being, and their relationship with God? Love looks beneath the surface to the soul.

Children need to *feel* loved—on their terms, not just the parents'. They need to know that their Mom and Dad care about them and want to spend time with them. This may include playing together, assisting with schoolwork, giving them affirming and encouraging words and touch, and listening with understanding. Part of this love includes grace—loving them in spite of the way they act and letting them *know* we love them. They aren't in a prison or a military training camp, they're in a home where they need to know grace, not just rules and laws.

The bottom line is that a child will more likely accept a parent's overall training process when that child is confident in the parent's love for them—and that means they must *experience* love in many positive ways, including grace.

• *Training should lovingly communicate clear expectations and the correction process to them.*

> *"Our fathers disciplined us for a little while as they thought best; but God disciplines us for our good, that we may share in his holiness. No discipline seems pleasant at the time, but painful. Later on, however, it produces a harvest of righteousness and peace for those who have been trained by it"* *(Hebrews 12:10-11).*

Many parents don't know their parenting goals. At best, their goals are related to wanting their kids to have a certain amount of money, get a good job, get married, and (at worst) stay out of jail. But Christian parents must know—and communicate clearly to their children—what they want their children to become, *especially* in terms of character and their spiritual life.

What kind of goals should we have for our children? I would suggest these four as priorities: (1) A love-relationship with God, (2) Respect for authority, (3) Sensitive love for others, and (4) Wisdom that understands successful living from God's perspective. This means we will regularly tell our children "God loves you," and "Loving God brings the greatest joy." (It's important not to force our children to either receive God's love or to give Him love, especially as they move into their teen years. Therefore, the question, "What would Jesus do?" should be used carefully, especially if our children are not clearly His willful followers.)

We will teach them to evaluate their actions by asking questions like, "Is it respectful?"and "Is it loving?" and "Is it wise?" Each of these involve shaping both their heart (desires) and mind (beliefs)—not just their behavior—recognizing that the heart is the "wellspring of life" (Proverbs 4:23).

Two parenting extremes are common in training children: *ignoring* their failures (being overly accepting) and *harping* on their failures (being overly critical). God's instructions for misbehaving children include a balanced approach that reflects both His holiness and His grace.

(1) Wise Instruction. Our children need to know what is right, what is wrong, *and why*. They especially need to know that these goals are *for their good*, which means we must explain why our rules (and God's!) are so beneficial to them and to others. This can be challenging at times. I remember my sons questioning our house rule about not wearing hats at the dinner table. In the ensuing discussion, I had no other arguments than "that's the way I was raised and it's the way I like to be shown respect"—not particularly attractive arguments for a youth! I could have played my "father" card and insisted on my way as a matter of principle, but eventually (it took me awhile) I chose to play the "humble servant of Jesus" card and I yielded to their preferences.

Our children should be clearly told what is expected of them (like "Respect your parents," "Be loving to others," "Be in bed by 8:30," "Clean your room every Saturday morning before you eat") and why it's in their best interest. These expectations should be made clear at the beginning of the training process, but they will often need to be re-communicated when misbehavior occurs.

(2) Gracious Overlooking. Part of the training and nurturing process will include overlooking their sin in particular instances.

> *"A man's wisdom gives him patience; it is to his glory to overlook an offense" (Proverbs 19:11).*

We may see a child's misbehavior or sin, but because of our "patience"—and so that our children experience grace from us and not just judgment—we won't always call attention to it. (After all, we wouldn't want all *our* sins pointed out to us every day!) In fact, it's good for our children to sometimes *know* we see their sin yet not call them on it, assuming our faces communicate loving acceptance and not disapproval or rejection. In this way our children can actually *experience* grace.

Obviously, it's not a loving thing to overlook their repeated patterns of sin or misbehavior. But for the sake of grace, and in order to train our own heart not to be overly critical, particular instances should sometimes be overlooked.

(3) Gentle Correction. When our children misbehave, they often need to be corrected, especially if a particular negative behavior pattern needs to be addressed consistently. But the most important word here is "gentle." We had our kids memorize this passage with us when they were young because we all needed to be more gentle in our reactions "A gentle answer turns away wrath, but a harsh word stirs up anger" (Proverbs 15:1). When a child is caught in sin, we "should restore him gently" (Galatians 6:1) and do it in ways that don't frustrate them (Ephesians 6:4). Gentleness refers to the words we use and especially to the tone of our voice. If we scold or yell or use harsh words, we're correcting without gentleness. This makes them feel unloved, which results in their hearts resisting our training and making their behavior even more difficult to shape.

(4) Appropriate Consequences. When repeated use of wise instruction, gracious overlooking, and gentle correction fail to correct behavior (which, by the way, should correct *most* misbehavior when coupled with heart-touching love), then consequences must be introduced. The next section elaborates on this training element.

• *Training should develop a clear discipline strategy of loving consequences.* Before I go any further, know this: consequences given with anger will usually not motivate a child's heart to change. At most, they *may* bring positive behavioral change, but the damage to the spirit is often severe and far-reaching into the future. I believe there are times when *controlled right-eous* anger can be helpful to communicate to the child how deeply a child's misbehavior affects the parent and when expressed *lovingly* and *sparingly* it can help bring the child to repentance. But it isn't always easy to control and the norm must be gentleness.

I'm ashamed of some of my own failures here as a young father. Though my parenting journal shows I was aware of my self-centeredness, I didn't fully realize the degree of training my heart and mind needed to undergo so that I could react to my twin sons' mischievous ways and my daughter's emotions in a peaceful and loving manner. Today I understand more fully how *child*-training is even more a process of *self*-training for a heart satisfied in God. *Angry* parenting is a sign of *misplaced affections*—wanting joy more from my children's response to me than from God.

The parenting guidance in this chapter flows from how God treats us and how law and grace are balanced in His dealings with us. In light of this, it must always be our desire that our children will want to please us *more out of love than out of fear.* However, fear of some negative consequences will often be needed, especially in the earlier years.

Thus, when the above three tools don't produce sufficient change in our children, we'll need to move to the stage of "Appropriate Consequences." This will often (though not always) involve an "If ____, then ___" statement. This motivational structure is used by God with us in Deuteronomy 28:1, 15; 30:15-20, and Matthew 6:14-15 and is appropriate for parenting as well.

(1) Select appropriate consequences that will help the child towards true repentance. Consequences are not primarily designed to punish our children, but to train their hearts and behaviors! Whatever we choose as a consequence, it should facilitate this goal and not just give them a negative experience. We want to teach them to do good—not just make them feel bad for doing wrong. Here are four types of consequences to consider.

Instructional Disciplines. These are responses to misbehavior that usually don't come in an "If/then" warning form but are used immediately after a mis-behavior. If delivered in an angry tone, they can feel like spontaneous punish-ments, but if delivered in gentleness and love, they can be an effective train-ing tool. For example, after a child repeatedly speaks disrespectfully to you, tell them to write a positive statement on paper ten times like, "I will speak respectfully to my parents because a submissive spirit is valuable to God and my life." A positive time-out is another option. (This has been developed by my friends Scott Turansky and Joanne Miller in their book *Home Improvement*, where they call it "take a break."[6]) It's like a normal time-out with two major exceptions: (1) The child is sent to an isolated place but may leave when they are repentant. (2) They must return to the parent after this self-reflection and repentance, stating three things: What they did wrong, why it was wrong, and what they will seek to do next time. Initially, they will probably not know some of these answers (especially the "why") but you as a parent will teach them and when they can say it back to you, they're done! These teach a positive conclusion which is helpful for training them (wise instruction) and the whole process clearly communicates your love to them.

Rewards. This is a prewarned "if/then" statement about the *positive* behavior we want to see and it *rewards* children for it. (God uses rewards with us—for example He promises it will "go well with us" if we honor our parents.) The benefits of this are that it trains our children to actually *do* what we desire ("If you go to bed when you're told without complaining for one straight week, then we'll buy your favorite dessert"). It's a positive experience for all, and it shows the child she *can* do it! The danger is that if it's used too much, the child isn't learning to do the good for the value of the good or out of respect for the parents. Used sparingly, it can be a helpful training tool.

Negative Experiences. "If you aren't in your bed in 5 minutes, there will be no computer games tomorrow." "If you fail to turn in your math homework again, you'll be grounded for the following two weekends." The key here is appropriate consequences. Possibilities include withholding desired things (privileges, TV, computer, phone, etc.) as well as inflicting undesired things (early to bed, extra chore, etc.). Equally important is gentleness in both the warning and the carrying out of these experiences.

An "Ultimate" Consequence. *Most* behaviors can be significantly modified with wise instruction, gentle correction, and the varied consequences outlined above if surrounded by love. If a defiant, rebellious spirit persists, the parent needs something that is used as an ultimate threat—something that hopefully they don't have to use very often but is used occasionally and brings enough fear into a child that they will conform at the mere mention of it. Each parent must determine what this is for each child at each level of development, and it's wise to find the threat that is the least violent (for the child's sake and yours). If you find that you must use spanking as that threat, I would suggest *one* firm stroke with a *flat object* (a ping pong paddle works fine) in such a way that pain is significantly inflicted. Comfort them if there is a repentant spirit; otherwise, leave them alone until they are ready to receive your love.

I had the privilege of helping a frazzled mother in our church gain control over her defiant three-year-old recently (sort of a "pastor/nanny to the rescue!"). It was through teaching the loving training process outlined above that she has gained greater control and respect, and love has grown between them.

Two final words about selecting the right consequence. First, it's often a good idea to run them by your kids to see if *they* think they're reasonable. This doesn't mean they have veto power over you, but it does mean you're seeking to enlist their participation in this process, and the more your children participate in the process of their change, the more they will accept it. When you invite your child into the process of identifying expectations and consequences, you are inviting your child into wisdom and respect. One more thing: if you realize you gave an inappropriate or a too-harsh consequence, *be humble enough to undo it*! God and your kids will honor you for it.

(2) Explain the consequences in advance, allowing them the opportunity to change. This is another commonly violated biblical child-raising principle. Think about it: would *you* like surprise punishments without warnings sprung on *you*? Surprise punishments are usually more emotional than wise, and they usually aren't constructive. They can also make for bitter children.

When you feel you need more than repeated wise instruction and gentle correction, give them a chance to change—with a gentle "if/then" statement. If they heed it, it's a win/win situation. You get the behavior you want (and hopefully *they* want) and they get to avoid the consequence!

(3) Negative consequences must be followed-through consistently. Children benefit from (and appreciate) consistency. Be careful not to train your children to respond to you only after the 3rd or 4th time, or only to a raised voice! Use the "if/then..." statement wisely, then consistently follow through if they don't correct their behavior. And do it with gentleness and love! (Appendix F is a "Parenting Self-Evaluation" to help you evaluate your parenting style in light of this chapter.)

Keep God's "big picture" desires for your family in clear view at all times.

It's so easy to get bogged down in the world of diapers, bedtime struggles, and school problems. Sometimes the word *survival* can be more on our minds than "the glory of God!" But, as we've seen, it's in the trials that God's glory is most clearly known and shown. The *coming, becoming,* and *love* process outlined in this book provides you with tools to be the best parent you can be in the midst of these trials.

These things are important because we don't just want to raise obedient children, we want them to be our friends as much as possible, so that we can laugh together, cry together, enjoy life together, and one day have the joy of seeing our children as spiritual brothers and sisters who follow Jesus with us.

Ultimately, we can't control our children's hearts. The best we can do is shape them and guide them. God and they must play their parts as well. Hey, *we're* still growing spiritually, so it shouldn't be too hard to free our children to grow, too.

I would say the two most common mistakes I see among Christian parents are their failure to *take time to train* and their failure to *submit their hearts to God's glory*. Effective, godly parenting will not happen if we see our children as inconveniences or interruptions to our daily agendas. Training will take time and effort. This process of training will likely take a few more minutes out of your day, but it will be the best investment you will ever make.

It will, inevitably, drive you to your need for God—who is the real longing of your soul (not your kids)! When parents fail to keep their priority the kingdom of God within them, they will easily drift and fail to allow God to be all He wants in their children *and in them!* As has been said, values are often more "caught than taught" by our children, which means *the model we live before them*—as individual parents and in our marriage—will be the *most powerful child-training* of all.

It will be caught when we apologize to our children when we sin against them through anger, disrespect, or neglect. It will be caught when our children see a peace in our hearts that comes from God—and certainly not from them! In the end our children will be *attracted* to God—not just steered to God!

John and Rose Marie Miller were heavily involved in Christian leadership and ministry and their children embraced it. But when their 18-year-old daughter, with eyes blazing, shouted at them, "Mom, Dad, I don't want your rules and morals. I don't want to act like a Christian anymore! And I'm not going to!" it shocked them.

Barbara had been a model Christian daughter. She had led several people to Christ as a teenager, she had boldly stood against drug use around her peers, and she had witnessed to the life-changing power of Christ in her life. But now she wanted fun and freedom, not rules.

John later realized that he and his wife had not helped their daughter examine her inner life of thoughts, desires, and motivations. They had seen signs of her lying and deceiving, her sensuality, her excuse-making, and blame-shifting (it was *always* someone else's fault) but, at most, they occasionally addressed her behavior, not her heart. He says, "We avoided the conflict that would have occurred if we had asked Barbara more probing questions about her values and motivations, what you might call her real wants."[7]

One of the most sobering moments for John came several years after her departure from Christ when he realized that Barbara needed to hear him confess his failures as a father to her. In Barbara's words, "I had rarely seen my father admit that he had done anything wrong. In our family, he mainly worked with us until we confessed *our* sins. That was what I had against him."

Finally, after several years into her third marriage, Barbara's resistance to Jesus melted. It was the result of enduring, unconditional love by her parents and her parents' church that made it possible. It was hearing her mother confess some personal sin that Barbara identified with personally that opened the door the whole way. In Barbara's words, "As I read about Jesus, I was overcome by his love for people. I would sit in my kitchen reading the Bible with tears streaming down my face. . . . I finally saw myself as a completely self-centered person. . . .I could tell God I was sorry and be forgiven. . . I realized that whether I wanted to or not, I did believe in Jesus and had to follow him."[8]

It's Never Too Late

It's never too late to honor your parents, even if they are miles from you or have passed away. It's never too late to get something right with a brother or sister. It's never too late to get a marriage back on track (and even divorce doesn't stop relational reconciliation). And it's never too late to love your kids—whatever their age—the way Jesus loves.

It's never too late because it's never too late to glorify God in your life. "Ichabod" can become "kabod"—experientially and to the people who see you in your family setting. Even if it means confession. Even if it means making some drastic changes. God's work in you is as fresh as the new day. It always begins in great hope—*right now!*

For Self-Reflection and Life Application

1. Think about the common reasons why families are experiencing such stress and crisis these days. To what extent do you believe the cause behind each is a lack of God-centeredness in the home. (Consider them one at a time.)?

2. What, if anything, has made it difficult for you to honor your parents? In light of this section, what is something you believe you should do to honor your parents more?

3. Reflect on your attitude towards any of your brothers and sisters (or inlaws). How (and why) might God want to glorify Himself more through your love towards them?

4. Discuss this concept of marital satisfaction. When might we expect too much from marriage, and when might we expect too little from God (through sources other than our mate)?

5. Which of the three "A God-Centered Husband or Wife Will . . ." sections speaks most to you and why?

6. God calls marriages to "regular God-glorifying practices." In that section of the chapter, what is God saying to you?

7. If you are a parent, take some time for self-reflection. What motives do you see that can block the purposes of God in the way you sometimes parent? (The chapter mentions pride, power, and personal peace, but don't be limited by these.)

8. Reflect on the challenges and importance of your God-given responsibility to protect and instruct your children. Also, how are you implementing the "Shema?"

9. What insights about training and nurturing children speak most strongly to you (whether your children are young or adults), and what step(s) would be wise for you to take to shape your training to be more constructive and like God?

10. Reflect on the two common mistakes seen among Christian parents (failure to take time to train and failure to submit their hearts to God's glory) shared at the close of the chapter. Do you see yourself in either of these? If so, what will you do to change?

11. If you realize you've made some significant parenting mistakes, what does God want you to do about them now?

---

[1] Donald Miller, *Blue Like Jazz,* Thomas Nelson Publishers, Nashville, 2003, p. 145-6.

[2] Gary Thomas, *Sacred Marriage,* Zondervan Publishing, Grand Rapids, 2000, p. 267.

[3] Larry Crabb, *The Marriage Builder*, Zondervan Publishing, Grand Rapids, 1982, p. 57.

[4] Kevin Huggins, *Parenting Adolescents,* Navpress, Colorado Springs, 1989, p. 20.

[5] This word appears in parenting texts like Hebrews 12:5-7 and Ephesians 6:4, as well as 2 Timothy 3:16, where Scripture is said to "train" us in righteousness.

[6] Scott Turansky, Joanne Miller, *Eight Tools for Effective Parenting*, Cook Communications Ministries, Colorado Springs, p. 53.

[7] C. John Miller and Barbara Miller Juliani, *Come Back, Barbara*, 2nd Edition, P&R Publishing, Phillipsburg, 1997, p. 29.

[8] Ibid., p. 145-6.

Chapter 11

Work and Money—Using Our Resources for the Glory of God

"Done!" he exclaimed. A smile formed on the man's face as he surveyed the intricate carvings in the wooden candlestick holders he'd been working on. They should look very nice in someone's living room.

He loaded his finished products into an open cart, hitched his horse, and set out for the first town. Soon his thoughts turned to his family. For the last several weeks he had made it his focused goal to love them at their place of need. It had required a lot of daily time with the King to fill his heart with His values and truth, but good things were coming from it. He especially valued his trips home from work as he quietly prepared to walk through the front door with the King and face whatever disaster, moods—or blessings—were behind it.

Last night had been a difficult one.

"We need to talk," his wife had said. "About money."

What a way to ruin a great evening, he thought. She was the conservative spender, worrying about the future and always trying to find ways to cut corners. Money, to her, was security. He, on the other hand, enjoyed nice things— especially new tools for his business. (He was still struggling about whether to return an unused carving knife he had bought impulsively just before going to Kingcity.) And, unlike her, he was more carefree in his approach to life.

"We've had a year-long drought," she said, her voice rising in concern. "People aren't buying handcrafted furniture like they used to. And we're just barely making it week to week. Something has got to change!"

That was last night. He glanced in the wagon behind him. It was an assortment of low-cost bowls, spoons, candlestick holders, and small toy figures. Few of them demonstrated his skill as a woodcarver. It was a bit humbling. He had to frequently remind himself that it was for the King he carved now, not for a big sale or the praise of people.

But he knew that this conversation wasn't just about money. It was about his personality. He wasn't a salesman—he was a woodcarver. And now, as a follower of the King, he especially didn't want to put pressure on people to buy something they shouldn't. Nevertheless, he also knew he needed to be more aggressive, in a good kind of way.

As his cart approached the first town, his old nemesis stirred within him— fear. He feared disappointing his wife. He feared rejection by the people. He feared financial failure. It all seemed so overwhelming and it took several minutes before he realized that he had been ignoring the King. Soon confession and surrender and trust had done their work and he was renewed again in the King's love.

He came to the first house, took a deep breath, praised the King, and with his bag of samples in hand, walked up to the front door.

"What do you want?" a middle-aged man asked gruffly from a nearby vegetable garden.

"I'm a woodcarver," the man replied cautiously, "and I'd like to show you some samples if you'd be interested."

"I'm not interested," came the terse response.

"That's fine," the man replied, half meaning it but half disappointed, too. Yet he had determined beforehand, on instructions by the King, to love whoever lived in this house, sale or no sale. And grumpy men needed special love. So he placed his bag on the ground, and with as much love as he could muster asked, "How's your garden growing?"

What happened next would be repeated in various forms through the remainder of his day—sometimes with sales and sometimes without. The King's love would touch the people the man touched. By day's end he gave away a small fish carving to a young boy, he listened gracefully to the complaints of a hard-to-please elderly woman (which required many silent conversations with the King throughout!), he played jump rope with a group of children, and he even brought up the topic of Kingcity and the King with one young man who seemed to be looking for something in his life. "Please come again!" they would often say. And he would.

It was a good day—all in the employment of the King.

Work—Celebrating God's Creative Energy

So what words come to your mind when you hear the word "work?" "Drudgery?" "Trapped?" "Obligation?" Do you think about it as a four-letter word that shouldn't be mentioned in public?

Some people work to live (going through the motions, seeing work as a necessary evil), and others live to work (being driven, and fighting the disease of workaholism).

Consider this biblical use of the word *work*:

"By the seventh day God had finished the work he had been doing; so on the seventh day he rested from all his work. And God blessed the seventh day and made it holy, because on it he rested from all the work of creating that he had done" *(Genesis 2:2-3).*

"God saw all that he had made, and it was very good" *(Genesis 1:31).*

Now, certainly, creating the universe and the earth was not hard work for God! I doubt He had to put in extra weekends to figure out the concept of space-time continuum or use trial and error until He found just the right cells to use in the eye that would record light and color to the brain. This stuff wasn't hard—but it *was* creative.

Then He turned His creative work over to humans. God tells both Adam and Eve to oversee the earth, and He put Adam in the garden to "work it and take care of it." So we are God's caretakers of his creation, using it for the good of all.

Notice who did the first work, though. God. Work isn't the result of sin entering the world. Work existed before the Fall. In fact, Scripture implies that work will continue in heaven—see Matthew 25:23. (I know that may sound like hell to some of you, but please keep reading!)

Work reflects the image of God. It's both *creative* and it's *good*. Think about that for a bit. Everything you do creates something. Maybe it creates helpful objects, a service to others, beauty, or knowledge in someone else or yourself. Your cooking creates, your lawn mowing creates, your employment creates—even reading this book creates. So work is clearly part of the "whatever you do" that reveals the glory of God.

In the last chapter we saw how God's greatness is known and shown in the family setting. Now we look at how God is to be glorified in our work, whether that's something you get a paycheck for or not. God wants us to *come*, *become*, and *love* in the creative places of our lives. "Your work is to take what God has made and shape it and use it to make him look great."[1]

For the purposes of this chapter, we're going to generally narrow our concept of creative work to our places of employment, since that's often the most difficult sphere of work for many people, and it's where we spend much of our day's energies.

So Why Do You Work?

If I asked you why you worked (vocationally), what would you say? Consider these three biblical reasons.

• *We work to provide for basic physical needs.*

> *"For even when we were with you, we gave you this rule: "If a man will not work, he shall not eat." We hear that some among you are idle. They are not busy; they are busybodies. Such people we command and urge in the Lord Jesus Christ to settle down and earn the bread they eat"* (2 Thessalonians 3:10-12).

1 Timothy 5:8 adds that we have a responsibility to provide for our family and relatives as well. Yes, pray for daily bread—but work to get it, too! Seek first the kingdom of God and know that He will take care of your essential needs (Matthew 6:33)—but still we are to "earn the bread we eat." This is not a command to place huge vocational burdens upon ourselves in order to have all we want. It's a command to work for our basic needs.

• *We work to serve others.* Jesus tells us, "Do not labor for the food that perishes, but for the food that endures to eternal life, which the Son of Man will give you" (John 6:27). In other words, there's more to life than material necessities, as valuable as they are. There are things that last for eternity. One of those eternal things is our service to others.

So how does your work benefit others? For some the benefits are obvious. They sell cars, make stuffed bears, build houses, or teach children. People are obviously benefiting. For others, however, it may not be so obvious. Their part be a mere support role—like a security guard in a fertilizer plant or an accountant for the airlines. And the people they ultimately serve may be living thousands of miles away. But someone *is* ultimately being served, and *they* are the reasons why we work.

It follows, then, that if you can't endorse what your creative work ultimately does, then you should probably consider changing jobs. This is really about love. If your work doesn't compassionately act in the best interest of others, then it's time to consider a switch.

• *Above all, we work to serve God—knowing and showing His greatness in what we do.* The wealthy and successful King Solomon warns us that ultimately work is "a chasing after the wind; nothing was gained under the sun" until he concluded in the final chapter that we must "Fear God and keep his commandments, for this is the whole duty of man" (Ecclesiastes 2:11; 12:13).

And that's the bottom line. We can't turn off the "glorify God" switch when we enter our places of employment. Could God possibly be irrelevant to something we give 20, 40, maybe 60 hours of our life to each week?

Probably the clearest passage in all the Bible regarding this is:

> *"Slaves, obey your earthly masters in everything; and do it,*
> *not only when their eye is on you and to win their favor, but*
> *with sincerity of heart and reverence for the Lord. Whatever*
> *you do, work at it with all your heart, as working for the Lord,*
> *not for men, since you know that you will receive an inheri-*
> *tance from the Lord as a reward.* It is the Lord Christ you are
> serving" [emphasis mine] *(Colossians 3:22-24).*

Phrase after phrase in this passage hammers home the truth that work is for God. Yes, we may have a boss, an employer, or a customer that we want to please, but the bottom line is that we live for the pleasure of God, "working for the Lord."

Between the years 1983 and 1997 I pastored half-time. My primary reason for half-time church ministry was so I could relate to the "real world" vocational challenges of the people I sought to shepherd, especially the men. The job I found fit the bill—sometimes better than I wanted! For ten of those years I worked half-time as a building superintendent and handyman in a large, old, office building. (A slight shift from electrical engineering and managing a Christian bookstore, but it provided the flexible hours I desired!) The owners had gone through six superintendents in the two years before I arrived, primarily due to the owners' fiery tempers, controlling personalities, and verbal abuse.

When I interviewed with them, I told them I didn't mean them any disrespect, but I felt they should know that, as a follower of Jesus, my ultimate boss was God. They said that was fine, but over those ten years I'm sure they questioned their decision at times.

Though they were often charming, their periodic abuse became a setting for God to be glorified *in* and *through* me as I practiced the trio of *come*, *become* and *love*. I must admit, not every day was ablaze with the glory of God in me. But, even in my darkest and most desperate moments, I knew God was glorified by my simple cries of "Help!" and "I'm sorry, Lord."

I like one of the chapter titles in John Piper's book, *Don't Waste Your Life*: "Making Much of Christ from 8 to 5."[2] That's what we are to do. We show up at our jobs to make much of Christ, in what He's doing *in* us and *through* us. This isn't some automatic thing. It's a consciously chosen reality that we make—often many times a day.

Whether we're a pastor, a missionary, an assembly line worker, or a computer programmer, our work is a holy calling. We are all "full-time Christian workers" glorifying the Master Worker "with sincerity of heart and reverence for the Lord."

Glorify God in the Product (Quality) of Our Work

Each of us has been given abilities by God. They may be common or they may be very unique. They may be related to our personalities, or to our voice, or to our "left brain" or "right brain." But whatever we've got, it's there because of some fundamental gift from God. And that means we owe Him gratitude.

God once warned the Israelites, "You may say to yourself, 'My power and the strength of my hands have produced this wealth for me.' But remember the LORD your God, for it is he who gives you the ability to produce wealth" (Deuteronomy 8:17-18). So if we're able to file efficiently, manage productively, hammer accurately, or design imaginatively, we owe God a big "thank you." If we don't, our pride will undermine His glory.

So what, exactly, does it mean to produce work for the glory of God? Quality work for *people* is obvious—some boss, company, or client usually tells us what quality is supposed to look like. Some jobs may even allow us the freedom to set our own standards. But what does it mean to do quality work for *God*?

Consider the following observations as they relate to your job.

• *We all have natural limitations.* Face it. We all have physical, mental, and temperamental limitations. We can press past some of them and perhaps improve our quality of work to some degree, but often we're going to hit a natural plateau and have to settle for B+ work (or even lower) in some area rather than A+.

World class athletes sometimes tell kids that they can do anything they set their minds to—but in reality it's an empty promise for most of them. (My dreams of Major League Baseball didn't get too far past the 4th grade.) As Proverbs 12:11 says, "He who works his land will have abundant food, but he who chases fantasies lacks judgment." For every person that fulfills his or her dreams of being president of the United States or owning their own company or going to the moon, there are thousands who gave their best but came up short—often very short. In fact, the work we most excel at may not even be marketable in the sense of a paid job. This means many of us may have to settle for doing *good* and adequate work for pay (because of our limitations), but pursue *excellent* work somewhere for free! And we do both for God!

- ***We all have time limitations.*** For most people, the pursuit of excellence in their work will require significant amounts of time—and the reality is that there are only so many hours in each day. If we're going to live a balanced life with job expectations, family commitments, church involvement, meaningful friendships, and rest and relaxation to renew our spirit and body, we won't have time to pursue excellence in very many things. And for some seasons of our lives, such as parenting young children, we'll be happy just to do "B" work in everything we do!

- ***Pursue high quality in some area of work.*** In the humorous and cynical workplace cartoon, *Dilbert*, Wally is known as the guy who excels in doing as little as possible—and being proud of it! At the opposite end of the spectrum are people whose personalities drive them to excel because of pride or power or the hope of financial gain.

We, however, are lovers and followers of Jesus. We work for God, glorifying Him in the *product* of our work. So we are responsible to use the abilities He has given us, and to use them well. Of all the work we do in a typical day, it would seem wise to pursue high quality in the vocational work we do, seeing that we do it for perhaps eight hours a day and we are financially compensated for it. Especially while we are at our jobs, we must give the best we have.

But there are still many choices to make, especially for how we use "non-job" time. Too often people give their best work energy to an employer and have little left over for the work of the church, their home, or their community. We must examine the available hours we have in a day and discern how best to use them in the pursuit of quality. For example, should I use free evening hours to pursue a higher-quality work in my vocation—or should it be given to the work of repainting that door trim on my house? Should I stop reading current event magazines in order to give more time to improve my guitar playing (or golf game)—or is it better to be more well rounded at several things than pursue excellence in one? These aren't easy questions, but know this: God is honored when you create well.

So to summarize what we've seen above, we can't be excellent in everything—and that's not a bad thing. Our limitations teach us to be humble. They teach us to need others. And God delights in glorifying Himself in our weaknesses (2 Corinthians 12:9-10).

Our inability to excel in everything will inevitably disappoint some people around us. They may want a higher standard from us than what we're capable of giving—or even willing to give. When this happens, we must remember Whom we work for. It's not that we don't want to please people, but we can't be ruled by their expectations. It's the Lord God we serve first, not people.

And He's full of mercy and grace (as Hebrews 4:15-16 celebrates). He's not a taskmaster! Hallelujah!

We'll likely *produce* poor quality, mediocre quality, and good quality in *many* things, and we'll *pursue* excellence in a *few* things. And we'll do it all for the glory of God. (This is really good news for all you average people out there. You are freed, at times, to be mediocre for Jesus!)

Glorify God in the Process (Attitudes) of Our Work

Drew met Michelle on a cruise around the Hawaiian islands. He was a gospel singer from Pennsylvania and part of our church. She was a waitress—and party girl—from Kauai. Their friendship ended up in her conversion to Jesus and their eventual marriage. Now she's getting her teaching degree and working part-time as a restaurant server. As a server, Michelle has a choice—either enter into the conversations that reflect her former life (plenty of opportunities!), or reflect her God. She's chosen to reflect her God. So she helps the food prep people when her tables are caught up. She cleans off her tables (it's not her job) when she can. She listens to people share their marital struggles and pain. Michelle takes Jesus to work because He's her life—and He wants to be in her friends' lives, too.

We glorify God in the *product* of our work, but we also glorify God in the *process* of our work—the attitudes and desires we bring to our creating and relating. Gordon Dahl once wrote, "Most Americans tend to worship their work, work at their play, and play at their worship."[3] There's a lot of truth there. And something is dreadfully wrong as well. When work is worshiped, God is dethroned from the heart.

It's also true, of course, that some *play* at their work, and their hearts are seduced by pleasure or laziness and they fail to see the glory of what God wants to do through them at their jobs. The text we looked at earlier, Colossians 3:22, makes it clear that God cares about the *way* we do our work, not just *what* we do at our work. We are to work with "sincerity of heart and reverence for the Lord." So getting a promotion or pay raise isn't sufficient. God's also checking our heart.

Paul Stevens asks an interesting question, "Do you find satisfaction in your work through God, or do you find satisfaction in God through your work?"[4] I personally think both of these have merit, but Stevens appropriately elevates the latter. God must be the central figure in our lives, not us. Work is just one means to know and show His glory.

So if you discover a cure for cancer, yet are consumed with pride or fail to love your spouse or fail to give gratitude to God, your work will not impress Him. God wants your heart, not just your hands and your brain.

Next to family relationships, our jobs are one of the most powerful forces to help us find God and be changed by Him. You may go to work to produce a certain quality of *product* (and rightly so), but God is primarily interested in producing a certain quality product *in you!*

Think about it. At our work we're often tempted by power, by riches, and by people's admiration. At our work we're tempted to frustration, anger, self-condemnation, fear, isolation, and bitterness. At our work we're tempted to find our identity in what we *do* rather than who we *are*—children of God and disciples of Jesus.

The apostle Paul, in 1 Corinthians 7:24 (NRSV) says, "In whatever condition you were called, brothers and sisters, there remain with God." So God can use you no matter what you do for your vocation. That doesn't mean you can't look for a new job, but Paul's point is that any challenge you face is not too difficult for you when you are *with God*. When you are with God, life—and your job—take on a very different perspective. Consider three areas:

• *Love*

I tend to be a task-oriented person. And task-oriented people like me must constantly remind ourselves that the people around us have souls. They are around us not just to help us accomplish our work-related goals, they are there as human beings made in the image of God who have feelings, longings, and unique sensitivities—and who have their own goals as well. They may work over you, or under you, or with you, or around you, but they deserve basic respect and love.

Of course, it's not just task-oriented people who need to remember this. People-oriented people need to remember too, because they sometimes *use* people for their *own* relationship needs, rather than acting in the best interests of those with whom they're speaking. If you find yourself talking a lot about your own kids or your own problems, you, too, may need to put on love at work.

We've already seen in Chapters 6 and 7 how love is to dominate the heart of the follower of Jesus, and this includes love in and to the world. "As we have opportunity, let us do good to all people..." (Galatians 6:10) In fact, our love is so unique that it loves people who don't love *us* (Luke 6:32, 35)! Sound at all like your workplace? In a work world where the rule of the jungle is to look out for "number one," Christ-followers are to display the supernatural love of God to people who want to use us, compete with us, look better than us, and stab us in the back when it suits their purposes!

Think of it this way. You arrive at your job and there, on your desk (locker, table, clipboard, or time clock card) is a memo: "Love your neighbor." The note is signed, "Your affectionate boss, Jesus." It's the same note every day, but you know every day brings new twists and opportunities. Yes, love will have its restrictions in our productivity-driven work culture, but company policy still usually permits encouraging words, understanding reactions, respectful disagreements, and forgiving people who hurt you!

Do your coworkers see you as a loving person? Would it surprise them to know you are a disciple of Jesus—or would they say, "I'm not surprised?" Here are four checkpoints to evaluate your workplace love: (1) Do you show interest in their personal lives and family? (2) Do you show compassion for their work struggles? (3) Do you commend people when they do something well? (4) Do you show love by not speaking negatively about people who aren't in your presence?

In a competitive culture, it's tempting to exploit people for personal gain. Proverbs 22:16 says, "He who oppresses the poor to increase his wealth and he who gives gifts to the rich—both come to poverty." Jeff is one of our church elders, but one of his greatest expressions of the kingdom of God in his life is the wholesale greenhouse business he co-owns. Jeff consciously seeks to make decisions about employee's benefits with love and respect in mind, even if it cuts into company overhead. Some of his employees have wives, children, and homes in Mexico, so when the men go back to their homeland for the winter, Jeff and/or his business partner travel to Mexico to visit them in their homes. Jeff works for Jesus–and obeys that memo on his desk!

• Integrity

I define *integrity* as "always doing what is right"—regardless of the implications. It's doing what's right even when it's inconvenient, risky, or unpopular. Even when people can't see you, as Colossians 3:22 said. People of integrity walk their talk in front of one hundred or none.

When we take a job for an employer, we say "I will do a certain kind of work in return for a certain compensation package." Our commitments usually include both quality and quantity, and failure to produce these is a lack of integrity. Some people may show up late to work, abuse coffee and lunch breaks, have extended personal conversations during company time, misuse the internet, or not give full mental and emotional energy to their job. But as followers of Jesus who live for the glory of God, we will fulfill the commitment to our employer.

This, of course, doesn't mean we must do everything a boss or company says. There have been several times in my nonchurch jobs that I've had to tell a superior I was sorry, but I couldn't do what he or she wanted me to do because it violated my convictions. Most respected me for it. But it can carry a cost at times. Fortunately, our ultimate Boss has promised to take care of our needs, so it gives us courage to sometimes respectfully say "no" to human bosses.

Another common workplace integrity issue is telling the truth. I like the story Nicki Gumbel, speaker in the Alpha course, tells of a man who worked for an executive. The executive had asked the man to lie for him on the phone and the man refused. This made the executive angry, but the man calmly responded, "If I can lie *for* you, then I'm also able to lie *to* you. And I will not do either." The executive saw his point and the man was a trusted employee for many years after.

Every time we lie we're being ruled by fear and not faith and placing our trust in our own verbal cleverness to protect us rather than in God. As we saw in Chapter 5, to trust God is not to expect protection from every hardship, but it is to trust God to love us no matter what. Even if we lose our job. Even if we don't get workman's compensation. Even if we lose our health insurance and have to move to find a new job and our kids have to go to a new school and they hate it. Even if . . .(you fill in the blank). Yes, we can glorify God even then!

> *"If you suffer for doing good and you endure it, this is commendable before God" (1 Peter 2:20).*

> *"The man of integrity walks securely, but he who takes crooked paths will be found out" (Proverbs 10:9).*

So live with integrity because it flows from the heart of God. *And* live with integrity because it's the ultimate place of security. Those who *don't* do right will eventually face the music.

• Don't Complain

"Do everything without complaining or arguing" (Philippians 2:14). Not complain? Ever? It's not that we can't disagree with someone's action, or object to injustice. To not complain means seeing life from God's perspective and in God's presence and realizing that in every undesirable situation God wants to be at work in *us*!

So instead of complaining, we can emphasize gratitude for the good we have. We can accept suffering as an opportunity to draw near to God and learn His peace. We can show people around us a peace that isn't based on bosses and raises but in God's life in us. As the statement under my brother Doug's E-mail signature says, "It is better to light a candle than to curse the darkness."

Take a Break—With God

Long before the disease of workaholism was identified, people needed to take a break. And from God's perspective, it's not just the high-achiever, task-driven, type-A personality that needs to take a break. We *all* do.

   • *We need a break to restore our bodies.* I love to accomplish things. I like the sense of completing a task, whether that task is a person helped, an idea fulfilled, a garage cleaned out, or a book read. Frankly, I don't usually think I *need* a rest. As long as I have variety, I can keep producing pretty long.

So when the concept of a forced rest (a Sabbath) is suggested, my personality resists it. But I've also learned to see the wisdom of it, and I'm glad God commanded it. (Yes, it is a command, not a suggestion!)

> *"Remember the Sabbath day by keeping it holy. Six days you shall labor and do all your work, but the seventh day is a Sabbath to the LORD your God. On it you shall not do any work" (Exodus 20:8-11).*

The Sabbath is a day to cease from physical work and experience emotional, mental, and physical rest and refreshment, mirroring God's rest from His creative work of making the world. We may want rules to define what is *work* and what isn't *work*, but that's down the wrong road again. We're in a love-relationship with God, not a courtroom.

Jesus reminds us that the "Sabbath was made for man, not man for the Sabbath" (Mark 2:27), so there's some flexibility here. The bottom line is that we need a break from work to be refreshed to do quality work and godly work to the glory of God. Forced rest encourages us to appreciate daisies as much as dollars, people as much as productivity, and silence as much as success.

   • *We need a break to be restored spiritually.* Actually, this reason is not as important as the physical rest reason because we're to be continually restored in God on a *daily* basis. Texts like Colossians 2:16-17 and Hebrews 4:3, 9-11 make it clear that we are not bound by legalistic "Sabbath days" because these are all "shadows" of the reality that "is found in Christ." The real Sabbath-rest for the people of God is in a love-relationship with Him. *Every* day of the week is holy. However, the reality is that sometimes we lose our focus, and a disciplined day in seven helps us refocus and be refreshed spiritually.

When we combine the physical Sabbath with a spiritual Sabbath, there are great benefits, even if we *are* making every day holy to God. We're reminded that our identity as God's people is more important than what we *do*; we reorient our values around God's rather than a boss's, or money, or productivity, or self; and we step back to value relationships—the church, family, and friends. But key to this is a disciplined and substantial time of spiritual restoration to God. Yes, it's taking a *break* from work, but it's also drawing *near* to God and His life.

This restoration doesn't need to happen on Sunday, or a set amount of hours. It's spiritually driven, not legalistically driven. But it should be intentional, so that a "free day" doesn't become mere recreation and TV and family time with little spiritual restoration of the soul.

Expect to Meet God

I don't know if the business woman of Proverbs 31:10-31 is for real, or just an ideal woman, but she sure sets the bar high! Her product and her process speak of God's presence in her life, with her grand achievement recorded in verse 30: "Charm is deceptive, and beauty is fleeting, but a woman who fears the Lord is to be praised." A God-ward heart is what makes a work site a holy place—where God is feared in reverent awe.

God wants to meet you there, *leading* you, *supporting* you, *changing* you, and *reaching out* to others through you, all in the context of work. The darker the place, the greater the potential glory! If it helps to put a subtle (or not so subtle) reminder somewhere in your car or at your job to remind you to see your work as God sees it, do it.

Paul Stevens had taught at a rural theological school in Kenya for three years. One of his students was a woman who had hoped to be a pastor, but when she graduated, she was placed as an overseer in a boarding school with three hundred girls. It was a 24 hours a day, 7 days a week job, with little recognition and little pay. Paul asked her, "Do you like your new job?" Her answer speaks to each of us: "I like it in Jesus."[5]

Money—Tests and Resources for the Kingdom

On my first date with Cathy, I took her to a drive-in theater, and proudly packed some of my mother's homemade applesauce and some of my own iced tea. What better way to impress a girl than to be creative, personal, and thrifty? It wasn't until years later that I discovered that she wasn't impressed that night (at least not with my frugality)! In fact, my thriftiness (she called it something like "cheap") actually was one of several reasons she had doubts about marrying me.

I've lightened up over the years. I actually suggest buying ice-cream cones every now and then rather than going home to eat from the half-gallon containers! But frankly, this loosening up has only served to complicate my life more. Previously I wouldn't spend money because I was cheap—or I "couldn't afford it." Decisions were easier. Now it's not so simple.

There are many areas of life that would benefit from asking the question, "How do I glorify God in *this*?" Work is one. Money is another. There's nothing like money to test the heart. That's why Jesus speaks about it more than any other topic. You'll recall that He used it as the litmus test in Mark 10 for the rich man's response to Him. Then a few verses later, Jesus says it's harder for a rich man to enter the kingdom of heaven than a camel to go through the eye of a needle! Why is money such a problem?

The Real and Present Danger of Being Mastered by Money and Possessions

The answer, as we have seen over and over again, is a matter of the heart. It's a matter of our affections and desires, values and goals. These are the real issues we face in life. They take us down the narrow road to eternal life, or the broad road to destruction.

Jesus puts it this way:

> *"Do not store up for yourselves treasures on earth, where moth and rust destroy, and where thieves break in and steal. But store up for yourselves treasures in heaven, where moth and rust do not destroy, and where thieves do not break in and steal. For where your treasure is, there your heart will be also"* (Matthew 6:19-21).

That's a clear description of money's power. It captures our hearts. It has power, like a magnet. It lures us like honey attracts bees. Jesus hammers this concept home a few verses later, shifting the metaphor from a treasure to a master.

> *"No one can serve two masters. Either he will hate the one and love the other, or he will be devoted to the one and despise the other. You cannot serve both God and Money"* (Matthew 6:24).

Money can easily become a master—which is a problem for the follower of Jesus who has said, and continues to say, "You are Lord." Two masters can't coexist. If money and wealth and "stuff" control us, then by definition, we can't be controlled by God. Only one can rule at a time. And God isn't interested in joint ownership.

Now this isn't an easy matter for people living in North America. Money has a lot to offer. It's lure can be strong to those with weak hearts or dull minds. Jesus doesn't tell us that money is bad—it just can't be a treasure. We are to "hate money" in comparison to our love for Him. It must not have any hold on us whatsoever.

Donny came to me a few years ago for counsel. All his life he'd loved restoring cars. He gave hundreds of hours and a lot of money to his hobby. But now he was trying to figure out the place it had in his life as a follower of Jesus. One thing he knew—it had too much hold on his heart, and his wallet. Today he still restores old cars, but it's no longer a treasure in comparison to Christ.

Jesus warns us: guard your heart against the power of money. It can grab the heart of anyone—poor, middle class, and wealthy alike. No one is immune. It can subtly seduce you, with eternal consequences:

> *"People who want to get rich fall into temptation and a trap and into many foolish and harmful desires that plunge men into ruin and destruction. For* the love of money is a root of all kinds of evil *[emphasis mine]. Some people, eager for money, have wandered from the faith and pierced themselves with many griefs" (1 Timothy 6:9-10).*

Money and possessions can be like the ring in J. R. R. Tolkien's *Lord of the Rings* trilogy. As Frodo wore it week after week, carrying it to Mount Doom to the fires of Mordor, it gradually began to control him. We may think we own money, but in reality it's often owning *us*. Though money isn't evil, "the love of money is a root of all kinds of evil."

It can feed pride (Look what I have!), self-trust (My investments will take care of me) and a never-ending thirst for more and more. Psalm 62:10 warns, "...though your riches increase, do not set your heart on them." If we do, we will pierce ourselves "with many griefs," chief of which is rejecting God's caring presence and substituting it for things that fade away—a most pitiful exchange (Hebrews 13:5).

Guard your heart against the love of money. There's a lot at stake.

But Isn't Wealth a Blessing From God?

An interesting thing has happened in America. Many have come to see money not as something to guard their hearts against but as a sign of God's blessing. They use Old Testament promises to Israel and apply them to the church, even though God's promises to Israel were largely tangible (specific land, good weather, good crops, etc.), and the promises He gives to the church are distinctly spiritual. Furthermore, the promises He gave to Israel were conditional upon their obedience not just their national identity as God's people. And the word *prosperous* in the Old Testament means "more-than-enough-to-live," not "rich." It's often the translation of the word *shalom*, which means "well-being," as in Jeremiah 29:11 where God tells Israel He has "'plans to *prosper* you and not harm you, plans to give you hope and a future.'"

God's categories aren't so neat as some would have them be. Many wicked people are rich (Psalm 73:12; James 5:1-6) and many godly Christians are poor (2 Corinthians 6:10; James 2:5). In fact, when we equate wealth with God's blessings, it's easy to be blind to any unjust means or greed that may have been present to acquire it.

Certainly, wealth *can* be a blessing from God (Psalm 112:3; Proverbs 10:22), but it may *not* be. If wealth was obtained through compassion, integrity, humility, contentment, mercy, and hard work—hard work that didn't neglect one's family and spiritual life in the process—then it is likely a blessing from God. Otherwise, it's likely a snare of the devil.

Jesus teaches that we are to pray for "daily bread," reminding us that He only guarantees enough to live for each day at a time. Later He says,

> *"But seek first his kingdom and his righteousness, and all these things* [food and clothing] *will be given to you as well"* *(Matthew 6:33).*

God's physical blessings to those who follow Jesus are pretty basic—food and clothing. We also see this in His promise to those who help the poor, in that God provides "all that you need" (2 Corinthians 9:8)—not all that we want. Jesus, Himself, modeled a life of simplicity, not of wealth.

So wealth is *not* automatically a sign of God's blessing, nor is it guaranteed to the righteous. But when we have it, God holds us responsible for what we do with it.

In the next two sections we're going to consider two building blocks for a strong biblical foundation to use money for the glory of God. The first has a lot to do with what we believe; the second more with what we want.

Whose Is It, Anyway?

The words we use in life teach our soul about what we think is true. So it's hard to talk about *my* house, *my* computer, *my* bank account, and *my* children without thinking that they really are *mine*. But there's more to it.

God owns the world He created (Psalm 24:1). He also owns you by your trust in Jesus (1 Corinthians 6:19-20). So, anything you own is His on two counts! Question: How does that make you feel? Think of all your stuff (let your mind roam from living room to garage to closets to the bank) and imagine God's name stamped on each and every item (sort of like when my mother sent me off to summer camp with "Freddie Miller" name tags on all my clothes!)

If I believe God loves me and is intent on my good, if I believe that I am capable of doing some pretty foolish things with what I own, and if I believe I'm here to glorify God, then my answer is, "I'm really glad God owns my possessions!" Of course, without those convictions, the idea of losing ownership doesn't feel so good at all.

But here's a twist. In Jesus' parables about the "minas" and "talents" (both are Roman units of money), He teaches that we are actually *caretakers* of God's property—and He expects us to use it well for *His* purposes (not ours), so at any time He can say, "Well done, good and faithful servant" (Matthew 25:23). That's the first thing we must believe—that *we are managers of God's property.*

This perspective can be a bit overwhelming when you think about it. It definitely requires a mental shift (and often a heart shift as well) if we're like most people who are quite sure that the car in the driveway with the registration in their name is theirs! It's God's. One event that reveals whether we believe this or not is when we experience loss of finances or property—when stocks dip, or when we see a new scratch on our (God's) car. How do we react? Are we more upset than God is?

God gives us a challenge. Care about money enough to manage it well for Him—but don't care so much about it that our hearts are tricked into a false treasure. Pursuing the glory of God helps keep the balance.

Enough!

A number of years ago, Cathy and I visited a Christian community called the Bruderhof. (Actually, it was a surprise trip for my wife, and she thought it was going to be a romantic getaway! So when we pulled up to a couple hundred people living in big apartment buildings in the Adirondack Mountains, all dressed in nineteenth-century German clothes, it was a bit of a shock to her. Let me just say I did *not* earn any romance points that weekend—but we both did have a great experience!)

The people there were an inspiration in simple living. They had little (and needed little), but joy abounded everywhere, from the faces of little children to the smiles of older folk in their 80s. This same experience was amplified in Zambia, Africa, where poor villagers in the bush gave us a live and scrawny chicken plus a large bag of groundnuts (peanuts) when we said good-bye. They had very, very little—but were very content.

> *"But godliness with contentment is great gain. For we brought nothing into the world, and we can take nothing out of it. But if we have food and clothing, we will be content with that" (1 Timothy 6:6-8).*

"Contentment is great gain." It's *good* for us. Having enough is part of the joy-filled Christian life. Would you call yourself a contented person? Can you go to bed at night and think, I have all I need, and if I never get a raise or promotion, if I never buy another gadget, if I don't remodel anything else in my home, if I don't buy anything else other than food and clothing and health essentials for the next ten years, I'd be fine. In fact, I'd be happy in my soul.

So how does one live in a consumer culture and still be a faithful, contented follower of Christ? It starts with godliness. When our hearts are occupied with God and His ways, *coming* to Him for all His riches in the spiritual realm, and *becoming* like Christ with a heart that is content and satisfied in God—then what the world has to offer loses its luster. We may admire, but our hearts don't desire and definitely don't need to acquire!

When I pack for a trip, I consider the weather and what I'll be doing there. But where *we're* going (heaven), we can't take any of our stuff with us. In fact, how we pack actually determines where we're going. Jesus' tells us to pack light with our possessions (remember He promises food and clothing) and to pack heavy with what lasts forever—people and our good deeds.

Lynn Miller, in his book *The Power of Enough* says, "Contentment is found in knowing that what things mean has nothing to do with who you are."[6] I am not the sum of my possessions. I am, in fact, the possession of God. And that truth allows me to say, "I don't need it, I don't want it, and even though I can afford it, I'm not going to get it." One way to teach our souls contentment is to fast for a time from the things we may think we "need"—like TV, shopping, eating out, new house furnishings, etc.

I faced this a few years ago when I saw a great deal on a tool assortment at Home Depot. I could think of a number of helpful uses for this kit and I knew I could afford it and I hadn't spent much on myself recently (the reasons to buy it were coming fast)! I spent a lot of time with God in that aisle. I probably stood in front of the display rack 10 minutes, trying to discern my heart and balancing stewardship (I can use it for God) with contentment (I don't need it). In the end, feeling my spirit needed practice in contentment most, I walked away.

G. K. Chesterton said, "There are two ways to get enough. One is to accumulate more and more. The other is to need less." He's right. Money loses its power when we say "Enough. I'm drawing the line in the sand right here. I don't need what's over there." So where's your line in the sand? When is enough really enough? Proverbs 23:4 says, "Do not wear yourself out to get rich; have the wisdom to show restraint." Identifying "enough" will free us from the cycle of needing to work longer and longer hours, with less time for God, family, and people.

The Power of Money for Good

We've seen the dangers of money and the things it can buy. It's time now to see the power of money for good. Prayerfully listen to the following text; it gives us a wealth of knowledge on wealth!

> *"Command those who are rich in this present world not to be arrogant nor to put their hope in wealth, which is so uncertain, but to put their hope in God, who richly provides us with everything for our enjoyment. Command them to do good, to be rich in good deeds, and to be generous and willing to share. In this way they will lay up treasure for themselves as a firm foundation for the coming age, so that they may take hold of the life that is truly life"* (1 Timothy 6:17—19).

The first thing we see in the above text is that it's okay to be rich! The only concern raised is that wealth can tempt a person to look to it for happiness rather than to God, who "gives everything for our enjoyment"—apart from wealth.

It's not that we can't enjoy life. (Chapter 12 will affirm pleasure!) But let's face reality here. God didn't "give" you that new set of golf clubs or that new patio furniture. A bunch of people made them and you bought them. God may have made the stars and flowers and people and the 113 molecular elements on this earth, but *people* make most of what we buy. That doesn't make them bad, but neither can we say that God "gives" us everything we buy! He could get blamed for a lot of junk and sin!

So how can we use our money for the glory of God?

• *To Meet Essential Needs.* Money is first of all used to purchase food, clothing, shelter, and basic health needs. Part of that is saving for our future basic needs when we are unable to earn income. How much to save is a delicate spiritual balance between not wanting to be a burden on our children or the church and trusting God for the future so we can freely share with those in need now.

• *To Facilitate our Individual Calling.* Money can be used to support the development of our vocation or to facilitate our participation in a particular ministry we feel called to. Perhaps it's taking courses, or purchasing books, tools, and equipment to do your ministry well. Our individual calling also has financial implications to the kind of home and car we need, the DVDs we rent, the clothes we buy, the computer we get, the magazines we subscribe to, etc. When we see our work and life in the context of the glory of God, especially in loving and serving people, we will use certain purchases to facilitate those ministries.

• *To Celebrate* quality and beauty and durability. God revealed His glory through a highly crafted tabernacle and temple, using skilled craftsmen with high-quality materials (Exodus 35:35). He didn't go the simple route. Once a year He ordered a huge feast to celebrate His provisions to them, telling them, "Use the silver to buy whatever you like: cattle, sheep, wine or other fermented drink, or anything you wish. Then you and your household shall eat there in the presence of the Lord your God and rejoice" (Deuteronomy 14:26). That's quite a party!

God is glorified when we celebrate the music from a grand piano, the beauty of an oil painting (and paying the person appropriately who painted it), the handcrafted beauty of an oak cabinet, or the lasting value of a quality automobile. But, of course, in order to make sure these aren't mere self-indulgences, it would also seem wise to place some limit on these kinds of celebration purchases in our lives, lest we fail to give priority to other matters that are especially on God's heart.

• *To Share With Those in Need. This* is what we are to be rich in according to the 1 Timothy 6 text—being "generous and willing to share." Generosity means giving beyond a token (more than a few bucks in the offering plate for that world hunger offering). Giving to the poor is worship to God. It cultivates love and compassion, both to people you will never meet as well as the needy in your own church. As Randy Alcorn notes in his little book, *The Treasure Principle*, "God prospers me not to raise my standard of living, but to raise my standard of giving."[7] Living this way is truly radical in our culture—and in the church. So "see that you also excel in this grace of giving" (2 Corinthians 8:7). When you give it away, it teaches your soul you don't need it. And you'll find that it's true.

• *To Support the Work of the Church.* The church teaches and equips its people for spiritual maturity, and it proclaims the Gospel to the world. It nurtures children, rescues marriages, encourages the hurting, builds loving friendships, and offers hope to the lost. The church and its parachurch, specialty ministries at home and abroad are worthy of financial support.

On Tithing and True Treasure

People often ask, "How much should I give away to God's work?" (In reality some are thinking, How little can I give away to please God so I can have as much left over as possible to spend on myself?) In answering this question, we must remember that *all* we have is God's, and all our life choices—including how we spend money—are submitted joyfully to Him.

Jesus once mentioned that the tithe (ten percent of one's income) was a good thing for the Jews of His day, but beyond that there's no instructive mention of it in the rest of the New Testament. But much *is* said about giving. Our giving is to be voluntary, generous, loving, proportionate to our income, and joyful (2 Corinthians 8 and 9). This is more in keeping God's disinterest with rules and His passion for a Spirit-filled heart that lives for His glory in all our affairs.

But for those just learning the life of the kingdom, a disciplined amount off the top has wisdom to it, and ten percent is a good place to begin. Though some may need to give less, most will be able to give much more. Besides, giving away our money is a powerful way to guard against it ruling our hearts, since the money given away would most likely have been spent on ourselves or our own family anyway!

1 Timothy 6 concludes with the affirmation that giving our money away is gaining us treasure where it counts—in the world to come. By doing this, we *"take hold of the life that is truly life."* What a wonderful phrase! Giving our money away to invest in people and the kingdom is *truly life*!

In what settings do you find yourself thinking, "This is the life?" Hopefully it includes times when you're giving your (God's) money away. This life of giving—of living on as little as we can to free up as much as we can for ministry—is where spiritual happiness is.

For Self-Reflection and Life Application

1. What do you think about the definition of *work* used here—"celebrating God's creative energy?" Do you think it's biblical? If so, how does it affect the way you look at the various kinds of work you do, whether vocational or otherwise?

2. What group of people do you serve in the primary work of your life (whether you are paid to do it or not)? How can this service mentality affect the way you go about your work?

3. In light of the section on the *product* of your work, what does it mean to *you* to glorify God with quality?

4. What do you most need to address concerning the *process* of your work so that your attitude and heart glorify God?

5. Are you comfortable with your practice of a body and spirit Sabbath and, if not, in what ways might you make it more effective?

6. Reflect on some of your encounters with the danger of money. What do you find you must guard your heart against when accumulating or using money?

7. In what ways do you think living in America has distorted many Christians' perspective on money?

8. Think about several recent or upcoming purchases. How does viewing your money and possessions as God's (and you merely His manager) affect the way you consider that expenditure?

9. Consider a few spheres of your life (like vocation, household furnishings, clothes, recreation, savings, electronics, etc.). How do you know when you've reached enough? Have you "drawn a line in the sand" anywhere in a particular area of your life—even for a period of time? If so, describe the benefits and challenges of that experience.

10. Reflect on each of the ways money has power for good. To what extent are these a part of your life, and to what extent do you find joy in them? Consider what your answers here are saying about your heart and mind as Jesus' disciple.

---

[1] John Piper, *Don't Waste Your Life,* Crossway Books, Wheaton, 2003, p. 139.

[2] Ibid., p. 131.

[3] Kenneth Boa and Gail Burnett, *Wisdom at Work,* NavPress, Colorado Springs, 2000, p. 95.

[4] Paul Stevens, *Disciplines for the Hungry Heart,* Harold Shaw Publishers, Wheaton, 1993, p. 6.

[5] Ibid., p. 3.

[6] Lynn A. Miller, *The Power of Enough,* Evangel Press, Nappanee, 2003, p. 23.

[7] Randy Alcorn, *The Treasure Principle*, Multnomah Publishers, Sisters, 2001, p. 73.

Chapter 12

Earthly Pleasure—Reclaiming Recreation, Media, Sports, and Sex

From the chair on his porch, the man listened as several birds, hidden from view, sang their songs into the wind. The cold air and the mostly cloudy sky didn't stop him from delighting in the world around him. He had come home a bit early from work because a shipment of wood had been delayed. The children would be back from school any minute but, in the meantime, he enjoyed his quiet in the King's world.

Soon his mind turned to fishing—and the desire for a new rod. Fishing was a way for the man to be alone, free from responsibilities. His family benefited from his catch (if he caught any!) but his primary motivation was the peace that came with it. A new rod would make it an even more pleasurable experience!

There were two small problems, though. First, he knew the King should be involved in this decision somehow but he wasn't sure how that should happen. And second, he hadn't mustered up the courage to talk to his wife about it yet. He was pretty sure she had other intentions for his hard-earned money! But if he brought it up at the right time, just maybe . . .

His daydreaming was interrupted by the sounds of his children walking up the road. "Daddy!" they yelled as they saw him in the chair. They normally had about an hour of chores to do before they were allowed to play, so when the man said, "Let's play hide and seek!" they squealed with delight.

The youngest girl, was volunteered by the others to be the first seeker. After about five minutes, she had found everyone except her father, who was still hidden. He had slipped under the front porch and slid behind the steps.

"Daddy, where are you?" she shouted in a singsong voice. He kept quiet. Another few minutes passed. "Daddy, where ARE you?" came her voice, this time with a bit more frustration in it. The man was pretty sure he had won this one.

As he was smiling to himself, all of a sudden the King was there. Not physically, of course, but there. This was one of the last places the man imagined he would encounter the King—lying in the dirt under the front porch!

He listened. What was on the King's heart? And why now? Then his daughter's clearly frustrated voice broke through the quiet. "Where ARE you, Daddy!" And it hit him. This game had become more about his fun than hers. He had lost focus on love.

He could sense the King's smile, and a different kind of joy formed in his heart. It wasn't the joy of victory—it was the joy of love. So how could he reclaim this event for love? An idea sprang to his mind.

"Meow!" All the children froze in their tracks. "Did you hear that?" they said.

"Woof! Woof!" came the strangest dog barks they had ever heard. His little girl beamed. "Daddy!" and they all began running in the direction of the sound. A few more animal sounds later and they were all rolling in laughter on the grass beside the porch.

That evening when the man and his wife were alone, he told her about the game—and the King's touch on his heart. "If I make animal noises will you come and find me when I need some help in the kitchen?" she asked with twinkling eyes. They both laughed.

He was sitting in his favorite chair, and what she did next was his second big surprise of the day. She walked over and sat in his lap, leaning against his chest. His arms wrapped gently around her and they sat in intimate silence for several minutes.

"Honey," she said softly, as she broke the stillness. "I'd like to go to Kingcity with you."

American Disciples of Jesus in Search of Pleasure

Recreational pleasure has become a standard part of the typical American lifestyle. We live for the weekend and fill our lives with all sorts of entertainment, from TV reality shows to sports, from computer games to the latest music CD. The question we pose in this chapter is how we are to live for the glory of God in our pursuit of earthly pleasures. These pleasures include these entertainment pursuits, but they also include the pleasures of fishing and reading novels, as well as scrapbooking and sex.

When God made the world, it was good. And that goodness continues as He "richly provides us with everything for our enjoyment" (1 Timothy 6:17). As we've seen, pleasure is good. The question isn't whether we should be happy or not—it's where our happiness comes from. And in America our choices are abundant.

I write this as a child of the United States of America. My interests and values and skills have been shaped by this culture. I didn't grow up walking an hour with my mother each morning to fetch water as in some countries—I turned on a faucet and it just came out. And I've never known life without electricity or telephones—imagining life without them is strange indeed.

These things inevitably shape me. The computer I'm using, the phone that's ringing, the football game playing downstairs, the cars sitting in my driveway, and my college education are all part of me. As I've reflected on what it means to be an American enjoying everything He provides for us, and relating this to my enjoyment of earthly pleasures as a follower of Jesus, several convictions have formed:

- *Our joy in God and the spiritual blessings of His kingdom are even more rich than any earthly pleasure God or man has given.* Earthly pleasures are wonderful, but they can be gone in an instant, including our eyesight, our house, good weather, and even our loved ones. But we have "every spiritual blessing in Christ" that lasts forever (Ephesians 1:3). And no earthly blessing can satisfy the deepest longings of the human soul like God does. The joyfulness of Christians around the globe who have few earthly pleasures are evidence that earthly blessings have their limitations.

- *Things people create are not necessarily gifts from God.* When I ask a child what he or she is thankful for from God, I inevitably hear them speak about dolls and toys and games. Adults often join them in this line of thinking, though with more expensive items! But, as we saw in the last chapter, just because people manufacture something, sell it, and we buy it, doesn't mean it came from God—especially in a culture that's driven by money, pleasure, and few values.

- *All we do must glorify God, and at least this will include coming, becoming and loving.* If I can't do these three in my enjoyment of earthly pleasure, either it's not worthy of my interest or I'm not ready to enjoy it.

Goodness Twisted

Something's gone terribly wrong. What started out as a good earth has turned bad. Not all bad, of course. But it's like a virus that's penetrated the human body. Every organ is affected in some way. Or perhaps *infected* is the better term. Life is harmed and the body becomes less than it was meant to be.

When God made the earth good, it was good not just to Him but to humans. It wasn't some abstract goodness discussed in a college philosophy class. This good world has been given for us to enjoy, and there's more wonder and beauty in it than we sometimes see.

When the lion Aslan is gloriously singing the land of Narnia into creation in C. S. Lewis' *The Magician's Nephew*, a watching cab driver from England (yes, a cab driver!) exclaims, "Glory be! I'd ha' been a better man all my life if I'd known there were things like this."[1] It was, indeed, a sight to behold. Soon some of the newly formed Narnian animals were given the gift of speech and they received their commissioning: "Creatures, I give you yourselves," said the strong, happy voice of Aslan. "I give to you forever this land of Narnia. I give you the woods, the fruits, the rivers. I give you the stars and I give you myself."[2]   God gave us the created world, fellow humans, and Himself, and each are intended to give us pleasure.

But this beauty has been marred. Because our hearts have been corrupted by sin, we see the world in a distorted view. Jesus says it this way:

> *"If your eyes are good, your whole body will be full of light. But if your eyes are bad, your whole body will be full of darkness. If then the light within you is darkness, how great is that darkness!" (Matthew 6:22-23)*

The way we look at a new car, a vacation brochure, or a beautiful kitchen can be seen through either a God-worshipping heart or a self-worshipping one. They can be enjoyed with God as our Treasure and Master, or they can be enjoyed as the treasure itself—then they become our master. Thus, our "eyes" determine how we "see" the world.

Then the world twists beauty even more. For example turning children's play into a "winning is everything" sport or like taking the fruit of the vine and making hard liquor. Or like taking the human body and displaying it to sexually excite outside of marriage. These are good things that have been distorted by hearts, then repackaged in a distorted form and marketed for pleasure. The result is that we must reclaim the goodness of God's pleasures.

Children of Light in Dark Places

> *"For you were once darkness, but now you are light in the Lord. Live as children of light (for the fruit of the light consists in all goodness, righteousness and truth) and find out what pleases the Lord. Have nothing to do with the fruitless deeds of darkness, but rather expose them. For it is shameful even to mention what the disobedient do in secret. But everything exposed by the light becomes visible, for it is light that makes everything visible. This is why it is said: 'Wake up, O sleeper, rise from the dead, and Christ will shine on you.' Be*

very careful, then, how you live—not as unwise but as wise,
making the most of every opportunity, because the days are
evil." (Ephesians 5:8-16)

If you didn't grow up from a young age loving and following Jesus, you
can likely identify with these words: "You were once darkness." You "followed the ways of this world and the ruler of the kingdom of the air," as Paul
says in Ephesians 2:2. Your ways may have been pretty evil or merely socially
acceptable evil, but either way they weren't the ways of God. But things have
changed. We're on the side of light now. We're "in the Lord." His Spirit lives
in us to change our values and empower us to live out those values—values
like "goodness, righteousness and truth" rather than fun, power, and sex.

This identity as "children of light" isn't something that's automatic. We
must intentionally live as children of light, which means we must "have nothing
to do with the fruitless deeds of darkness." Love the good. Hate evil. The one
attracts us, the other distances us. Both require intentionality. They don't just
happen.

We are not even to mention these "deeds of darkness" because they're so evil.
They shouldn't become "no big deal" in our homes—or on our TVs. Don't even
joke about them. Humor tends to put a pretty face on evil. It makes it seem harmless—and it isn't. When my sons were young, we prohibited them from play that
pretended to shoot people, including "bad guys." It wasn't that we feared they
would become violent criminals. It was because we wanted them to be sensitive,
compassionate, and loving. Pretend violence doesn't train a heart in love. It
trains a heart in revenge, judging, and earthly power. Why would we want to
think these values are cute and harmless in our children if we want them to
develop tastes for the kingdom of God where power is not in weapons and mar-
tial arts but in truth and love and courageous holiness?

After we reject evil, we're then called to "expose" it—take it out of its glitzy
wrapping and let people see what it *really* is. Let people see the damage and
pain it causes in real life—and believe me, there's more pain out there from the
pursuit of pleasure than we care to admit. Prime-time television is *not* real life!

Ephesians 4:17-22 and 5:11 give us directions in our efforts to pull back the
curtain on evil and darkness. We must expose its *futility*, *addictive* nature,
deceitfulness, and *fruitlessness*. We can use these arguments to help our spiritual brothers and sisters stay far away from these things and also to help pull
them and unbelievers we know out of the sewage—even sometimes ourselves.

But beyond our arguments will be the "light" of Christ. The closer we get
to Him the more we "wake up" and see the darkness for what it is. We'll be
wise (seeing life from His perspective and not getting sucked into the

darkness) and making "the most of every opportunity" to expose evil's darkness and show the better way of Jesus' light. As a woman told me recently in describing her increasing freedom from the world's power, "I just stay close to Jesus all day long and it's not that hard."

So this chapter has a threefold purpose: (1) *to expose the darkness around us for what it is in common pursuits of pleasure,* (2) *to help us live wisely and purely as light in these places,* and (3) *to help us know when and how to take back the good things of God and restore them to their beauty.* We must "find out what pleases the Lord" in all things. This is the ministry of redemption— untwisting the evil and reclaiming goodness. It's hard work and can be painfully slow at times, but for those God has called, it's a ray of light (and thus an offer of Christ) to our world.

Somewhere Between Legalism and Looseness

Both Cathy and I were raised in churches where a deck of playing cards was seen as sinful. The two reasons I remember hearing most were that they were associated with gambling and that the face cards (king, queen, and jack) were depicting historical people who were bad people. So we played a lot of Rook. One day I went off to college and learned pinochle! It didn't involve gambling and the characters on those cards didn't look bad to *me*, so I felt free to change what some said was sinful to them to something good (I used cards to connect to guys in my freshman dorm.)

Now it's very possible that somewhere in the past it may not have been a good thing for particular Christians to play games with a standard deck of cards. Perhaps it would have fit into the "have nothing to do with the fruitless deeds of darkness" warning we saw above, especially if their Uncle Pete was gambling away his earnings while drinking with his womanizing buddies! But the cards themselves were never the real problem. For Cathy and me today, they're just cards with pictures and symbols on them—period. The only power they have is the power our hearts give them.

Every generation has to grapple with how to be holy. And it's natural for people to make personal rules for themselves and for their children to stay pure. This can often be a good thing. For example, prohibiting R-rated movies may be helpful, but if the rules become more important than the heart's pursuit of holiness, children may continue the law but without the spirit behind the rule—or they may reject God because they rejected a human rule they associated with Him.

If there's one thing that comes out loud and clear in Jesus' teaching, especially in the Sermon on the Mount, it's that God looks at the heart, not human rules. He looks at *why* we do something, not so much *what* we do (though there are some actions that are dark no matter what the motive behind them may be, like sex before marriage even if two people love each other or like getting drunk even if we're celebrating our wedding anniversary together!)

Let's consider a man named Chuck. Chuck has made a rule about not drinking alcohol because he has a desire to not be tempted towards abuse. Proverbs 20:1 is his text: "Wine is a mocker and beer a brawler." Chuck's rule pleases God. But legalism comes when Chuck thinks *all* people shouldn't drink alcohol or when his kids adapt his *rules* without a desire to *please God* or when he judges Charlie for having an occasional beer (who uses Psalm 104:15 as *his* text—God made "wine that gladdens the heart of man.")

In these kinds of situations, the apostle Paul advises that everyone's actions must be done "to the Lord" (Romans 14:6) and that is sufficient. As you can imagine, this principle will inevitably bring a lot of variety among Christians! Nevertheless, in "disputable matters" (Romans 14:1) we should not judge a person if they're doing something with a heart to please God. However, if someone uses their freedom in an area that is explicitly forbidden in Scripture (and thus their error is indisputable), then we'll need to go in love to that person and address the concern.

Of course, this kind of freedom can bring some difficult challenges to us. What one person does "to the Lord" can make another person quite uncomfortable. Standards of female modesty are an example of this and so are the kinds of toys our children play with. Again, Paul's criteria of accepting love (Romans 14:15-21) must guide us, and honest and humble dialog in community must lead the way. But we don't need to get everyone to conform to *our* standards.

Let's be frank. Our problem isn't usually that everyone is pursuing pleasure "to the Lord." Too often we pursue pleasure "to ourselves"! Not only that, but our fellow Christian friends often look the other way because they don't want to be accused of being judgmental (and they don't want others telling *them* what to do either!) So like Israel, many people do what is "right in their own eyes" (Judges 21:25 NRSV). The danger is no longer legalism but looseness. Accountability is lost to the god of tolerance. Instead of "judgmentalism," the problem is individualism. Both obscure the glory of God.

It's my desire to find a middle way here and answer the question, "What do recreation and earthly pleasures look like to the follower of Jesus whose heart beats for the glory of God?"

Biblical Criteria for Enjoying Earthly Pleasure

Before we examine several specific pleasures our culture serves up for us, let's consider some relevant guidance God gives us in handling pleasure. As we've already affirmed, pleasure is a gift from God. In particular, food, drink, work, wealth, and possessions are all described as gifts from God (Ecclesiastes 3:13, 5:19). On the other hand, Paul warns us that "At one time we too were . . . deceived and enslaved by all kinds of passions and pleasures" (Titus 3:3). How can we enjoy what God has given without being deceived and enslaved?

1. Set Your Highest Affections on God (The "Affection" Criteria). "In the last days. . . people will be . . . lovers of pleasure rather than lovers of God" (2 Timothy 3:1-4). This is about what we love most; what captures our heart. Even if a particular pleasure isn't bad in itself, it could be bad if it competes with God and His kingdom in us. *Coming* and *becoming* must be foremost in our hearts. The question we must ask ourselves, then, is: Can I do this activity while at the same time pursuing my foundational calling of a love-relationship with God that's centered in His glory?

2. Don't Adopt the World's Values and Thinking (The "Values" Criteria).

> *"Do not conform any longer to the pattern of this world, but be transformed by the renewing of your mind" (Romans 12:2; also Colossians 3:2).*

> *"For everything in the world—the cravings of sinful man, the lust of his eyes and the boasting of what he has and does—comes not from the Father but from the world" (1 John 2:16).*

The world has its ideas about what is right and wrong, true and false. Some may come from God—and some may not. In light of the texts above, there's a good chance they *don't.* That means we must constantly evaluate whether evil has crept into our lives from the things around us. It may be work to think on what is "true" and "right" and "lovely" (Philippians 4:8) in a particular setting, but it's *necessary* work. The question we must ask ourselves, then, is: Does participating in this activity require me to embrace any values and beliefs of the world that are in conflict with God's?

3. Don't Neglect Love and Relationships (The "Love" Criteria).

> *"Be imitators of God, therefore, as dearly loved children and live a life of love" (Ephesians 5:1-2).*

We've been created to love and to be loved (Chapter 8). So even though some solitude is appropriate, love must be a life-priority. Some leisure events are very individualistic, and they can take large amounts of time away from family, church ministry and relationships, and even non-Christian friendships. Furthermore, we must realize that every financial expense we make will often mean less resources available to love the poor and support the church and missionaries. So a helpful question is: Does this activity keep me away from important relationships and love?

4. Examine the Benefit—Beyond Mere Pleasure (The "Benefit" Criteria). "'Everything is permissible for me'—but not everything is beneficial" (1 Corinthians 6:12). The fact that something is enjoyable or fun can't be a sufficient reason to do it. It may, in fact, be quite harmful—to our body, to our soul, or to others. But it's not just whether it's harmful; the question is whether it brings good into our lives. Does it refresh? Educate? Inspire? Create? Equip? Mature? Unite? Celebrate? Nurture spirituality? Or to condense it into one question, Is this activity beneficial to me, so that it promotes God's purposes for my life?

5. Examine Your Freedom (The "Control" Criteria). "'Everything is permissible for me'—but I will not be mastered by anything" (1 Corinthians 6:12). Some activities can be addictive. They can control us and we become their slaves. This is why Jesus tells us that His followers can only have one Master—Him. So we must ask ourselves, Does this activity control me, or am I able to lay it down at any moment or even for an indefinite period of time, if God should ask me to?

6. Seek Rest and Refreshment in Order to Live Faithfully to God in Your Life (The "Rest" Criteria). We looked at this in our consideration of the Sabbath in the last chapter. Many Christians have a tendency to "work at their play," with the result being mental, physical, and spiritual exhaustion that hinders the quality of their lives. So consider this question: Does this activity hinder my ability to faithfully engage the people and responsibilities and callings of my life to the glory of God?

These six questions can help us in evaluating whether every pleasurable thing we do is done to the glory of God. They guard us from being swept along by dictums like "Everyone does it," "There are worse things I can do," and "It's okay if I can afford it." Something deeper and more beautiful must shape the heart of the follower of Jesus than these.

Let's now turn our attention to some common areas of pleasure in our culture that warrant a closer look.

The Pleasure of Media

When I was growing up, my dad was a supervisor at RCA. That meant we were one of the first families around to get a color television set. We were so excited—even though the only programming available in color was the evening news! But soon *cartoons* would follow!

Some people I know have little interest in TV. I'm not one of them. Add cable television and a remote control and I can be entertained quite easily for hours at a time, if I have nothing more important to do—and if I don't keep a sense of the kingdom of God about me.

Much of today's generation can't imagine life without TV. (Even in Mexico I saw people living in city shacks, but TVs glowed through their windows!) It relaxes us, informs us, and stimulates us in ways previously unknown. If we throw in computers, video games, and music to the mix, our culture is immersed in entertainment pleasure.

Cathy and I have usually been one of the last among our friends to add the latest home entertainment device to our home, but one-by-one they usually come. Soon they'll all be integrated through a home computer so any song, any movie, any program, any information, can be accessed at any time! (And no, that's *not* heaven!)

It seems to me most inventions that bring good also bring the potential for harm. Something may be gained, but something is usually lost as well. Radios brought music and news, but they also brought sexual lyrics and arrogant, crass talk shows. Computers brought the ease of word processing and Internet research tools, but they also brought violent games and ready access to pornography. Media can either be a tool of God or Satan.

One of the real strengths of media is its ability to convey the human drama. Whether it's a news report on a natural disaster, a movie that stirs our hearts to the possibility of love, or a sitcom that humorously exposes our own self-centeredness, media brings life to the surface. In *The Sacred Romance*, authors John Eldredge and Brent Curtis put it this way: "Art, poetry, beauty, mystery, ecstasy: These are what rouse the heart. Indeed, they are the language that must be spoken if one wishes to communicate with the heart. It is why Jesus so often taught and related to people by telling stories and asking questions. His desire was not just to engage their intellects but to capture their hearts."[3]

Television, film, and the Internet have joined with the older forms of literature, theater, and music to express the human heart. And behind it all is the whispering of God, for people write out of their souls, and their souls speak about spiritual longings.

For example:

- *Dramas* look at the challenges that face the human heart and can serve as glimpses of our need for personal and interpersonal wholeness that only God can provide in Christ and His church.

- *Adventures* involve achieving a goal against formidable odds and mirror our soul's longing to victoriously battle against sin and evil, culminating in our future reward and victory in heaven. (This is why I enjoy films like the "Lord of the Rings" trilogy—because its harsh physical battles symbolize the harsh spiritual battles I fight for righteousness and peace.)

- *Mysteries* discover something that is unknown or uncertain, and are glimpses of our soul's longing to know eternal truth and the satisfaction of understanding what was previously unknown about God, ourselves, and His creation.

- *Romances* are experiences of human love and can serve as glimpses into our longing for perfect human love and ultimately the satisfaction of God's love.

- *Comedies* confront our human weaknesses and pain through exaggeration or contrast and are glimpses of our soul's longing to feel significant, to experience acceptance in light of our weaknesses, and to find happiness in the midst of pain.

- *Fantasies* stir our longings for joy and wonder and a "happy ever after" meaning to life, which can serve as glimpses of the kingdom of God that He offers substantially here on earth and in fullness in the new heaven and earth to come, where He Himself is the center.

Some films, like *Les Miserables* and *The Mission*, proclaim divine truth clearly and explicitly. God is front and center. Others, like *Sound of Music* and *The Lord of the Rings* proclaim divine truth clearly but implicitly. God isn't mentioned, but some deeper reality is there. Other films proclaim divine truth more subtly and perhaps only partially, like a painful portrayal of life without God, or perhaps a hope is stirred that becomes an object lesson on spiritual truth. *Dr. Zhivago*, *Field of Dreams*, and the *Star Wars* series are examples of these.

As much as I love learning and being entertained, I can appreciate those who conclude that TV and film are not worth the cost. "Kill your TV" they advise. Or, "Television is a Destroyer. . . the very little good that can be extracted from TV does not make up for the overwhelming harm it has wrought."[4] Who can argue that seeing repeated sensual and sexual encounters outside of marriage, the use of violence to stop the bad guys, and godless solutions to life don't have a negative effect on one's spirit? Who can argue that hours of kingdom time can be wasted in front of a TV or a computer terminal—time that could better be used for solitude with God, Scripture or spiritual reading, relationship building, serving someone, thinking, enjoying nature, creating, repairing, or learning?

Douglas LeBlanc observes: "Certainly few of us will go to our deathbeds wishing we had watched more television. Nevertheless, some of us may wish we had spent more time thinking critically about the TV we *did* watch'"[5] Yes, visual media can be a powerful reminder to us of spiritual realities, driving us to deeper devotion, praise, courage, and love. But if we watch TV mindlessly without "taking every thought obedient to Christ," TV can be a form of idolatry and escapism, where our shallow relationship with God (and people) is compensated by entering into the false realities of the screen.

So what is our role in "exposing the deeds of darkness" depicted on our screens? I admire those who seek to redeem the media by writing and producing quality stories with godly values, but most of us are left with two realistic choices as disciples of Jesus: flee it or discern it.

If we choose discerning it, I would encourage applying the six "Biblical Criteria for Enjoying Earthly Pleasure" in the previous section with great courage. For example, if you watch movies or TV programs with a spouse, family, or friends, why not discuss them together using the lens of Jesus? (Are we concerned this would then "spoil" the entertainment value?) If we can't *come, become,* and *love* in this setting for God's glory, perhaps we've bowed at the idol of earthly pleasures.

Recently I had to excuse myself from a program where a character depicted evil too intensely for me to watch. I've also had to guard my exposure to certain kinds of sexuality. Yes, I can critique the bad and rejoice in the truth, but some battles may be too intense even for that. So fleeing must be an option, even if others around me don't join me.

Of course, TV and film can provide a wonderful shared experience with family and friends. But it can also be a substitute for conversation. (Let's face it: It's often easier to watch three hours of TV in an evening than it is to sensitively inquire into your spouse's or kids' hearts or to humbly share about the state of your own soul.)

As we raised our children, Cathy and I would often unplug the TV for periods of time. One year it went into a closet the whole summer. It's amazing what creative and relational things kids can find to do after a few minutes of being *bored* without TV! I often take "fasts" from TV or my car radio, reminding my soul that life with God is satisfying without needing all the details about the latest news, needing to experience another sports event, or needing to use the TV as a form of relaxation.

The Pleasure of Sport

More money and time is spent in the pursuit of sport in America than in any other nation. When you add up all the youth sports, scholastic sports, professional sports, recreational sports, and all the spectating that happens in stands and on recliners and sofas, sports bring pleasure (or at least the *pursuit* of pleasure!) to millions.

I love sports. From my early days of tackle football in the front lawn with the neighborhood kids, to Little League baseball, intramural high school basketball and college lacrosse, I've spent many hours in the joy of playing. Even today I love a good table tennis game with my brother and sons. The challenge of performance and the satisfaction of success attract me.

As with action movies, I see a basic longing in my soul to overcome and succeed against obstacles. Though we may not always be consciously aware of it, I believe sport and competition reflect the deeper human longing to fight against evil and our desire for greatness—in God.Not only is sport a reflection of spiritual realities, but I believe sport itself can be played to the glory of God—and not just when we win. In fact, it's very possible that God can receive more glory in our losing than in our winning. Think about it. Who tends to be glorified in a win? The winners. But there's no human glory in losing—except if the loser demonstrates peace, love, and joy in the loss. Then *God* can be the one who is known and shown as very great!

To keep sport from being an idol and a snare to the Christian, consider these questions, which are expansions of several of the six criteria previously mentioned:

• ***Where is your heart?*** A few years ago I yielded to pressure and played on our church's slow-pitch softball team. I love the guys, so why not? In the first game of the season I managed to make several easy fielding errors (where did my 21-year-old body go, anyway?) and I didn't contribute a whole lot at the bat. I felt I had let the team down (and myself)—and, of course, it didn't help my attitude that some people from church were spectators and watching my stellar performance! I found myself withdrawing into a pity-party a few yards from the bench.

Later at home, my son Jeff courageously observed that it was only a game and the guys weren't nearly as concerned about my play as I was. (I think in some way he was also a little embarrassed for me because I had failed to practice what I preached and tried to model throughout his childhood.)

As I reflected on my heart, I realized I had placed my worth in my ability to perform well, and, in particular, I had wanted my church to look up to me on the softball field. But playing second base, batting eighth, and making errors didn't exactly feed my self-worth! I had so much wanted to quit, but I realized that this place of humility was probably what God wanted for me, assuming the guys really *wanted* me to play! (Spiritual growth can be a little painful at times! One of my favorite "*becoming* like Jesus" settings is the golf course, where my drives can vary from two hundred yards to twenty! "God, make me a humble man!")

Sport can feed sin—like pride, selfish ambitions, fear, and a performance-based self-worth. These aren't the values of the King we serve. Our motivations can't be to hear the praise of others or to feed the self-worth of being better than someone else.

It's often said that sport can teach children character. It's true. The problem is, what *kind* of character? A cooperative attitude or a need-to-be-first attitude? Discipline or pride in self? Handling disappointment or feeling like a failure in the eyes of a coach? Character can go both ways.

One of the ways I've decided I must live out this life with God in sport is to laugh at my mistakes—or at least smile! That smile reminds me that I have limitations, that my worth comes from God, and that He loves me no matter what I do. Smiling smirks at the idol of pride that wants to set up camp in my heart—and it welcomes God to be my life.

So what place should the goal of winning have in a Christian's heart? As the apostle recognized, in a race "only one gets the prize" (1 Corinthians 9:24), referring to the fact that the very structure of most sports allows for only one winner. Everyone else loses, no matter how well they play. Certainly, there's nothing about sports that would incline God to care who wins. (As we already saw, He can be glorified in losing as well as winning.) His idea of success is a godly heart. Winning an athletic contest may be a measure of skill on a particular day (though not always!), but it has little to say about what's really important and truly satisfying as followers of Jesus. If we're going to guard our heart in competitive events so that pride doesn't lead to boasting or self-pity, then it would be well to give our best, enjoy the challenge, and find our joy in God regardless of the outcome.

• *How is love being shown?* Can a disciple of Jesus really "hate the New York Yankees" or desire his church volleyball opponent to miss-hit a serve? Can we so easily ignore 1 Corinthians 16:14—"Do everything out of love"— just because we play sports? (Does God give a "love exemption" for athletes?) Think about it this way: If we are to love our enemies, shouldn't we at least love our *competitors*? For many sports enthusiasts, one of the biggest disconnects of the soul from God is how it relates to love.

One of my memories of the church I grew up in was seeing my pastor try to strike out young kids at a church picnic and then throw a temper tantrum when one of his pitches was called a ball. Neither the children or the umpire felt a lot of love that day.

There are two ways I've sought to keep love a central part of sport. The first is to compliment opponents on their good play during the game. "Nice shot." "Good block." (Complimenting also guards my own soul from pride!)

The second way comes from Romans 12: "Rejoice with those who rejoice; mourn with those who mourn" (Romans 12:15). If I can live by this command when I watch a college lacrosse game my kids are playing in or when I play a family card game, then there's a good chance I'm glorifying God in it. To enter into a person's emotional world long enough to identify with what he or she is experiencing is part of compassionately acting in their best interest. They're not just an athlete or an opponent—they're a human being made in the image of God.

I love the Peanuts cartoon that shows Linus excitedly describing a televised football game in which a team had just made a last-second, come-from-behind win and the fans were going crazy. "It was fantastic," he says. In the last frame Charlie Brown looks at him and says, "How did the other team feel?" Christians should ask that same question and respond accordingly.

I realize, however, that the principle of love in sport is not always so simple. My brother Doug has coached at youth, high school, and college levels, and he knows the challenges of love in organized sport. He teaches a yearly college course called "God, Goals & Glory—the changing spirit of the games we play," to help students think about these kinds of questions. As he points out, when someone enters into a game setting, he or she is really agreeing to compete under a set of rules that say, "You're loving me if you try to play better than me. I *want* you to try to stop me. It's in my best interest, because I want to be challenged and it motivates me to improve." Unfortunately, competitive love is easily twisted when our pride and loveless hearts take over. But for the follower of Jesus, love *can* be married to competitive sport.

As the man in the parable became aware under the porch, love must find a way because love is always at the heart of the King. Each competitive setting—from family board games to professional sports—will need to find its own expressions of love. It may be compliments, or a sense of empathy, or not taking advantage of an opponent's weaknesses. When our children were young, we sought to minimize self-centeredness and hurt feelings in games by having a rule that whoever lost would get hugs from the rest of the players! Losing was not the end of the world!

So as you reflect on the effect of sport in your own life, what do you see? How do you handle your emotions before games, during games, and after games? What do they tell you? (If you're a coach, you may want to contact me for a copy of "Verbal Guidelines for Christian Coaches.") I've known one group of Christians who decided not to play basketball for awhile because their hearts weren't being ruled by God and love was scarce. After a "basketball fast" for a few months they were able to begin again with the right heart.

If you're a disciple of Jesus who pursues pleasure in sport, you don't have the option of putting God on a shelf when you pick up a ball or watch a team compete. *Come. Become.* If you can do it in sport, you can probably do it anywhere! Yes, guard your heart from being mastered by it, especially in the many hours it can take out of your life. But you will know the joy of the Lord if, instead of living for the glory of the game, you live for the glory of God.

The Pleasure of Sex

Our culture isn't the first one to overdose on sex. Many ancient societies were equally obsessed with it, but western culture has taken it to new levels with the advent of magazines, television, and the Internet. Now all sorts of sexually implicit and explicit scenes can be accessed in the privacy of one's own home or room. The increasing casual display of a woman's body in our culture just adds gasoline to the fire.

Perhaps we shouldn't be too surprised. God designed the human body to be pleasurable in sight, in touch, and in sexual union. Biblical passages such as Proverbs 5:18-19 and Song of Songs 7 celebrate these realities in surprising detail. And 1 Corinthians 7:4 affirms that "The wife's body does not belong to her alone but also to her husband. In the same way, the husband's body does not belong to him alone but also to his wife." This is about mutual pleasure, where both are focused more on giving than getting—a delicate love-dance if there ever was one.

But there's the question our culture is raising: Why does it have to be limited to a "husband" and "wife?" Why does God give this wonderful gift and then put limits on it? The reason is that *sex is designed by God to nourish the life-long relational union of a man and a woman through its intimacy and pleasure and is designed to provide a secure and nurturing setting in which to raise and love any children that come from it.* Without limits, sex not only fails to do what God designed it to do, it fuels all kinds of relational harm.

In light of these God-designed purposes for sex, four primary distortions emerge:

1. Sex is distorted when it occurs outside the male/female relationship— either in the same-sex relationship of homosexuality or in the self-sex non-relationship of masturbation. This same-sex prohibition has been challenged by many, but the facts of sex organ biology, the need for procreation, the absence of any positive same-sex endorsement in the Bible, and the clarity of Romans 1:24-28 in calling it sin, all affirm the traditional argument. Masturbation—which is usually fueled by self, lust, and addictive qualities— can't be God's design for sex either.

2. Sex is distorted when it occurs outside of marital commitment—in sex before marriage, in adultery when married, or in pornographic sex of the heart and mind.

> *"It is God's will that you should be sanctified: that you should avoid sexual immorality; that each of you should learn to control his own body in a way that is holy and honorable, not in passionate lust like the heathen, who do not know God"* *(Thessalonians 4:3-5).*

> *"But I tell you that anyone who looks at a woman lustfully has already committed adultery with her in his heart"* *(Matthew 5:28).*

The media knows that Americans don't like to delay gratification of pleasure, so it bombards us with passion-sex—sex without commitment, without deep knowing, without responsibility. Movies don't show the loneliness, rejection, shame, and shallow relationships that accompany passion-sex. But passion-sex isn't just a hormone problem, it's a heart problem. It's about what we *want.* Do we want to first glorify and please God, or do we want to please ourselves or another person?

This applies not only to sex but to lust as well. I've talked to scores of men who have been damaged by their lust—most of whom never act out with another woman, but the fantasies and lingering looks that feed sexual desire are very, very real. Looking for the purposes of sexual gratification undermines marital love, hurts wives (just ask her), and controls the heart. According to Jesus, sexual sin (of either male or female) begins in the heart and the head—not the bed.

3. Sex is distorted when it pursues self-pleasure more than loving the whole person in relationship. When sex is self-driven it fails to walk in love. There's nothing wrong with asking a mate for pleasure, but it must never be demanded and it must never be isolated from giving love—desiring what is in his/her best interest. This love will not only include what gives a spouse physical pleasure, but also what gives them relational pleasure—and, what's good for them spiritually as well. So even in a dating relationship, this kind of love will motivate a couple to delay sex until marriage because true love desires the other's spiritual purity and priority love for God.

4. Sex is distorted when it rejects the responsibility to love and raise children. The reality is that God intended sex to result in children. (I know this may sound strange to some readers but it's true!) The advent of "the pill" in the 1960's has helped disconnect sex from child-bearing and parenting responsibilities and has allowed sex to become mostly about pleasure. I don't believe conception control is wrong, but we certainly mustn't believe that sex is primarily about self-seeking irresponsible pleasure. Sex is supposed to include lifelong love-commitments that are prepared to care for children together.

These four distortions highlight the need for limits to safeguard God's purpose for sex. For many of us, these are sufficient. God has spoken. We see the dangers of sex wrenched out of marriage. We're persuaded that sexual union is God's seal for marital commitment and that it acts out on a physical level what is to be happening on a soul level (what other species unite face-to-face?). These limits made sense to Cathy and me and they were sufficient to keep us and millions of other disciples of Jesus sexually pure before marriage.

But some may still wonder, "If I'm in love, and I believe this person is probably going to be my mate someday (whether I'm 16, 26, or 46), why wait for marriage?" Consider the following wisdom behind God's "rules." Perhaps they will help you fight off the pressures of our culture, or even help you persuade someone you know who isn't persuaded merely by God's Word.

• ***Sexual purity helps cultivate a balanced and lasting relationship not based on physical attraction.*** The reality is that most dating relationships don't last—and the non-lasting depth to these relationships would most likely have been revealed if the physical component hadn't dominated so much. The couple would have been forced to find affection and attraction through other dimensions of the relationship—like intellectual, social, emotional, and spiritual components. So not only can sex mask over the weaknesses in a relationship, it can also tempt someone to stay in a relationship when it should be ended.

• *Sexual purity thinks beyond short-term realities and feelings.* "Am I sleeping with someone else's future marital partner?" "Would my future mate want me to be sexually active now?" "Do we want to have sex if we know we're not going to be together a year from now?"

• *Sexual purity enhances sexual relations with a future marriage partner.* Many people wish they had waited until marriage for sex; few wish they had been *more* active. Sexual control before marriage is a gift to a future mate because it tells your partner that if you're able to wait *now*, you'll be able to have sexual control *after* marriage as well. It's a gift to a future mate that says, "I've kept myself only for you." It also frees a person from distorted techniques, attitudes, and comparisons developed from self-centered recreational sex.

• *Sexual purity guards against sexual addiction.* Recreational or self-sex that is separated from self-control can easily evolve into addictive sex—and getting married usually doesn't fix the problem.

• *Sexual purity guards against dehumanizing women and making them property of men.* To view or touch a woman for the purposes of sexual excitement is to make her an object—even if she gives permission. To give women the full dignity they are worth means to relate to them as a whole person, with longings, needs, friends, family, fears, and a soul that needs God.

• *Sexual purity frees from the consequences of an unwanted pregnancy.* Children are supposed to be a blessing. When they're seen as an intrusion or a burden, something is very wrong.

• *Sexual purity greatly decreases the threat of STD's.* There are over 12 million sexually-transmitted diseases each year in America. Some are curable; some aren't. Some can be stopped by condoms; some can't be. When people have sex, they're exposing themselves to all the people their partner has had sex with, and all *their* partners, and the chain goes on and on. The best safe sex is between two people who are virgins.

• *Sexual purity enables spiritual fruitfulness.* How we handle sex is a sign of the spiritual orientation of our hearts. When sexual pleasure and pleasing another person are more important than love for God, that idolatry undermines spiritual fruit in our lives (2 Peter 2:18-19). I've heard it from so many. God can't fully bless someone who deliberately sins. In fact, continued sexual immorality puts the soul in eternal danger (Ephesians 5:5; Hebrews 13:4).

C. S. Lewis has said that when we opt for sexual pleasure apart from God's purposes, we choose too *little* pleasure, not too much! Pleasure is more than orgasm or sensual passion. It's also the happiness of being faithful to God, the joy of mutual commitment through relational struggles, the satisfying experience of spiritual transformation that true love requires, and the joy of naked intimacy when two souls are open and trusting.

So how is this godly pleasure attained in our sex-addictive culture? It always starts with the heart and mind—wanting to glorify God and thinking on righteous things. It means fleeing temptation—even radically if necessary—so that the places you go and the things you see don't distract you from your goal of sexual purity.

Sexual sin has a slippery slope. Sensual touching is intended by God to be foreplay for marital sex, not recreational passion. As 1 Corinthians 10:12 says, "If you think you are standing firm, be careful that you don't fall!" This means we all need to set clear standards for ourselves so we are *far* from sin. To "flee sexual immorality" (1 Corinthians 6:18) and live so that there "not be even a hint" of it in our lives (Ephesians 5:3) means setting standards far from sex, not just at the edge.

Christian women, in particular, have a responsibility to not tempt men by their dress. They are to dress modestly (1 Timothy 2:9), not only because their bodies belong to their present or future husbands, but because they should show kindness to the many men who struggle with impure thoughts. Invite men to see your heart, not your body.

And a word to men: If you find yourself pursuing visual images of women for the purpose of sexual excitement, you need to seek spiritual accountability with other men who will pursue the *come-become-love* pattern with you to sexual freedom. Lust need not control you. There are also helpful, online discipleship courses available designed to overcome sexual addictions.

If we are to pursue sexual pleasure to the glory of God, we will need to be willing to critique our modern dating practices and especially the role of romantic affection in it. We must be willing to protest the provocative messages of romance novels, MTV, and lingerie companies that use sensuality to market their products. (I personally boycott several.) Sexual pleasure is good—but it's not necessary for happiness. God can give you a new heart.

Other Pleasure-Pursuits

There are other pursuits of earthly pleasure, of course. Most have their appropriate place in this world, if submitted to God. Take physical appearance, for example. Many people spend a significant amount of time and money to find joy in having a particular facial appearance, hairstyle, body shape, or clothes adornment. Some of this can be justified by the desire for health, but pride can easily come close behind. Proverbs 31:30 says, "Charm is deceptive and beauty is fleeting; but a woman who fears the Lord is to be praised." That keeps priorities where they should be.

If a woman's or man's sense of self-worth is tied more to their appearance than to their character with God (as 1 Peter 3:1-4 warns against), then perhaps the time and money given to this pursuit should be re-examined. To feel good about oneself through external means is not inherently bad—it can be part of creating and celebrating beauty. But to *need* to feel good about oneself through external means can't be the heart of the disciple of Jesus.

The appearance of our homes is another pleasure-pursuit for many. I enjoy creating beauty around my home. Planting bulbs, perennials, and annual flowers amidst bushes and ornamental grasses is a way for me to celebrate God's world. But is pride my real motive? Do I want the praise of others? Do I want my house to look *better* than someone else's? Is the expenditure of money and time in this pursuit neglecting the needs of others?

This is a challenging one for me personally. I recently put in a small patio that cost me about $500. It adds to my home's beauty and ease of upkeep, but I also had to ask myself if I'm being generous to the needs in our church and the world. Cathy, too, will often wait many years to replace a worn carpet or add a new piece of furniture just to make sure her heart doesn't *need* it.

One of our family's earthly pleasures is taking a vacation or weekend away. The change of pace from responsibilities and telephones is a welcome break, especially because it relationally reconnects us as a married couple or as a family, sometimes including extended family or personal friendships as well. We've laughed, learned, and adventured together at Disney World, marveled at the wonder and simplicity of God's creation from simple campgrounds to the Grand Canyon, and relaxed at beach houses with books, games, and good videos.

But always we must take God in our hearts. How sad it is to have a getaway and pack our days so full of activities that we rarely draw near to Him. Times away should be times to reconnect with God and family, making relationships a priority—especially the quality of those friendships. Car rides filled with hurtful words, hotel rooms filled with arguments, and campground sites marked by frustration don't glorify God. But these times *can* be relationally and spiritually rich if we intentionally *come, become,* and *love* throughout.

Another pleasure-pursuit is the world of hobbies and interests. Cooking, carpentry, hunting or fishing, scrapbooking, sewing, art, playing a musical instrument or singing, and restoring old cars bring joy to many. Again, the issue is not eliminating a good thing, but surrendering a good thing to God using the criteria He has given us as His followers.

We are blessed in this world with many pleasures. *Abundantly* blessed. Some are from God. Others are created by people. But with all these pleasures comes a responsibility—to enjoy them under the rule of Christ. It's only then that they can give their greatest pleasure, satisfying to both body and soul.

For Self-Reflection and Life Application

1. What does it mean to you that God "richly provides us with everything for our enjoyment" according to 1 Timothy 6:17? What does it *not* mean?

2. You are a child of light according to Ephesians 5:8-16. How do you practice this identity in the midst of your pleasure interests?

3. Have you ever tried to rescue someone from the futility, addiction, deception, and fruitlessness of the pleasures of a particular sin? What arguments did you use? What was successful and what wasn't?

4. What issues have come up in your own life that stretched you to be either less legalistic (not so judgmental and rigid) or less liberal (more accountable and pure)?

5. Pick one pursuit of pleasure in your life and evaluate it in light of the six "Bible Criteria for Pursuing Earthly Pleasure."

6. In light of this chapter's discussion of the pleasure of media, what, if anything, do you believe you should do to submit it more to the glory of God? How might this change bring you *more* pleasure?

7. Repeat question 6 in light of sport.

8. Repeat question 6 in light of sexual pleasure.

9. Consider other pursuits of pleasure in your life and how they can be more fully surrendered to Christ in thought, desire, and action.

[1] C. S. Lewis, *The Magician's Nephew* Macmillan Publishing Co., New York, 1955, p. 100.
[2] Ibid., p. 118.
[3] Brent Curtis and John Eldredge, *The Sacred Romance*, Thomas Nelson Publishers, Nashville, 1997, p. 6.
[4] Preston Jones, "Con: Dumping TV," Christianity Today.
[5] Douglas L. LeBlanc, "Two Cheers for TV," *Christianity Today International/Books and Culture Magazine* 1998.

Chapter 13

The Church—The Glory of God on Earth

That was a night to remember. The man could hardly believe his ears when his wife told him she'd like to go to Kingcity with him. It had been over four months since he had come back from there. Four months of loving and failing and drawing near to the King—and then loving some more. He was aware of the transformation that was taking place within him, and he knew his wife saw it, too. But when she said, "I want to go to Kingcity with you," he wasn't prepared for it. Tears glistened in his eyes as he held her close and, with his face buried in her hair, gave praise to the King for the privilege of having His life formed in him. It was a special night.

It took them a couple of days to arrange for care for their children and to deal with some loose ends about his business, but soon the night before their departure arrived. The children had already gone to be with some friends so the house was quiet. The two of them sat across from each other as gas lanterns cast a yellow glow across the room.

"What was it like?" she asked. He knew what she meant. He let out a long breath as if to calm his nerves. He had longed to tell her so many times before, and now that she finally asked, he didn't want to say anything that would make her change her mind with the trip only hours away.

"Imagine yourself being all dirty and weary and hot and you come upon a waterfall. And you walk in. It's just the right temperature to cool you off, and just the right power to massage your muscles, and completely clean to quench your thirst. That's the King—and Kingcity." And with that, he told her about the woman on the road, his first encounter with the people, his first sight of the King, the wonderful people he met there and, of course, the moment when he fully surrendered to the King.

"I've been reading more of the Breath recently," she said. "I don't know why I didn't see it before, but it describes you . . . and the people of Kingcity." She paused a moment. "I want it too."

With that expression of surrender, the man led his wife into the beginning of a love-relationship with the King. It was the happiest night of their lives, as two people became one.

Several days later they arrived hand-in-hand at the outskirts of Kingcity. Over the last ten miles they had encountered many citizens who greeted them warmly, several even offering them a place to stay. They accepted with great joy. But when they came over the crest in the hill, their hearts beat faster. The city was absolutely beautiful. "I didn't know a place like this existed!" she said to the man. He nodded understandingly.

They were quickly incorporated into the city's life. Each was given work to do and friendships grew easily, not only at their work, but during meals they shared with residents. Their highlights, of course, were meeting with the King when he came to their neighborhood, and meeting with groups of citizens who gathered to know the King's greatness in them.

One day as they walked together through the fields outside the city, she turned to the man with a smile. "You know, these people certainly aren't perfect, but they are real. And they're loving. And—they love the King so much. I can see why."

"Have you noticed their boils disappearing?" the man noted. "Even over the last few days I've seen fewer on our host's face. And that man who's been here 40 years—he's practically boil-free." They both glanced at their arms and smiled because the boils were beginning to leave their bodies as well.

"Thanks for bringing me here. Since experiencing this, I know we can't go back to life as it once was. I never want to be far from Kingcity again." His wife's voice was filled with joy.

"He's making all things new," the man nodded. Their arms linked behind each other and they stopped walking. Their voices turned to the King in thanksgiving and love. They both thought about friends who they wanted to bring here to the King—to His life. This was what it was all about.

Bigger Than Just You and God

When I look up at the stars and galaxies on a cloudless, moonless night, I marvel at the glory of God. When I ponder the intricacies of the human body—from the wondrous complexity of the eye to the millions of blood cells that gather to heal the cut on my profusely-bleeding finger, I am awed by the glory of God. But even more amazing and glorious is what God does in human relationships that have bowed their knee to Him.

It started with Israel, when God picked Abraham to bless his offspring and to reveal Himself to the world. He gave them miracles, His law, atonement for their sins, the tabernacle, godly leaders, and prophets. There was much divine glory in those things, but it wasn't enough to keep them from straying away from God's heart.

In time God sent Jesus. His plan wasn't to merely forgive millions of people so they wouldn't go to hell—it was to create a people: "But you are a chosen people, a royal priesthood, a holy nation, a people belonging to God, that you may declare the praises of him who called you out of darkness into his wonderful light" (1 Peter 2:9). Now comprised of both Jews and non-Jews, He would write His law on His people's hearts and minds. He would pour His Spirit upon all those who put their trust in His Son.

The result? They would exist for "the praise of his glory" (Ephesians 1:14). In the Old Testament it was the tabernacle and the Jerusalem temple that were symbols of God's glory. Now it is the church—not the buildings we meet in but the people He lives in!

> *"To him be* glory in the church [emphasis mine] *and in Christ Jesus throughout all generations, for ever and ever!" (Ephesians 3:21).*

We are the greatness of God!

For some of you reading these words, this description may seem more ideal than real. You look around at your church and you don't exactly feel the glow. The closest you get to brilliance is the annual candlelight service on Christmas Eve, and the closest you come to greatness is eating Mrs. Jones' apple pies at potluck dinners!

Yet the message of the Bible is that God wants to light us up! Christians are the light of the world, the glory of God and, as we saw in Chapter 9, together we are to shine like stars in the universe, holding out the Word of Life.

It's not primarily by the quality of our worship teams, our state-of-the-art video projection system, or the size of our church parking lot by which God is glorified among us (though these all may contribute to some degree). Whether your church is 25 people meeting in a school gym or 25,000 people meeting in multiple services in a coliseum, the display of God's greatness is about the quality of our gathered spiritual lives.

For all its quirks, personalities, embarrassments, and blunders, the Church is still the glory of God. You and I get to make it that way—by His grace!

Who's The Head of *Your* Church?

What do you think of when you think of the church? Hopefully not a building—or at least not *primarily* a building. Meeting places for Christians weren't built until over 200 years after Jesus. Homes and the outdoors worked just fine.

Church—perhaps you thought of an assembly of Christians. That's how the New Testament uses the word. But I'd like to suggest a slightly different image for you. Picture an assembly of Christians with Jesus Christ standing at their center. Not the pastor, the church board, or even an open Bible. Jesus—the Lord and Savior, Vine and Shepherd, Bread and Life, and Living Word of the Church.

This may seem obvious, but in practice it's not. Neither Jesus nor His earthly replacement, the Holy Spirit, are visible to our human eyes. That means we can tend to fix our eyes on what is seen—like a pastor or the Bible—rather than what's not seen. But it's Jesus who we must fix our eyes on. He is always at the center of the church, whether during a sermon, a practice session of the worship team, or a committee meeting on the misuse of the church kitchen. Every leader and every follower reports *directly to Him* on the organizational chart!

Now this brings up an interesting question: How, then, do we see this Jesus—and see Him accurately? Philip Yancey wrote a book entitled *The Jesus I Never Knew* (the book my cousin Bob read that helped him return to Jesus). Perhaps you, too, need to see the *real* Jesus, not the one filtered through so many churches.

So who *is* He to *your* church? Consider Ephesians 1:

> *"And God placed all things under his feet and appointed him*
> *to be head over everything for the church" (Ephesians 1:22).*

This is the Jesus of authority. All things are placed "under his feet." It's what we often think of when we think of the word *head* (as in "he's the head of a corporation"). After all, Jesus gives us commandments, not suggestions. He's our Master and Lord. He calls us to obey Him.

And this has significant implications. He's given us clear expectations about the permanence of marriage, not loving money, practicing forgiveness, and love with one another. These aren't options for the church and its leaders. He's the King. In fact, "You are not your own; you were bought at a price" (1 Corinthians 6:19-20). Yes, we may need to use grace and patience in helping some people obey, but there must be no doubt where we're heading, and Who is in charge.

The word *head*, however, means more than authority.

> *"And he is the head of the body, the church; he is the begin-*
> *ning and the firstborn from among the dead, so that in every-*
> *thing he might have the supremacy" (Colossians 1:18).*

This is the Jesus of honor. He is supreme. First among all rulers and powers. The early Christians gave their lives to be devoured by lions because they wouldn't call Caesar "God." Caesar wanted to have the place of highest honor, but for the follower of Jesus, He alone is prominent and preeminent. He is our *head*—as in the *head* of a mountain, where the summit is the mountain's honor or the *head* of the table, where it is seen as a position of honor.

In practice this means we give Him praise. And it means we pray a lot—at our board meetings, in our home groups, when we're trying to comfort or advise someone in a crisis. He must be placed front and center. And we must be willing to get out of the way if necessary.

There's still another meaning to *head* in the New Testament.

> *"Instead, speaking the truth in love, we will in all things grow up into him who is the Head, that is, Christ. From him the whole body . . . grows and builds itself up in love" (Ephesians 4:15-16).*

This is the Jesus who is the source. When we speak of the *head* of a river, we speak of its source—where the water originates from upstream. This is Paul's use here. We "grow up into him" so that we can grow "from him." The closer we get to Jesus, the more He feeds us with His life.

When a church sees Jesus as its source it can't just do Bible study. Right doctrine isn't spiritual maturity (in fact, it's a lot easier for some to read a book on theology than to volunteer to care for children in the church nursery). To worship Jesus as source is to cling to Him as life-giving Vine and to eat from Him as life-giving Bread. This is about faith, not just facts; transformation, not just information. Most Christians don't need more Bible study—they just need to live in the simple reality of what they hear from their leaders and already know from God.

For Jesus to be our source we must also make Him the first person we go to when we're troubled, not the last one. He tells us in Matthew 11:28, "Come to me, all you who are weary and heavy laden." So do that. Do it when the overhead guy mixes up the song lyrics; do it when that parent is slow to take their crying child out of the auditorium; do it when the pastor doesn't visit you in the hospital. He's your source, so run to Him first and fast—for all He's promised to be for you.

Why *Do* We Go to Church?

Why does your church exist? We've already noted from Ephesians 3:21 that the purpose of the church is to glorify God. So people should go away from our worship gatherings and our small groups and our business meetings and say, "Wow, God sure is great!"

Perhaps the clearest passage in the New Testament on the purpose of the church is in Ephesians 4:

> *"It was he who gave some to be apostles, some to be prophets, some to be evangelists, and some to be pastors and teachers, to prepare God's people for works of service, so that the body of Christ may be built up until we all reach unity in the faith and in the knowledge of the Son of God and become mature, attaining to the whole measure of the fullness of Christ. . . From him the whole body, joined and held together by every supporting ligament, grows and builds itself up in love, as each part does its work" (Ephesians 4:11-13, 16).*

The church is clearly about the business of knowing and showing the greatness of God here on earth. Note each of our trilogy here. The church is to "reach the knowledge of the Son of God" (referring not to information but to relational knowing)—that's *come*. It is to "*become* mature, attaining to the whole measure of the fullness of Christ." And it is to grow and build itself up "in *love*."

This is why God has given the church pastors, teachers, and other gifted servants—to prepare, or equip, the church to serve one another so that these three will happen. Leaders are to stimulate the church in such a way that whatever people do during the week (from having informal conversations to putting money into the offering plate) they are *becoming* spiritually mature—*becoming* like Jesus. Is that how *your* church functions? I hope so.

Sometimes I'll hear someone say: "The church is the only organization that exists primarily for nonmembers." But that's not what Ephesians 4 says. The church exists for you and me—and the glory of God. Yes, we have a message of truth and love to proclaim to the world, but one of the primary ways this is done (as we saw in Chapter 9) is to cultivate a church that lives in the reality of the risen Christ.

Here, But Not Yet

One of the tensions I felt in writing the parable throughout this book was choosing when to show the ideal and when to show the real. Too much ideal might not connect to you, the reader, resulting in a dream-like spirituality. But too much of the imperfection of the Christian walk might not stir the reader to greater things, which is what Jesus did with His parables.

This tension is real and it's real in the Bible. On one hand we have passages like:

*"For in Christ all the fullness of the deity lives in bodily form,
and you have been given fullness in Christ" (Colossians 2:9-10).*

On the other hand we read,

*"You are still worldly. For since there is jealousy and quarrel-
ing among you, are you not worldly? Are you not acting like
mere men?" (1 Corinthians 3:3).*

I wish I could say my experience was different, but I can't. I've known wonderful times of "fullness in Christ" with my spiritual brothers and sisters. And I've also seen them acting very "worldly . . . like mere men." I've been loved to the point of tears, and I've been criticized to the point of tears. I've seen relationships mended in humble obedience to Christ, and I've seen relationships torn apart in prideful self-righteousness. The glory of the church— and the agony of the church. My guess is that you can relate.

Theologians describe this tension as "fulfillment without consummation," or "here, but not yet." Jesus illustrated this with many parables about the kingdom He was establishing. One speaks of yeast that slowly permeates the whole dough to cause it to rise. A substantial degree of spiritual fullness *has come*—but it often grows slowly, and it's often experienced imperfectly and without consistency. That's why it's "here, but not yet."

The problem I see in the church is that we too often settle into the "not yet" reality without living the "it's here" reality. We hide behind our immaturity with slogans like "I'm not perfect, just forgiven," or we excuse our struggles with sin because we're waiting for heaven.

The reality is that "our old self was crucified with [Jesus] so that the body of sin might be done away with, that we should no longer be slaves to sin. . . . Count yourselves dead to sin but alive to God in Christ Jesus" (Romans 6:6, 11). The normal Christian life and the normal Christian church should know this in substantial measure. No excuses. Especially no blaming God ("I've asked, but He hasn't answered," or "God's in control. I'm just waiting on His timing.") The Bible puts the ball in our court, not primarily God's. He's ready to make it happen any time we're ready. We are *not* slaves to sin anymore.

Yes, there *will* be days when we're more aware of the "not yet" than the "here"—both in us and in the church around us. Sometimes church life will be a mess and, when that happens, several things must happen to not just accept this as normal (even if it *seems* normal to you): (1) Examine your own heart, and in the face of God deal with anything you may be contributing to the problem; (2) Determine to be part of the solution and not part of the problem—especially in the purity of your love; and (3) Look forward to the new heaven and earth where messiness will be no more, and the church will be the pure bride prepared for her Husband!

In the pages that follow, I want to describe the church as God meant it to be. God's Word says these are substantially attainable, and I've experienced them—sometimes for only brief periods—but real experiences, nevertheless. They rarely come without struggle, but few good things in life do.

The Glory of Our Unity

You may not be aware of this, but being on a church worship team isn't always fun. Musicians can have very different ideas about what kind of sound they're looking for and about what level of excellence they want to attain. Different personalities add further "interest" to a practice session.

I've had the privilege over the years of helping musicians get along together (including at times getting along with me!). But because they were committed followers of Jesus more than musicians, I've also had the privilege of seeing hearts become more like Jesus in the process. Egos humbled. Sensitive personalities putting on love. These men and women were willing to work to be one.

Jesus said,

> *"I have given them the glory that you gave me, that they may be one as we are one: I in them and you in me. May they be brought to complete unity to let the world know that you sent me and have loved them even as you have loved me" (John 17:22-23).*

God is glorified by our unity. This isn't a unity of agreement about every item of doctrine, or about what color the church nursery should be. It's the unity that Jesus and His Father have "as we are one," which is a unity described as being "in" each other. It's a relational unity, sharing the same heart, same purpose, same goals, same love. It's not conformity; it's communion.

How does this unity happen? How can such a diverse group as the church (and it is diverse!) all share the same heart together? It happens when they're united not by worship styles, baptism doctrines, or knowledge of the Bible but when their hearts are captured by Jesus.

A common marriage counseling diagram is a triangle with God at the top and the husband and wife at each of the bottom corners. The closer the couple moves toward God in this diagram, the closer they get to one another. That's the way it is in the church. But it requires dying to self—something many aren't willing to do.

Years ago I volunteered to mediate between two groups of people in an area church that were splitting over a leadership and building dispute. There was no bad guy but their hurts and pride had made it very difficult to appreciate each other's perspective. One group's lawyers prohibited face-to-face dialog between the key players (not exactly a recipe for mutual understanding!), and the other group hired a new pastor whose righteous rhetoric only fanned the flames of resentment. After almost a year of listening, phone calls, meetings, and being accused by both groups as siding with the other group, bankruptcy was filed and resolutions fell to the courts. I was worn out and grieved. It was one more example to the world that Christians are no different than anyone else.

Fortunately, not all conflicts end this way. The denomination I currently serve in strives hard to model biblical unity founded on spiritual realities. Its eighth core value is "Pursuing Peace: We value all human life and promote forgiveness, understanding, reconciliation, and nonviolent resolution of conflict." If we value these kinds of things, something different happens between us. Our personal hurts and opinions won't control us. We'll be more passionate about the purposes of Christ than about our own—and we'll also be able to tell the difference!

As I write these words, however, I recall how I failed just last night in a leadership meeting. I moved to analysis in a conversation before listening deeply. God convicted me this morning and I apologized to this brother. He graciously accepted it.

"Not to us, but to Your name be the glory" (Psalm 115:1). John 17 unity in the local church (and between Christians in different local churches) happens when we make much of Christ and little of ourselves. It's a never-ending surrender to God, laying down the need to be affirmed or understood by people and laying down the need to straighten other people out. The only need we must have is to be known by God and to know God—to know and show Him as great. The church isn't primarily unified around a pastor's vision or preaching skills, and it's not unified around the collective pride in our church facility. It's unified around our common life in Christ.

A few years ago our congregation addressed a very controversial topic together. After a year's worth of biblical papers and discussions, the decision-making meeting arrived. Passionate spokespeople were on both sides—and my view lost by two votes. A few relationships were a little strained for awhile, but the church leaders urged the people to work hard at unity in Christ, despite their strong convictions. Paul said it well: "Make every effort to keep the unity of the Spirit in the bond of peace" (Ephesians 4:3).

Yes, there are issues that could be so important that it might be better for people to meet in different congregations so that their differences don't distract each of them from their primary mission of following Jesus. But every possible effort should be given to be "perfectly united in mind and thought" (1 Corinthians 1:10) on matters of faith and practice. And when it isn't resolved, the Baptists, Lutherans, Presbyterians, Assembly of God, Catholics, and Brethren in Christ must proclaim their essential unity in Jesus Christ as their common Lord, Savior, and God.

Cathy and I, along with our children, have visited a number of residential Christian communities over the years, where hundreds of followers of Jesus share all things in common, including finances. They aren't utopias, but they *are* beautiful. I believe *non*residential communities (like the typical local church) can be beautiful, too. "How good and pleasant it is when brothers live together in unity!" (Psalm 133:1).

It's this kind of reality that Jesus says will "let the world know that you sent me and have loved them." This is because unity isn't natural—unless God has come among us.

The Glory of Our Shared Spiritual Growth

About every other week I meet with two other discipleship partners for spiritual reflection, encouragement, and accountability. In these times we share about *coming*, *becoming*, and *loving* at very personal levels, which includes our jobs and marriages. Over the last few years these partners have included Paul, Doug, Drew, Keith, and Steve. Together we have pursued the glory of God using the spiritual discipline of Hebrews 3:

> *"See to it, brothers, that none of you has a sinful, unbelieving heart that turns away from the living God. But encourage one another daily, as long as it is called Today, so that none of you may be hardened by sin's deceitfulness" (Hebrews 3:12-13).*

We need one another. Really. And that's not an easy pill to swallow in our self-dependent age. Somehow it seems like we're admitting to being weak people, like we're in need of a therapy group or something. Yet that is just the point—we *are* weaker than we want to admit.

If all you want out of God is a weekly sermon, a few songs, a nice prayer, an active children's program, and a good pot luck dinner every now and then, corporate worship services will do just fine. But if you have affirmed that the goal of your life is to glorify God as a lover and follower of Jesus Christ, then *you need people*. You need people to listen to your soul. And you need people to speak to your soul. Or to put it another way, you need people to be Jesus to you in the flesh. That's why we're called the *body* of Christ.

In Christian pollster George Barna's *Growing True Disciples,* he concludes, "Most disappointing is a widespread lifestyle among Christians that fails to demonstrate the practical realities of the Christian faith."[11] To what extent does your church produce people who actually follow Jesus with increasing devotion and obedience? Are the young adults able to look to the middle-age and senior adults and see mature disciples that inspire them?

For most people, sermons, singing, and suppers don't produce disciples. They need settings in which Hebrews 3:13 happens—where people actually encourage one another to overcome sin. *Encouragement* in the Bible isn't just nodding sympathetically to someone's struggles, or saying "I'll pray for you" when a friend unloads about her parenting frustrations. It's speaking words that promote the glory of God in that person—helping them *come, become,* and *love.* And this requires face-to-face encounters. In other words, *small groups.*

"The small group was the basic unit of the church's life during its first two centuries."[2] In groups people can know each other—their personalities, habits, limitations, and sins. In small groups friendships are focused on a few, rather than scattered over the many. In small groups accountability is possible and sin can lovingly and redemptively be addressed.

Of course, small groups don't automatically result in spiritual growth. But with the right structure, expectations, and resources, they can become an experience of Jesus among us. This will happen, not just by our friendships with one another, but by our intentional pursuit of holiness. We thus rise "to become a holy temple in the Lord" (Ephesians 2:21). A good group meeting isn't measured by how much we learned, or how much we laughed—it's determined by how much we've loved and grown to be like Jesus. That includes overcoming sin.

Small groups can come in all shapes and sizes. They can be Bible study driven, ministry-task driven, discipleship driven, or family-support driven. They can happen in a church softball team or while cooking together for a Christmas banquet. They can even happen in one-on-one chats after the morning worship service.

Behind the variety, God is looking for people who will intentionally speak into the spiritual lives of one another—and who will encourage others to speak into their lives.

> *"Let the word of Christ dwell in you richly as you teach and admonish one another with all wisdom" (Colossians 3:16).*

The Glory of Our Shared Love

A lot of attention has already been given to love in this book, but we can't talk about the glory of God in the church without highlighting it again. In Ephesians 4:16 we saw that love is what connects us to one another and allows the church to grow up spiritually. Note that this is the kind of love that comes *from him*.

There have been many times when I've wanted to withdraw from a church relationship because it was either too painful, too humbling, or too much work. But love (compassionately acting in their best interest) overcomes the resistance as I *come* to God to purify my heart, to catch His vision for *His* church, and to empower me to reach out and touch someone again by His grace. As a disciple of Jesus, I pledge not to be ruled by self-protection (keeping my distance from people so they can't hurt me again) but by the Lord of the Church.

The "faces of love" we looked at in Chapter 8 are as basic in the church as breathing: deeds of kindness and mercy; acceptance, understanding, and forgiveness; edifying speech; and honoring one another. Through all of these, however, is the highest call of love—to help each other glorify God. When this happens God is doubly glorified. *We* glorify God by giving love. And the *recipient* glorifies God by being led to *come*, *become*, or *love* in some way.

Dolores is an example of this. She writes notes of spiritual encouragement to people (what a blessing to receive one of these!). She listens to people's pain with compassion, while ever gently pointing them to God and His life for them. She and her husband Dave extend hospitality to people in their home, and their fellowship is like being with Jesus because you know you've been loved in His name.

What a difference love makes in a church! What glory is given to God when people walk into a church gathering and greet others instead of waiting to be greeted. What happiness in God is known when hurting people are compassionately pointed to God as their life, rather than just listened to. What greatness of God is seen when nursery slots are always lovingly filled—with volunteers waiting in the wings.

Ephesians 4:16 ends with the phrase, "as each part does its work." One of my greatest joys as a pastor is to see people assume responsibility to love without a leader tapping them on the shoulder first!

There's a story about four people named Everybody, Somebody, Anybody, and Nobody. An important job needed to be done in the church and Everybody was asked to do it. Everybody was sure Somebody would do it. Anybody could have done it, but Nobody did it. Somebody got angry about that, because it was Everybody's job. Everybody thought Anybody could do it but

Nobody realized that Everybody wouldn't do it. It ended up that Everybody blamed Somebody when Nobody did what Anybody could have done!

This happens in the life of the church more than most people realize. There's also the "20/80 rule," where 20% of the people do 80% of the work. This is a problem not just because the 20% are often overworked, but because they're doing what God wants "Somebody Else" to do, and that means "Somebody Else" is missing out on the spiritual glory that comes from servant love.

Bill Hybels, pastor of Willow Creek Community Church, likes to say, "There's nothing like the local church when the local church is working right." And this involves "having the right people in the right places for the right reasons."

In a healthy church, everybody has their place—and they're in that place because they want to love in the name of Jesus. From Jeff, the drummer, and Jocilyn, the kids' teacher, to Fran, the bulletin folder, and Mark, the fix-it guy, the church is alive in love for the glory of God. Whether the love flows through our special gifts and abilities or through the "every-Christian" kind of love of affirmation and correction, God is glorified by love.

The Glory of Being Family

I often have to remind myself that the church is family. The larger a church gets, it's harder to remember that. Values like quality, efficiency, and professionalism become important, but never forget—we're family. Remember that the next time the words on the screen don't match what you're singing. Remember when people ramble a bit during a testimony time. Remember when a child (or adult) forgets his lines in the Christmas drama.

A few years ago I preached on sex and decided to have an after-the-sermon question time during the service. One was memorable. A woman asked for my advice about whether her husband should get a vasectomy! Her husband's face got very red. Mine may have, too. But, hey, we're family!

> *"You are no longer foreigners and aliens, but fellow citizens with God's people and members of God's household"* *(Ephesians 2:19).*

Families expect crazy things to happen. They also learn to laugh. A sign of a healthy church is one that can laugh at itself (and I've shared some great laughs with the two churches I've pastored!). We can laugh because we're comfortable with imperfect people. Of course we won't laugh *at* them, but we can let them know that their mistakes are okay with us! We're family.

Also, families stick together even if everyone isn't best friends. In a family you may smile at your grandmother's repeated stories, and you may wish

Uncle Barry wouldn't be so gross. But families don't give you the cold shoulder just because you're a little different—at least healthy families don't.

This isn't an appeal for loose cannons and sloppy ministry. It's merely a plea for accepting one another, looking past "B" performances, and seeing the heart. It's being glad that the next time I say something stupid from the pulpit, blank out on a friend's name, or stand someone up for breakfast, the grace of being family will glorify God.

Philip Yancey says this family characteristic requires us "to voluntarily choose to band together with a strange menagerie because of a common bond in Jesus Christ."[3] Have you made this vow? "Henri Nouwen once defined a community as 'a place where the person you least want to live with always lives.'"[4] Welcome to the church! It's good for you—and for them.

The Glory of Our Fellowship

The biblical word "fellowship" means "to share in common." What do we share in common? Our life in God together.

> *"We proclaim to you what we have seen and heard, so that you also may have fellowship with us. And our fellowship is with the Father and with his Son, Jesus Christ" (1 John 1:3).*

> *"And the fellowship of the Holy Spirit be with you all"* (2 Corinthians 13:14).

This is a spiritual "communion" (a fitting word used in 1 Corinthians 10:16 that describes what happens when we take the Lord's Table together—and it's also the same Greek word translated "fellowship" elsewhere in the New Testament). It's two fellows in the same ship, sharing our spiritual journey together.

I love being around followers and lovers of Jesus. Whether their theology is fundamentalist, charismatic, reformed, or anabaptist (or combinations), when God is worshiped in humble love, it's a delight to be together. Sure, I sometimes have to push through certain clichés and perceived imbalances, but at the core we share Jesus together, and that's enough.

At our local ministerium we practice this monthly. We focus on and celebrate our common calling as shepherds of His Church. For that hour we lay aside our baptism differences, church structure differences, and our theological distinctives and affirm that we love the same Lord. It's great. And it shows that God is great.

To have fellowship in God together means I admit and enjoy that our diversity enriches my experience of God. I can't think of one person in my church of 250 that I'm not happy to know. Each has something special to proclaim about God's life.

When our twins were born 10 weeks premature and the church provided meals for us and care for our $2^1/_2$-year-old daughter, we knew we shared a common Lord. And when we made the difficult decision to leave the church I helped plant and say good-bye to scores of wonderful friendships we had established over 20 years of ministry, we knew we shared a common Lord. Words of affirmation united our hearts to Jesus and to one another in deep gratitude.

Fellowship says, "Come you who are broken and wounded and taste of God's grace in my company." A few years ago I visited one of our church's home groups and I heard people share stories of being raised in condemning and judgmental homes or churches—but having now experienced love and acceptance in the church. That is the fellowship of the Lord.

The Glory of Our Shared Witness

As we saw in Chapter 9, God intends our witness to be corporate. It was that way with Israel and it's now that way with the church. What we do *together in relationship* is a powerful witness to the greatness of God. We are witnesses who *experience* the reality of God among us as He rules in our hearts. So whether people see the church *gathered* (like at a worship service) or see the church *scattered* (like at our homes or our jobs) they will *see God.*

Even though most churches don't structure their weekly worship service primarily for outreach, it would still be wise to ask what non-Christians might experience if and when they visit. This would be at least one application of Paul's instruction to us, "Be wise in the way you act toward outsiders; make the most of every opportunity" (Colossians 4:5).

So when unbelievers come through our doors, what *do* they see?

Lee Strobel, in his book, *Inside the Mind of Unchurched Harry and Mary*, suggests a number of ways churches can connect to many of today's unchurched without compromising the message of the Gospel. Some are: give them some space (they don't want to "belong" right away); give them creativity (they don't want to be bored); give them quality (it says our message is quality, too); give them something that touches their heart (they want their longings to be stirred to hope); and give them relevance (so that it touches them where they live each day).[5] If we have churches like this, lost people may just return—and bring a friend—and ultimately find that the good news of Jesus speaks to their longings and needs in a powerful way.

Another relevant question to ask is whether our church members feel like our worship service is a place they would *want* to bring an unchurched friend. Will they feel pressure to give money? Will the greeters be formal and impersonal? Will the pastor use in-house vocabulary that makes them feel like an outsider? A church doesn't need to have their worship service be seeker-*driven* in order to be seeker-*sensitive*.

The church must also provide settings of relevancy that engage their member's friends in the process of exploring the Gospel. These might include classes on parenting and finances, sports nights or fishing trips, recovery groups, concerts, drama plays, or community dinners.

One task of the church (specifically leaders) is to partner with its people in communicating the Gospel to their friends out in the world. This is equipping the church to be *scattered*. So the question isn't just, "How can we get them here?" but "How can we *go to them*?"—and do it effectively. Evangelism training sessions, literature resources, sermons on CDs, informative web pages, prayer support, and accountability partners that help members keep a pure and bold witness are all equipping strategies to proclaim a message of life to the lost for the glory of our King.

A story is told of a mother and her small child who were in a church with stained-glass windows. The child was fascinated with them. "Who are those people painted on the windows?" the boy asked. "Those are saints," his mother replied. When he went home, he told his father that he had seen the saints in the church. "Who are the saints?" his dad asked. "Saints are people the light shines through," the boy said. They are.

Structuring for New Wineskins

When Carol felt God leading her to start a home fellowship group in her home, it was a huge step. She had only reaffirmed her faith about four years previously, and she certainly wasn't a Bible teacher. Praying out loud made her very uncomfortable. But she had a gift of hospitality, and a video curriculum helped take some of the leadership burden off her, so she decided to step out in faith. To her surprise, her group ended up being people like her— somewhat shy when it came to speaking about their faith. Knowing her own reluctance to oral prayer, she decided to make praying out loud part of their group's expectation. They would pray around the circle, and each would pray at least one sentence. A year later, those sentence prayers have all become paragraphs! Carol's leadership is a wonderful example of using new structures (small groups, prayer circles, video curriculum) for the new things God wants to do among us.

I don't believe we have to pattern all our meetings after the structures of the New Testament church. This would deny how the Spirit adapts eternal truths to specific cultures. But there are some elements that seem to go beyond time and culture, and if we fail to implement these structures in some way, the life of God will be hindered in His church. It would be like asking a business to be successful without using advertising, banks, telephones, and computers. Some structures are necessary for life. I believe these three are essential:

• *Plural spiritual leadership.* Everywhere you look in the New Testament there are teams of spiritually-focused people leading the work of the church. Jesus selected 12 apostles. And they later ruled in plurality with elders in Jerusalem (Acts 15:2). Furthermore, Paul and Barnabas appointed elders (plural) in each church (Acts 14:23).

Though I prefer the biblical term "elders,"[6] the function is more important than the terminology. These leaders are to nurture, rule, protect, and equip the church for spiritual life under the Chief Shepherd and Overseer, Jesus. According to 1 Timothy 3 and Titus 2, the essential requirements for these church leaders are spiritual maturity and the ability to teach God's Word to another. Business and administrative skills may be helpful, but only if these spiritual criteria are met first.

Leadership is to be done in plurality because *all* now have the Spirit—not just a single Moses, Joshua, or a David. Some Spirit-indwelt team-members will likely be more gifted in preaching and teaching than others, and some will be more gifted as vision casters, as shepherds, as evangelists, or as team facilitators. In addition, some may be *paid* to minister in the church and others will not be. But together, these leaders discern and implement the Shepherd's heart for His flock.

When a church is led by a spiritual team, pride is more guarded, decision-making is wiser, and sin is more likely held accountable. Though scripture speaks about these teams mostly in terms of overall leadership, these principles of plurality are applicable to sub-ministries of the church as well.

Together, the church leadership team's highest priority is to ask what the Head, Jesus, would desire with *His* church. Their priority isn't to please people, or grow numerically, or to keep a smooth organizational machine going. It's to glorify God through the church as a spiritual community of Christ-followers. Recently our elders decided to have our congregation divide into loose prayer groups during a morning worship service in place of our normal prayer led by a single person. We know that it makes some people uncomfortable (and we've done all we can to minimize that) but, in the end, we felt this was a step towards spiritual maturity for our people. It was what Jesus wanted.

• ***Care for the tangible needs of the church.*** In Acts 6 the church structured itself to care for Greek widows who were missing out in the food distributions. Six were called to oversee this ministry—six who were "full of the Spirit and wisdom." In our church we call these individuals deacons.[7] They are a team of individuals who oversee practical people-concerns related to finances, health, jobs, and family. They do some of the work, but often they coordinate others in helping to respond to the church's tangible needs. We also have an Administrative Team that handles all financial and property matters. Like the deacons, they are accountable to the elders. Both free the elders to stay focused on the spiritual life of the church.

• *Gatherings for personal accountability and encouragement.* In the New Testament people usually lived within walking distance of one another, and the pace of life was much slower. For today's church, we need structures that facilitate meaningful face-to-face conversations about life, God, and spiritual growth. Without small group structures, people will usually not see one another—and even less speak about their spiritual lives in terms of accountability ("How's your patience with your four-year-old going?") and encouragement ("The next time your kids do that, try to stay consciously surrendered to God and see them with eyes of compassion rather than as intrusions.") If we don't create these personal growth settings, they will likely not happen with most people.

There are certainly other structures that are helpful, and many are uniquely needed to support a church's ministry callings. But these three would seem essential to "doing church" to the glory of God.

A Note to Church Leaders

Many years ago, during one particularly-difficult season of church life, I was given a little book called *The Three Kings* by Gene Edwards to read. It's a historical allegory of Saul, David, and Absalom and their dysfunctional power struggles. The theme of the book is that leaders need to be broken before they can be used, which often means releasing control even if God has given us authority by our positions. I remember crying as I encountered these truths because in my desire to not have messy things happen in the flock (and with me) I realized that my care for the church had, at times, been too controlling and overprotective. That was a turning point for me. I told God that I really did want to be a broken man more than a "successful" man, and on that day I took a significant step in dying to success in human terms.

But that didn't stop church life from being messy. If our hearts aren't pure before God, we will certainly contribute to the mess. I've done my share. It

fills me with grief whenever I think about it. If our hearts as leaders aren't living out the reality of the beatitudes as described in Chapter 1, then our
responses will be contaminated every time we receive criticism about our
leadership, every time there's a board meeting disagreement, and every time
we face a difficult personality challenge. Without a priority given to relationship (*coming*) and righteousness (*becoming* and *love*), we will certainly hinder our people from following Jesus well. We can't expect their spirituality to
be much greater than our own.

Leading a church is the most challenging thing I've ever attempted to do,
particularly in finding the balance between listening and leading. On the one
hand, the people of the church should be honored as Spirit-indwelt people and
brought into decision-making. On the other hand, open discussion can cause
sides to form, immaturity to be vocal, and a lot of energy to be spent. In a similar tension, leaders desire to please their flock. But sometimes we must make
choices that are often unpopular. "Servant leadership" is a great term and I
believe in it, but living it out is immensely challenging!

Paul instructs his pupil, Timothy, with these words: "Watch your life and
doctrine closely" (1 Timothy 4:16). The best way to do this is to invite a man
or woman of God into your life who has the heart of a pastor (inquires into
your heart, empathizes with your struggles) but the courage of a prophet (able
to speak spiritual truth to you even if it's unpopular). I thank God for the men
like this in my life. They are more valuable than gold.

In addition, to watch life and doctrine closely, a leader must maintain regular times of self-reflection in the presence of God. Using the themes of this
book would be one way to keep your heart and mind drenched in the life of
God for you. Also reading books like *Authentic Leadership* by Bill Hybels or
In the Name of Jesus by Henri Nouwen can help keep your spirit accountable
to the One you serve.

A woman in our church grew up as a "PK"—pastor's kid—in a growing
church in the 1950s. When tensions began to grow over certain standards of
holiness in the church (like playing sports on Sunday and going to movies),
her dad became a lightening rod for criticism. Denominational leaders only
fueled the division, so when her dad was disaffirmed by the congregation as
their pastor, it left her angry and disillusioned about church leaders for years.
By God's grace, the ten churches she has been part of since then have each
contributed different levels of healing, and thankfully, our church and a
"Celebrate Recovery" ministry here have further helped her. But it's been a
long and often hard road.

We leaders have the potential to bless and the potential to hurt. I'm glad
that my three children have weathered church hurts without losing their love

for the church. It speaks well of the churches they have experienced. And I hope and pray that the list is small of the people who would point to me as the cause of their lack of love for the church of Jesus Christ.

The church is God's treasured possession. And, my fellow leader, it's entrusted to you and me. That's a weighty thought. Some pastors have a view of God's sovereignty that says God will accomplish His purposes in our churches with or without us. I don't see that in the Scriptures. The pain, apostasy, conflicts, and power struggles I see point to a battle for purity. Yes, at the end of the age God will have His pure bride. But what we do—or don't do—here on earth makes a huge difference. To those who have been given much, much will be required (Luke 12:48). I tremble in holy fear. And I cling to His grace.

Accept the Adventure

Over the last 25 years, I've had the privilege of giving pastoral leadership to two churches. They have been wonderful congregations (and substantially-real communities). In these churches I have known some of my greatest joy: life-changing conversions, restored marriages, spiritually stimulating discussions, deep laughter, affectionate embraces, intergenerational soccer games, heart-felt worship and prayer meetings, people liberated from anger and worry, invigorating missions trips with paint rollers and mortar trowels, musicians that touch my spirit, offerings that met goals, and the blessing of making a difference in people's lives. It's been a profound privilege and wonder, all under the loving rule of the Head of the Church.

I've also had my share of pain: people leaving for other churches, marriages not making it despite hours and years of working together, and people falling away from Christ. There have been critical words given without humility or love, unresolved disagreements with brothers and sisters I loved deeply even after every effort was made, and personality challenges. I've often felt judged and misunderstood. "Why do I do this to myself?" I've sometimes asked. Because God chooses to glorify Himself through jars of clay. And my joy is tied to His glory.

In the words of someone who has given his life to forming Christian community, "One of the important characteristics of true Christian community is the presence of struggle. It's impossible to live a brotherly life together without struggle, which sometimes become 'crises.' . . . If one sets out to live together according to God's will, there are going to be problems, and the problems must be faced, and facing the problems always means struggle—*always.*"[8]

This means work. It takes spiritual effort to see the pride that hinders us from seeing our own weaknesses. That pride also hinders us from seeing the good in others. Our struggle isn't primarily against one another—it's against sin and disunity and indifference. I've found that one of the greatest joys in the Christian life is to wrestle through a struggle together and, in the process, experience the presence of Jesus who binds us together at places deeper than our issue.

(I want to say a heartfelt "thank you" to those men and women who have done this with me. Words cannot express what your perseverance, grace, and Godward hearts have meant to me.)

Mr. Bilbo Baggins is short with large, hairy feet, a stout build, a good-natured face, and always maintains a well-kept, comfortable hole in the ground. Bilbo is a hobbit—the creation of J. R. R. Tolkien in *The Hobbit*. For their many positive traits, hobbits hate adventures. They pride themselves in not doing anything unexpected.

When the wizard Gandalf dropped by unexpectedly at Bilbo's hole and told him, "I am looking for someone to share in an adventure that I am arranging, and it's very difficult to find anyone," Bilbo answered, "I should think so—in these parts! We are plain folk and have no use for adventures. Nasty disturbing uncomfortable things! Make you late for dinner! I can't think what anybody sees in them."

Gandalf informs Bilbo that it is *he* who he wants for this adventure. Bilbo replies, "Sorry! I don't want any adventures, thank you. Not today. Good morning!"[9]

Eventually, and reluctantly, Bilbo agrees to embark on this adventure along with some disagreeable dwarves. And what adventures he had, defeating creatures like trolls, goblins, and Smaug, the dragon. After narrowly escaping death, Bilbo returned home a very different hobbit. He began writing poetry and having elves, dwarves, and wizards for guests (which caused him to lose respect in the eyes of other hobbits). And, though few believed his tales, he remained happy to the end of his days.

Adventure is the most appropriate word to describe what God has for us, both individually and corporately. A most unusual adventure it is—weakness and meekness are necessary qualifications. These adventurers are, "sorrowful, yet always rejoicing; poor, yet making many rich; having nothing, and yet possessing everything" (2 Corinthians 6:10).

Like Bilbo Baggins, it will do no good to complain about your church. God has work for you. You and God are on an adventure—an adventure with fellow faithful disciples of Jesus, sometimes with a handful and sometimes with thousands.

There is a beatitudes-kind of glory in this adventure. And the church is the treasure chest of God's riches. In the church you and I are wealthy. Ours is a glorious inheritance (Ephesians 1:18). Paul wrote,

> *"Therefore, my dear brothers,* stand firm. Let nothing move you. *Always give yourselves fully to the work of the Lord, because you know that your labor in the Lord* is not in vain"* [emphasis mine] *(1 Corinthians 15:58).*

Seize the day. Seize the adventure. Don't flinch in conflict. Keep your eyes fixed on Jesus. Fight in humble love for the glory of the church of Jesus! His glory on earth awaits.

For Self-Reflection and Life Application

1. Describe some personal experiences of knowing God's greatness in the churches you've been a part of.

2. In what ways do you personally look to Jesus as the Head of your church? In what ways do you find yourself looking elsewhere?

3. How does the purpose of the church, according to Ephesians 4:11-16, fit with *your* motives for going to church?

4. Describe some of your "not yet" (imperfect) experiences of church life. To what extent have you settled for normalcy at this level?

5. How should the fact that Christ is in us make a difference when we have a disagreement or conflict with another?

6. What people have intentionally encouraged you to love and follow Jesus? Who have you intentionally spiritually encouraged?

7. What works of love are you doing in the church? Are you balanced (involved enough, but not over-involved?)

8. When do you most need to remember that your church is family?

9. What does your church do well in partnering with its people for the communication of the Gospel to the world? How might it improve?

10. Evaluate your church structures. Do they aid—or hinder—the work of God as described in the Scriptures?

11. How do you react to the idea of church life being an adventure with God?

12. For review: What parts of the parable spoke most to you throughout this book?

---

[1] George Barna, *Growing True Disciples*, WaterBrook Press, Colorado Springs, 2001, p. 83.

[2] Howard Snyder, *The Problem of Wineskins*, InterVarsity Press, Downers Grove, 1975, p. 139.

[3] Philip Yancey, *Church: Why Bother?*, Zondervan Publishing house, Grand Rapids, 1998, p. 63.

[4] Ibid., p. 64.

[5] Lee Strobel, *Inside the Mind of Unchurched Harry and Mary*, Zondervan Publishing House, Grand Rapids, 1993, pp. 170-220.

[6] The terms *elders*, *overseers*, and pastors/shepherds are used to describe different facets of the same leadership office in the New Testament church, as both Acts 20:17, 28 and 1 Peter 5:1-2 show. The terms *church board* or *team* are all words borrowed from secular models and can be helpful, but they must not subvert the purposes and processes of a Christ-submitted fellowship of leaders.

[7] *Deacons* comes from the Greek word, *diakonein* in Acts 6:2, translated "wait on tables" in the NIV (though the apostles are said to be engaged in the *diakonia* ("service" or "ministry" of the word). *Deacons* also comes from 1 Timothy 3:8, again a translation of the word *servants*.

[8] Merrill Mow, *Torches Rekindled*, Plough Publishing House, Ulster Park, 1989, p. 47.

[9] J. R. R. Tolkein, *The Hobbit*, Ballantine Books, New York, 1966, pp. 18-19.

An Afterword

I am walking this path with you. The convictions of this book are rooted in God's Word and, for the most part, they are my personal experiences as well. In some of these things I am a spiritual adult. That isn't to say I'm perfect, but I can say generally with the apostle Paul, "Follow my example as I follow the example of Christ" (1 Corinthians 11:1). But in some things, I know I'm still a teen—and in a few I'm still a child. So in the words of those entering into the final land of Narnia in C. S. Lewis' Chronicles, "Higher up and further in!" God is pursuing us, and we surrender to that pursuit, moving further and further into the fullness of His love and life.

This verse from the Bible's grand conclusion sums up well what we have considered together in these pages:

> *"Let us rejoice and be glad and give him glory! For the wedding of the Lamb has come, and his bride has made herself ready" (Revelation 19:7).*

In a first century wedding a man and woman were betrothed before marriage—which is more serious than our modern day engagement. Betrothal was commitment without living together and without sexual union. And that is the picture of our relationship with Christ.

This means first, that as Christ's promised bride we have *come* to Him and entered into an intimate love-relationship with Him. The French Benedictine monk Bernard, who lived about 1000 years ago, is credited with the words to hymns like, "Jesus, the very thought of thee, with sweetness fills my breast; but sweeter far thy face to see, and in thy presence rest" and "Jesus, thou joy of loving hearts, thou fount of life, thou light of men; from the best bliss that earth imparts, we turn unfilled to thee again."

This is what this book has been about—a God-centered joy. In elaborating on Song of Songs 1:2, Bernard described three kinds of kisses we might give to God: kissing His feet, which expresses humility; kissing His hands, which expresses dependency; and kissing His lips, which expresses joy and intimacy. This describes well our love-relationship with Him.

Second, betrothal to Christ means we have made a commitment to love Him exclusively. There's no fooling around. As William Barclay writes, "If God is the lover and we are the loved ones, it means that sin is not a breach of the law but a crime against love. The sinner does not so much break God's law as he breaks God's heart" *(Jesus As They Saw Him).*

Third, as Christ's promised bride, we want to please Him with holiness. We want to "Become" like Jesus, and in particular live a life of "Love." That is His greatest joy, and ours—a pure bride.

And finally, as Christ's betrothed bride, we look forward with great anticipation to the actual wedding celebration and union to come. Our betrothed status will become marriage, complete with all the intimacy that comes with that day. Then forever we will be face-to-face with the one who made us, loved us, forgave us, and changed us!

In the closing words of Revelation, we read, "The Spirit and the bride say, 'Come.' And let everyone who hears say, 'Come.' And let everyone who is thirsty come. Let anyone who wishes take the water of life as a gift" (Revelation 22:17, NRSV).

So the invitation is there. For the glory of God, for the exaltation of Jesus, and for your joy, God says, "Come." *Come* to know His greatness. *Come* to show His greatness. In every moment, in every situation of life, *come*—and be changed.

This is an invitation from God to you to embrace the radical lifestyle of living daily life drenched in God. And why would we want to live it any other way? This, indeed, is *life*!

Your fellow lover and follower of Jesus,

Fred Miller

(If you would like to share your thoughts, questions, or personal journey with God, I'd love to hear from you. Visit my web site at www.fredmillerglorifygod.com for contact information, a free small group study guide for this book, as well as other downloadable resources on loving and following Jesus in all of life.)

Appendixes

To further enrich your study.

The following Appendixes may
be copied for personal or classroom use.
Please include: "Used by permission
of Evangel Publishing House."

APPENDIX A

I Need You . . .I Praise You. . .

I need You . . .

For forgiveness and salvation - rescuing me from the penalty and the power
of my sins.

For the confidence of having eternal life and the hope of heaven.

To give me the gift of Your Spirit when I receive the gift of Your Son by
faith.

I need You . . .

To knock on the door of my heart to remind me about Your desire to spend
    time with me.

To reveal Yourself to me.

To slow me down so I can hear Your voice.

To make me dissatisfied with imitations of Your goodness.

To teach me Your ways.

To give me meaning and purpose to my life.

To satisfy my deepest needs and longings.

To show me what it means for me to glorify You in everything I do.

To welcome me when I fail and doubt.

To comfort me, encourage me, heal me, accept me, cleanse me, and love me.

To turn trials into treasures, pain into patience, and disappointments into Your
    appointments.

To make my worship genuine and my devotion full of zeal.

To help me know life in all its fullest.

I need You . . .

To show me the sins I must confess and repent of.

To expose my self-centeredness.

To help me hate my sin and hunger for holiness.

To create the fruit of the Spirit in me—love, joy, peace, patience, kindness,
    goodness, faithfulness, gentleness, and self-control.

To renew my mind with Your truth and to expose the false values and beliefs
    I have developed.

To give me an unshakable trust in You for Your care for me in all
    circumstances.

To give me wisdom to know how to please You in a sinful and complex world.

To show me a portion of Your goodness when circumstances are hard and
    painful.

To help me desire the best for others at all times.

To give me love for those who are hard to love.

To help me speak respectfully to every family member I live with.

To help me deny myself daily for the sake of Christ.

To teach me to live as a servant in my family, community, and church.

To help me put others ahead of my own desires.

To help me guard myself against frustration, anger, sarcasm, and criticism of those who are close to me.

To help me see the idols in my life—whoever and whatever competes for my love for You.

To expose my pride, my fears, my anxieties, my lust for control, and my longing for worldly pleasure.

To show me how my words and actions affect others.

To make me slow to speak and quick to listen.

To help me not blame others for the way I feel.

To help me live at my job as if Jesus was beside me at all times.

To help me forgive those who offend me—not allowing any barrier to grow between us.

To keep me from fearing what people think about me.

To help me not need people's approval.

To help me have the courage to correct a brother or sister who is regularly sinning.

For the discipline to say "no" to temptation and to stay far from it.

To help me express my opinions humbly.

To help me willingly and effectively use my spiritual gifts in the church.

To help me not love money—and to enjoy giving it away.

To help me share my possessions with others without control.

To help me not covet what others have—and to be content.

To help me treat all people equally, regardless of personality, age, race, or social position.

I need You . . .

To give me a compassionate heart for people who don't know Christ.

To help me glorify You to a watching world.

To help me show the reality of Christ through my life.

To help me live as salt and light in a decaying and dark society.

To help me build genuine friendships with non-Christians.

To help me share my faith with gentleness and clarity.

For the boldness to speak about my faith to others.

To encourage me to use my home for hospitality—not just family.

To give me a heart for the poor and disadvantaged.
To remind me to pray for my unsaved neighbors.
To give me the courage to invite my acquaintances to church.
To teach me my part in supporting world missions.

I praise You . . .

For loving me enough to send Your Son to die for me.
For Your gift of forgiveness of sins and eternal life.
For the Holy Spirit who immerses me in Your life.

I praise You . . .
For your kingdom that supercedes all earthly kingdoms.
For Your grace that extends love to me even when I sin.
For Your goodness that never fails.
For Your sovereign, ultimate control over all things.
For Your power that can change me and others.
For Your holiness and Your perfect moral righteousness.
For being the kind of God who delights in my company.
For the hope of eternal life and the anticipation of seeing Jesus face-to-face
        someday.

I praise You . . .
For Your creative works.
For the gift of music, song, musicians, and instruments.
For birds that sing, brooks that bubble, oceans that crash, and nights that
        are still and silent.
For stars that twinkle, clouds that hover, and the sun that warms and shines.
For flowers that color my day, for forests that quiet my spirit, and for animals
        that reflect your creativity.
For the wonder of my body—every cell, organ, tissue, bone, nerve, and DNA.
For my mind, will, creativity, feelings, and longings.
For my spirit that enables me to commune with You.
For my unique body, personality, talents, and passions.
For smell, taste, touch, sight, and hearing.
For those who reveal You despite their limitations and handicaps.
For the diversity of races and cultures.
For the smiles, laughter, curiosity, and innocence of children.
For the dignity, wisdom, and endurance of old age.

I praise You . . .
For sending Jesus as my example to show me how I should live in this world.
For giving me full—or substantial—victory over specific sins.
For the power not to have to sin.
For changing my heart to be conformed to Your heart, altering my desires,
	values, attitudes, and motives.
For the beauty and pleasure of living by Your holiness.
For the delight of doing Your will.
For giving me Your Word.
For renewing my mind with Your life-giving truth.
For Christian literature, music, radio, TV, and other Christ-centered ministries
	that have encouraged me.
For pastors, teachers, parents, and grandparents who have taught me
	Your Word and life.
For the grace to say "no" to temptations.
For the hard times that have deepened and matured my faith.
That I am not the way I used to be.
That I am not a prisoner of my past.
For humbling me so that I need You when I mess up.
For breaking my pride and exposing my selfish heart.
For teaching me how to truly love others.
For giving me your peace amidst trials.
For daily making me more and more like Jesus.

I praise You . . .
For loving me through people who love You.
For my spiritual family that is bound by faith and eternal love.
For people who have accepted me even when I have sinned against them.
For people who have overlooked my lack of love towards them.
For those who have prayed for me.
For those who have corrected me when I sinned.
For those who have listened when I cried.
For those who have shared my burdens and my joys.
For those who have helped me in very tangible ways.
For those who have ministered to my spouse and my children.
For the glory of Your church.
For the many gifts of Your people that have assisted me in growing to
	spiritual maturity.

I praise You . . .
For earthly family members to love—and sometimes to be loved by.
For a government that allows the Gospel to be freely spread.
For times of persecution that purify my faith.
For as many years as You give me to live on Your earth.
For my very life!

Fred Miller 2/99

APPENDIX B
SPIRITUAL TRANSFORMATION GOALS
Common Desires and Behaviors that God Desires to Transform Through a Love-Relationship With Jesus

Select one (or two) of the following things that you will seek God's help with over the next year. (Some may have roots in multiple heart-categories A-D.) Reflect on how these may show up in family life, work, recreation, church, or in private. This change-process will require **Surrender** *of your heart & life to Him,* **Insight** *about your sin,* **Repentance** *of your sin,* **Grace** *from God to conquer your sin, and* **Perseverance** *to continue amidst resistance. Identifying some of God's key means of grace to you (prayer, Scripture, fellowship, solitude, worship, confession, spiritual reading, service, etc.) will also be an important part of this journey to freedom.*

"For the glory of God and my ultimate joy, I desire . . ."

A. Less pride and a greater trust in my worth being in God's purposes and love for me. (See Pss. 10:4; 36:2; 115:1; Prov. 18:12; Jer. 9:23-24; Matt. 20:25-28; Luke 9:23-25; Phil. 2:3-8; James 3:13-18; 4:6, 10)

___❑ A1. To be less *opinionated* or argumentative; more humble and a better listener

___❑ A2. To have less need to *be right* in a conversation; more meek in assessing myself and more willing to admit some level of wrong

___❑ A3. To be less hesitant to say *"I'm sorry"* ; more quick to acknowledge hurt done to others, even if hurt was unintentional; free from the need to add a "but..." as a means of defense.

___❑ A4. To have less need to *control people* and get my own way; more submissive, flexible, and sensitive

___❑ A5. To be less resistant to people in *authority* over me (boss, church leaders, government, parents, teachers); more willing to do what others want me to do with a willing spirit.

___❑ A6. To have less need for *respect* from my children, spouse or work associates; more secure and humble

___❑ A7. To have less need to use wit or *humor* to feel important; more humble and sensitive in using humor

___❑ A8. To be less concerned about my personal or home *appearance*; more self-confident in who I am in God's eyes

___❑ A9. To have less need to *perform* perfectly (games, sports, music, academics, speaking, etc.); more honest and accepting about my human limitations

___❑ A10. To have less need to *brag* or talk about what I've done; more humility in how I think about my accomplishments

B. Less anxiety and fear and more trust in God for my happiness and security
(See Pss. 27:1-3; 56:3-4; 112:7-8; Prov. 3:5-6; Isa. 26:3; 41:10; Matt. 6:25, 31-34; Phil. 4:6-7; 2 Tim. 1:7; 1 Peter 5:6-7)

___❑ B1. To be less fearful or *anxious* about what might happen; more peaceful about the future and willing to take risks in the presence of God as my loving Father

___❏ B2. To be less dependent upon what people think about me, to not need their *approval*; to be more self-confident

___❏ B3. To be less preoccupied with *difficult realities* in my life; more focused on the benefits of suffering and on what God is doing and will do in the midst of them

___❏ B4. To have less need for *financial security* in the future; more contentment in God's care for my basic needs

___❏ B5. To be less *protective of my children*; to free them more to experience life in God through trials

___❏ B6. To be less *negative* and pessimistic about life and people; more positive

___❏ B7. To be less inclined to *stretch the truth* or lie; more honest and truthful

C. Less self-centeredness and more love (and more satisfaction in God's love for me) (See Matthew 22:37-40; Luke 6:27-36; John 13:12-14; 34-35; Rom. 2:8; 12:9-21; 1 Cor. 13:4-7; Phil. 2:3-4; Col. 3:14; 1 John 3:14-18)

___❏ C1. To be less *frustrated*, irritated, or angry with the people around me; more patient, compassionate, and understanding of people and confident of God's love

___❏ C2. To be less *demanding* that people lovingly consider my needs; more considerate of others' needs, and content with God's spiritual blessings through Christ

___❏ C3. To be less *withdrawn* when around others; more involved, risking and vulnerable in my conversation.

___❏ C4. To be less *critical* of others; more understanding, accepting and content

___❏ C5. To be less bitter and *resentful*; more forgiving and understanding

___❏ C6. To be less *dominating* in conversations; more honoring to others, showing more interest in their lives and thoughts and feelings

___❏ C7. To be less *blunt* and direct; be more gentle and sensitive

___❏ C8. To do less *gossiping*; be more quiet, protecting the reputation of others

___❏ C9. To be less focused on my *own interests*; spend more time and energy responding to the needs of others in kindness

D. Less rule by earthly pleasures and more focus on pleasure in God
(Pss 16:8-11; 34:8-10; 37:4; Isa. 55:1-3; Jer. 2:11-14; Matt. 6:19-21, 24; 7:11; John 15:9-11; 1 Cor. 6:12; Phil. 3:7-11; 2 Tim. 2:22; 3:2-4; 1 John 2:15-16)

___❏ D1. To be less controlled by *entertainment*-TV, sports, videos, computer, games, etc.; more balanced in life and discerning about what my heart delights in

___❏ D2. To be less controlled by *money*, shopping, clothes, home, and possessions; more content and a better financial manager of the resources God has entrusted to me

___❏ D3. To be less focused on *personal and family desires*; more free to give to the ministries of the church and the needs of the poor and the world

___❏ D4. To be less controlled by impure *sexual desires*; more pure in thought and action

___❏ D5. To be less ruled by *food*; more content with "daily bread" and moderation

___❏ D6. To be less ruled by *alcohol, drugs, or cigarettes*; more peaceful and free to live a Spirit-led life, satisfied with God's goodness

"God, I not only turn from my sin, but I turn to You to have my desires satisfied!"

"Oh God, glorify yourself in me, not for my will but Yours I plea.
Give me your love and truth anew, in all I want, think, say and do."

Fred Miller; 1/28/05

APPENDIX C

A Prayer Seeking Freedom From Depression

Dear God, *You are good.*
And You are good to me! Yes, me! (Psalm 34:8-10)
Even when feelings of regret or disappointment whisper in my head
I know You love me, just as I am. (Psalm 13:1-6)
And, even when You seem so far away, I know You are near—
watching me, supporting me, helping me through this pain
(Psalm 139:1-10).
Therefore I will expectantly wait on Your love (Psalm 5:3),
which wants to change the things I want, the things I believe,
and the things I do and say, thus making me more open to
knowing Your joy and presence again (Psalm 51:12).

Lord, help me stop rehearsing these thoughts of sadness and regret,
free me from my self-centered preoccupation with them,
and deliver me from the bondage they have on my emotions
and productivity (Psalm 42:1-5).
When I feel sorry for myself, or for those I think I may have hurt in
some way, remind me that Your "power is made perfect in
weakness," therefore I will "delight in weaknesses, in insults,
in hardships, in persecutions, in difficulties.
For when I am weak, then I am strong" (2 Corinthians 12:9-10).
So I confess to you, Lord, that when I feel sorry for myself
and continually dwell on my disappointments,
I am sinning against You,
because I have looked more to people and circumstances for
happiness than to You. (Lamentations 3:19-24).
Remind me, O Father, that "Not to us, O Lord, not to us
but to your name be the glory" (Psalm 115:1).

Lord, I accept my difficult circumstances as part of Your love for me,
because they help me deepen my faith and character (James 1:2-4).
I surrender my unique personality to You, because You gave it to me
and want to be glorified through it (Psalm 139:13-14).
I surrender my human weaknesses and limitations to You,
because they help keep me humble and resist pride from
growing in my heart (Matthew 5:5).

I want my greatest joy to be in You and Your grace for me—
      not in my accomplishments and successes (Philippians 3:7-8).

So God, teach me the beauty of Your ways:
      To rejoice in Your forgiveness when I sin (1 John 1:9).
      To rejoice in Your acceptance when I am not perfect (Romans 15:7).
      To not dwell on the past, but on my present and future with
      Christ (Philippians 3:13-14).
      To not dwell on negative things but to keep my mind on that
      which is good (Philippians 4:8).
      To give thanks in all circumstances, finding something to be
      thankful for (1 Thessalonians 5:18).
      To allow earthly disappointments to move me to spiritual
      hunger (Colossians 3:1-2).
      To find life-purpose through loving the people around me in
      meaningful ways (1 Corinthians 13:1-3; Matthew 25:35-40).
      To believe that You will reward my faith and obedience with
      peace (Philippians 4:6-7);
      and
      To be confident that all things work together for good to those
      who love You (Romans 8:28).

I pray this for the glory of Jesus to be known and shown in my life, Amen.

Fred Miller; 1/28/03

APPENDIX D

DISCIPLESHIP PARTNERS

A Simple, Grassroots Plan for Making Disciples of Jesus Christ

HOW THE GROUPS WORK

• "Discipleship Partners" are comprised of two or three individuals of the same gender who meet weekly, bi-weekly, or monthly for one to two hours for the *primary purpose* of stimulating each other to be *faithful, everyday disciples of Jesus Christ*. New groups are formed either through birthing new groups or through dividing existing groups and inviting new people.

• Each meeting includes three "disciple-making" elements:

1. Scripture Reflection: Reading a Bible chapter each session and then sharing *applications* to your lives. (Emphasis should be on what God is *saying to you* through His Word — not extensive doctrinal discussions.)

2. Life Reflection: Asking one another to reflect on his/her life as a disciple of Jesus, using any of the general *"come, become, love" goals,* the *six applications*, or the *listed focuses*. Each of these levels is designed to stimulate a balanced life with God. (These reflections should be directed to your daily life, not to the above Scripture-readings.) One person usually begins by directing one partner to any of the categories above. (That is: "Jim, how are you doing with *coming* to God?" or "Sue, share about *becoming* like Jesus in your heart, specifically around relationships at home.") After responding, that person directs the next partner to a different one (or the same one), and the process continues until the time allotted for this is finished. Partners may also choose categories *they* would like to reflect on. Don't be rigid with the process. You may even think of new categories or questions.

3. Prayer: Praying for one another in simple, informal, conversational style.

• A Facilitator should be chosen from the group to *schedule* your meeting times and to *transition* the group into all three of the activities above in the time you have allotted, especially if you have a time of informal fellowship in the beginning (which is valuable but will not in itself produce transformation as a disciple.) A typical hour and a half might be: thirty minutes informal fellowship, twenty-five minutes Scripture Reflection, twenty-five minutes Discipleship Reflection, and ten minutes Prayer.

50 SCRIPTURES TO CHANGE YOUR LIFE

Use this variety of biblical nourishment including: inspiration, instruction, and exhortation to *hear from God*. Read from top to bottom in columns. When completed, read again or use different portions.

Psalm 62	Psalm 19	Psalm 34	Psalm 91	Psalm 139
John 15	Matt. 6	Matt. 7	John 17	1 John 3
Eph. 1	Eph. 42	Cor. 5	1 John 1	Deut. 5
Psalm 23	Psalm 27	Psalm 42	Psalm 103	2 Peter 1
Matt. 5	John 14	John 16	1 Peter 1	Ro. 6
Psalm 1	James 4	1 Cor. 13	Phil. 4	Matt. 13
Col. 3	Psalm 32	Deut. 6	Luke 6	Psalm 145
Psalm 51	Ro. 12	Heb. 12	Isaiah 58	1 Tim. 6
Ro. 8	Lam. 3	Psalm 77	Eph. 5	Prov. 15
Isaiah 55	Rev. 3	James 1	1 Cor. 14	Rev. 21

LIFE REFLECTIONS FOR DISCIPLES OF JESUS

Disciples pursue the "life purpose" of *glorifying God* (1 Corinthians 10:31), which involves a God-centered desire to know and show His greatness and worth in everything we want, think, say, and do. In practice, this will include reflecting on **three goals** - how we are *coming, becoming, and loving*:

"COME" . . . to God to love Him, know Him, be satisfied by Him, trust Him, hear Him, confess to Him, ask Him, praise Him.

1. Fellowship—*Reflect on your response to God's moment-by-moment invitation to have a love-relationship with you Revelations 3:20.*

- *Consider frequency of conversation*
- *Honesty; transparency*
- *Surrendering ambitions & priorities?*
- *Meditating/reflecting on your life in His presence?*
- *Degree of satisfaction*
- *Coming in trials & joys?*
- *Listening? . . . Learning?*
- *Asking?*

2. Gratitude—*Reflect on how God has shown His goodness to you recently Psalm 34:8-9.*

- *Creation*
- *Church*
- *Answers to prayer*
- *Earthly blessings*
- *In failures, needs, and trials*
- *Spiritual successes and privileges*

"BECOME" . . . like Christ in holiness, humility, purity, attitude, and spiritual maturity—in heart, mind, words, and deeds.

3. Heart—*Reflect on what God is revealing to you about the desires, thoughts, and trust behind your actions Psalm 139:23-24.*

- *Seeking God's best, others' best or self?*
- *Contentment or frustration, impatience?*
- *Submission or control?*
- *Sorrow about sin?*
- *Who or what are you trusting in? (See Psalm 62)*
- *Humility or pride?*
- *Peace or fear, anxiety, worry?*
- *Confessed sin to God and others?*

4. Obedience—*Reflect on how you are living obediently to Jesus in the daily issues of your life Galatians 2:20.*

- *In Marriage*
- *Relationships*
- *Parenting*
- *Sexuality*
- *Job*
- *Time*
- *Money*
- *Sports*
- *Church ministry*
- *Leisure activity*

"LOVE" . . . through Christ to every person we encounter in life, especially to family, church, and non-Christians we know.

5. Relationships—*Reflect on how you have compassionately acted (or not acted) for the good of others around you Philippians 2:1-5.*

- *Words, deeds, and attitudes*
- *Honor/Respect*
- *Kindness*
- *Understanding*
- *Gossip?*
- *Forgiveness*
- *Acceptance*
- *All people*

6. Outreach—*Reflect on how you have directed your love to non-Christians you know.* Colossians 4:5-6

- *"Prayer? . . . Care (felt needs)? . . . Share (the Truth)?" process*
- *Family*
- *Work associates*
- *Neighbors*
- *Friends*
- *Enemies*

APPENDIX E

REFLECTIONS AND SCRIPTURE FOR
"WHEN RELATIONSHIPS ARE DISAPPOINTING"

• Questions to ask while meditating on God's Word (below) to you:

(1) For whose glory do I live—God's or my own?

(2) What sins of behavior and heart (attitudes and desires) is God revealing to me right now? Will I repent of them? (That is, confess them to God and those I hurt . . . be sorrowful about them . . . and turn away from them?)

(3) What promise or spiritual truth does God want me to trust Him for right now?

(4) What does love look like towards those around me right now?

• **Lamentations 3:20-26** ". . . my soul is downcast within me. Yet this I call to mind and therefore I have hope: Because of the Lord's great love we are not consumed, for his compassions never fail. They are new every morning; great is your faithfulness. I say to myself, "The LORD is my portion; therefore I will wait for him." The LORD is good to those whose hope is in him, to the one who seeks him; it is good to wait quietly for the salvation of the LORD."

• **Psalm 13** "How long, O LORD? Will you forget me forever? How long will you hide your face from me? How long must I wrestle with my thoughts and every day have sorrow in my heart? How long will my enemy triumph over me? Look on me and answer, O LORD my God. Give light to my eyes, or I will sleep in death; my enemy will say, "I have overcome him," and my foes will rejoice when I fall. But I trust in your unfailing love; my heart rejoices in your salvation. I will sing to the LORD, for he has been good to me."

• **Psalm 62** "My soul finds rest in God alone; my salvation comes from him. He alone is my rock and my salvation; he is my fortress, I will never be shaken. . . My salvation and my honor depend on God; he is my mighty rock, my refuge. Trust in him at all times, O people; pour out your hearts to him, for God is our refuge. . . Do not trust in extortion or take pride in stolen goods; though your riches increase, do not set your heart on them. One thing God has spoken, two things have I heard: that you, O God, are strong, and that you, O Lord, are loving. Surely you will reward each person according to what he has done."

- **Psalm 34:18-19** "The LORD is close to the brokenhearted and saves those who are crushed in spirit. A righteous man may have many troubles, but the LORD delivers him from them all;"
- **Psalm 139:23-24** "Search me, O God, and know my heart; test me and know my anxious thoughts. See if there is any offensive way in me, and lead me in the way everlasting."
- **Psalm 43:3** "Send forth your light and your truth, let them guide me; let them bring me to your holy mountain, to the place where you dwell."
- **Psalm 32:3-5** "When I kept silent, my bones wasted away through my groaning all day long. For day and night your hand was heavy upon me; my strength was sapped as in the heat of summer. Then I acknowledged my sin to you and did not cover up my iniquity. I said, "I will confess my transgressions to the LORD"— and you forgave the guilt of my sin."
- **Jeremiah 17:5-8** "Cursed is the one who trusts in man, who depends on flesh for his strength and whose heart turns away from the LORD. He will be like a bush in the wastelands; he will not see prosperity when it comes. He will dwell in the parched places of the desert, in a salt land where no one lives. But blessed is the man who trusts in the LORD, whose confidence is in him. He will be like a tree planted by the water that sends out its roots by the stream. It does not fear when heat comes; its leaves are always green. It has no worries in a year of drought and never fails to bear   fruit."
- **1 Corinthians 10:24** "Nobody should seek his own good, but the good of others."
- **Philippians 2:3-4** "Do nothing out of selfish ambition or vain conceit, but in humility consider others better than yourselves. Each of you should look not only to your own interests, but also to the interests of others."
- **2 Timothy 3:2-4** "People will be lovers of themselves, lovers of money, boastful, proud, abusive, disobedient to their parents, ungrateful, unholy, without love, unforgiving, slanderous, without self-control, brutal, not lovers of the good, treacherous, rash, conceited, lovers of pleasure rather than lovers of God—"
- **Ephesians 4:31-5:2** "Get rid of all bitterness, rage and anger, brawling and slander, along with every form of malice. Be kind and compassionate to one another, forgiving each other, just as in Christ God forgave you. Be imitators of God, therefore, as dearly loved children and live a life of love, just as Christ loved us and gave himself up for us as a fragrant offering and sacrifice to God."
- **Romans 15:7** "Accept one another, then, just as Christ accepted you, in order to bring praise to God."

Fred Miller; 11/01

APPENDIX F
A PARENTING SELF-EVALUATION

1 is lowest value; 5 is highest.

1. I regularly spend time with my children in ways that *they* experience as positive and loving, such that we are being drawn relationally close together.

1   2   3   4   5

2. I regularly affirm and praise my children for things they do right, especially for character qualities like kindness, respect, truthfulness, obedience, and humility.

1   2   3   4   5

3. I have clear behavior expectations in mind for my children that are appropriate to their age and temperament.

1   2   3   4   5

4. My children clearly know what my expectations for them are.

1   2   3   4   5

5. My children accept and appreciate the wisdom of my expectations for them.

1   2   3   4   5

6. When I want to give a command to my children, I am sensitive to any emotions and distractions they might have at the time that could cause them to resist immediate obedience—and I express my expectations accordingly.

1   2   3   4   5

7. I am aware of any self-centered motives in myself (frustration, anger, needing to be in control or have my own way, pride, etc.) that can frustrate and emotionally hurt my children, and I am taking steps to change.

1   2   3   4   5

8. When I give a firm, loving, and clear command to my children (without raising my voice), they obey the first (or at least the second) time I speak to them.

1   2   3   4   5

9. I lovingly overlook *some* of their misbehavior (not reacting in any way) so that they feel loved unconditionally and so my own heart is trained in acceptance.

1   2   3   4   5

10. I address unloving and unkind attitudes in my children (like selfish or mean play with other siblings or children, or when they call people names) by verbally *instructing them* about love and kindness.

1   2   3   4   5

11. I address disrespectful attitudes in my children (like when they say "no" to parents or those in authority, or when they talk back with an attitude) by lovingly *instructing them* about appropriate respect.

   1   2   3   4   5

12. I respond to their misbehavior and negative attitudes by *correcting them* with a calm, gentle, and respectful—but firm—voice (not yelling).

   1   2   3   4   5

13. If my children repeatedly disobey me, I give them a chance to change their behavior by explaining that the next time they misbehave in this way a particular negative consequence will occur (rather than giving surprise, impulsive punishments).

   1   2   3   4   5

14. When I give a potential consequence (or threat) to my children, I follow through with it (assuming it was an appropriate consequence to begin with).

   1   2   3   4   5

15. When I discipline my children by sending them to a time-out or a particular room, I help them understand what they did wrong, why it was wrong, and what they should do next time (in other words, guide them through repentance).

   1   2   3   4   5

16. I have an "ultimate consequence" that I can use effectively when my child is persistently defiant and is unresponsive to my authority and minor discipline.

   1   2   3   4   5

17. My spouse and I agree on what is "misbehavior" and how to deal with it.

   1   2   3   4   5

18. When my spouse and I are together with our children, I take initiative in training and disciplining them and don't relinquish this to my spouse.

   1   2   3   4   5

19. I regularly speak to and/or read to my children about Jesus, pray with or for them, or help them embrace God's love and truth in their daily lives.

   1   2   3   4   5